Nicholson

GUIDE TO
SCOTLAND

Robert Nicholson Publications

P9-DTC-122

Also in this series:

Nicholson's Guide to England and Wales

A Nicholson Guide

First published 1981

© **Robert Nicholson Publications Limited 1981**

Original cartography: Fairey Surveys Limited,
Maidenhead to © design by Robert Nicholson
Publications Limited. Maps revised by Geographia
Limited, London.
Maps based upon the Ordnance Survey with the
sanction of Her Majesty's Stationery Office.
Crown copyright reserved.

New text, revision and drawings: Richard Reid

The publishers would like to thank the
following for photographs provided:
The Scottish Tourist Board
The National Trust For Scotland
Fife Tourist Authority
City of Glasgow District Council
Information Bureau
The Scotsman Publications Ltd
The Tweedale Press Group
Interteam McCann for William Grant
& Sons Ltd

Robert Nicholson Publications Limited
17–21 Conway Street
London W1P 5HL

Typeset and printed in England by
E. T. Heron & Co Limited, Essex and London.

ISBN 0 905522 51 6

Contents

How to Use this Guide

Scotland has been divided into three distinct areas: the Scottish
Lowlands and Border Country incorporating Glasgow and
Edinburgh; Scottish Highlands and central Islands; Northern
Scotland including the Outer Hebrides, Orkney and Shetland
Islands. Each section is conveniently separated into a wide range
of topics to cover all interests and each entry is clearly map
referenced to make planning an itinerary easy.

The full colour touring maps at the front have been numbered 1,
2, and 3 to reflect the guide's defined regions. To see exactly how
the area divisions work, refer to the diagrammatic map on the
next page.

Scottish Boundaries

In 1974 new regions of Scotland were created, which absorbed all
the existing counties. Although the old counties have ceased to
exist for administrative purposes, they are still recognised by the
GPO and often used in postal addresses. To avoid confusion, the
name of the region is included immediately after each place name
in the text and the county name is shown in italics on the next
line.

For practical purposes, only the old county names appear next to
places listed in the index.

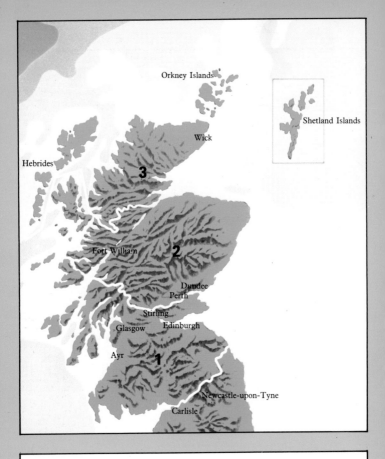

Map key

	Motorway and junction number	
	A road primary route	
	A road	
	B road	
	Other roads	
	Main railway	
	Private railway	
	Canal	
	River	

Height above sea level in feet

	3000 and above
	1000 – 3000
	200 – 1000
	0 – 200

·1334 Spot height

Built up area

County boundaries

Nicholson's guide area boundaries

⌐8⌐ Page number of adjoining map

Scale 1:1050 000

0	25	50 Miles

0	40	80 Kilometres

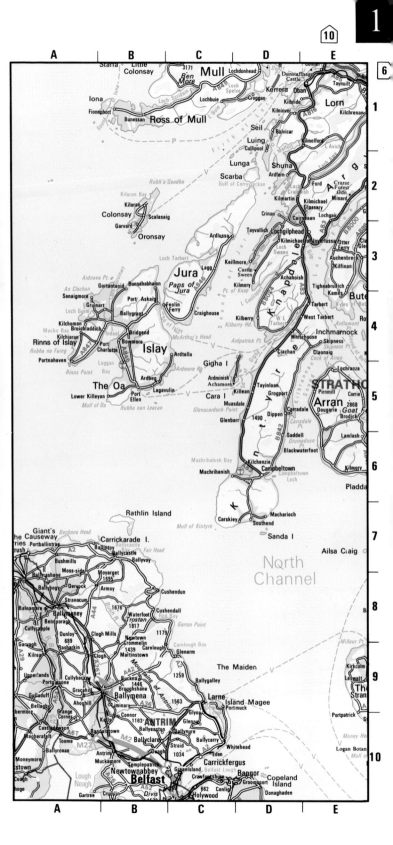

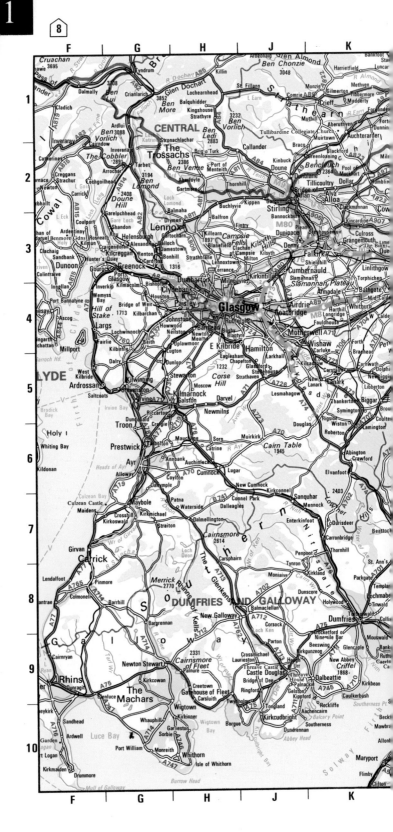

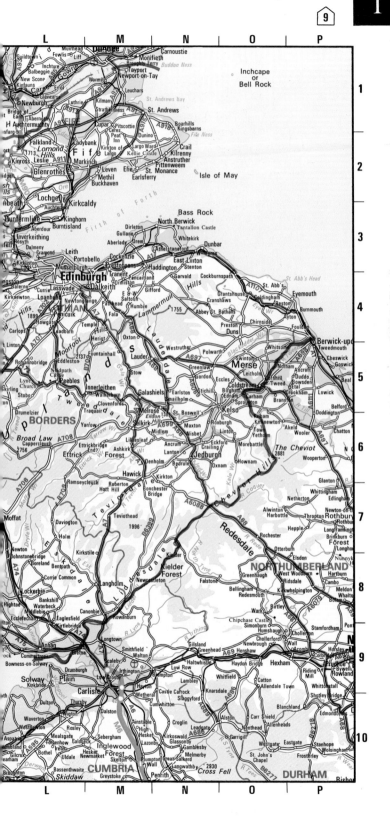

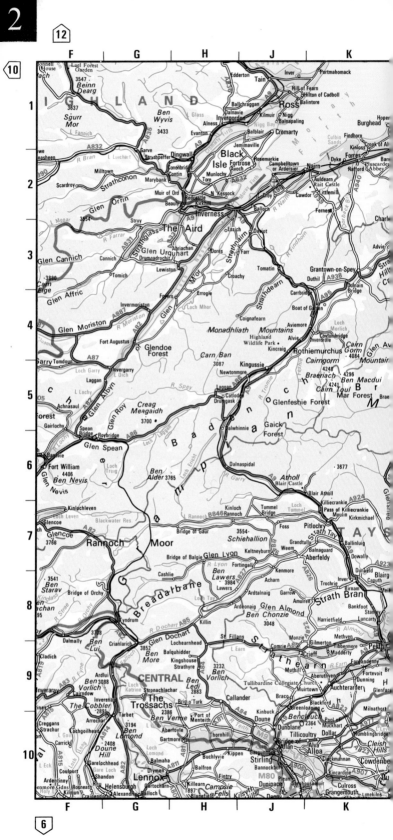

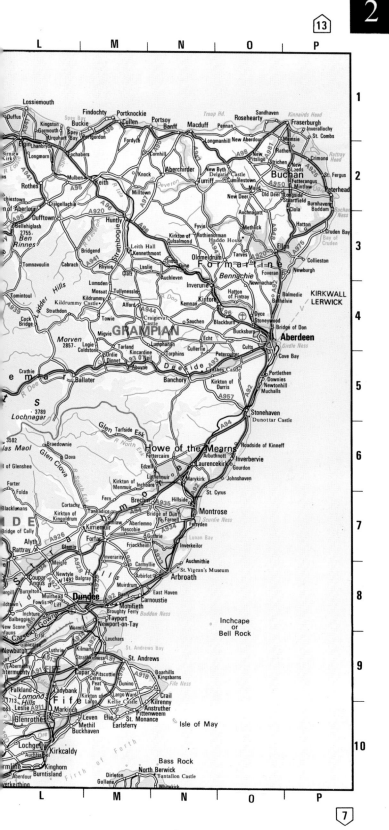

L   M   N   O   P

1

2

3

4

5

6

7

8

9

10

Lossiemouth
Duffus
Kingston
Garmouth
Urquhart
Birnie
Kirk
Elgin
Longmorn
Spey Bay
Buckie
Findochty Portknockie
Portsoy Banff Macduff
Cullen
Fordyce
Spey Portgordon
Lochabers
Troup Hd.
Pennan
Sandhaven
Rosehearty
Kinnairds Head
Fraserburgh
Inverallochy
St. Combs
Longmanhill New Aberdour
Crimond
Rattray Head

Rothes
Mulben
Keith
Craigellachie
Dufftown
Knock
Cornhill
Aberchirder
New Byth
Delgatie Castle
Turriff
Cuminestown
Strichen
Memsie
Rathen
New Pitsligo
New Leeds
St. Fergus
Peterhead
Fettercairn
Mintlaw
BUCHAN
A950

chiestown
n of Aberlour
Bellehiglash
Ben Rinnes
2755
Tomnavoulin
Cabrach
Huntly
Strathbogie
Milltown
Old Deer
Maud
New Deer
Longside
Stuartfield
Clola
Auchnagatt
Boddam
Burnhaven
Buchan Ness

Bridgend
Leith Hall
Kennethmont
Kirkton of Culsalmond
Rothienorman
Haddo House
Fyvie
Methlick
Tarves
Oldmeldrum
Ellon
Cruden Bay
Bay of Cruden

Tomintoul
Rhynie
Leslie
Clatt
Auchleven
Insch
Oyne
Bennachie
FORMARTINE
Collieston
Newburgh

Ladder Hills
Lumsden
Mossat
Tullynessle
Kildrummy
Castle
Strathdon
Alford
Towie
Kildrummy
Inverurie
Kirkton of
Kemnay
Hatton of Fintray
Newmachar
Balmedie
Belhelvie
KIRKWALL
LERWICK

Cock Bridge
Migvie
Craigievar Castle
Sauchen
Blackburn
A96
Dyce
Stoneywood

Crathie
Morven
2857
Logie
Coldstone
Tarland
Kincardine
O'Neil
Lumphanan
Torphins
Cullerlie
Bridge of Don
Aberdeen
Girdle Ness

Ballater
Aboyne
GRAMPIAN
Echt
Bucksburn
Cults
Cove Bay

Lochnagar
3789
R Dee
Deeside
Banchory
Crathes Castle
Kirkton of Durris
Peterculter
Portlethen
Downies
Newtonhill
Muchalls

3502
las Maol
Braedownie
Clova
Glen
Tarfside
Esk
R North
Fettercairn
Howe of the Mearns
Stonehaven
Dunottar Castle
A957
Roadside of Kinneff

of Glenshee
Glen Clova
Edzell
Littlemuir
Arbuthnott
Laurencekirk
Inverbervie
Gourdon

Forter
Folda
Kirkton of Menmuir
Inchbare
Fern
Marykirk
Johnshaven

Blacklunans
Cortachy
Kirkton of Kingoldrum
Tannadice
Brechin
A935
Hillside
St. Cyrus
Bridge of Dun

IDE
Bridge of Cally
Kirriemuir
Tanlaw
Aberlemno
Rescobie
Farnell
Montrose
Scurdie Ness

Alyth
Rattray
Glamis
Forfar
Friockheim
Guthrie
Inverkeilor
Lunan Bay

Coupar Angus
Newtyle
W 1492
Balgray
Inverarity
Carmyllie
Auchmithie
St. Vigean's Museum

Meigle
Muirhead
Airliot
Arbroath

cargill
Burrelton
Fowlis
Liff
Muirdrum
East Haven
Carnoustie

ildtown
Inchture
Balbeggie
New Scone
fauns
Dundee
Monifieth
Broughty Ferry
Buddon Ness

Newburgh
Carse
Gleneagles
Tayport
Newport-on-Tay
Inchcape
or
Bell Rock

Abernethy
rthermuchty
Luthrie
Kilman
Leuchars
St. Andrews Bay

FIFE
Cupar
Strathkinness
St. Andrews
Boarhills
Kingsbarns
Fife Ness

Falkland
Lomond Hills
1713
oss
Ladybank
Ceres
Pitscottie
Peat Inn
Dunino
Crail

Glenrothes
Leslie
Markinch
Kirkton of Largo
Kellie Castle
Kilrenny
Anstruther
Pittenweem

Lochgell
Leven
Elie
St. Monance
Earlsferry
Isle of May

Kirkcaldy
Methil
Buckhaven

Auchtertool
Kinghorn
Burntisland
Bass Rock
North Berwick

rmline
Aberdour
Dirleton
Gullane
Tantallon Castle

verkeithing
Whitekirk

L   M   N   O   P

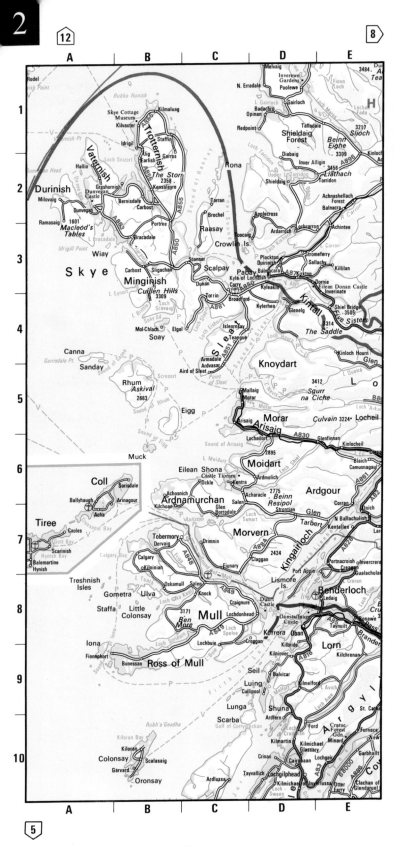

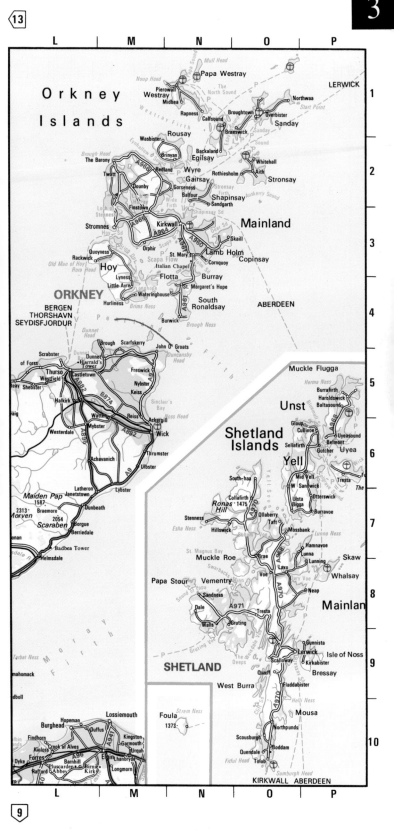

Orkney Islands

LERWICK

Papa Westray
Noup Head
Pierowall
Westray
Midbea
Rapness
Calfsound
Broughtown
Overbister
Northwaa
Start Point
Sanday
Braeswick
Wasbister
Rousay
Brough Head
The Barony
Brinyan
Backaland
Egilsay
Whitehall
Redland
Wyre
Rothiesholm
Aith
Stronsay
Twatt
Downby
Gairsay
Gorseness
Balfour
Shapinsay
Sandgarth
Mainland
Finstown
Wide Firth
Stromness
Kirkwall
A964
Skaill
Orphir
St. Mary
Lamb Holm
Copinsay
Quoyness
Rackwick
Cornquoy
Hoy
Italian Chapel
Flotta
Burray
Lyness
St. Margaret's Hope
Little Ayre
Waterhinghouse
South
Hurliness
Ronaldsay
Burwick

ORKNEY
BERGEN
THORSHAVN
SEYDISFJORDUR

ABERDEEN

Dunnet
Brough
Scarfskerry
John O' Groats
Head
Scrabster
of Forss
Thurso
Dunnet
Harrald's
Tower
Freswick
Westfield
Castletown
Nybster
Reay Shebster
Keiss
Halkirk
Watten
Reiss
Westerdale
Mybster
Ackergill
Achavanich
Wick
Thrumster
Ulbster
Latheron
Lybster
Maiden Pap
Janetstown
1587
Dunbeath
Braemore
2313
2054
Borgue
Morven
Scaraben
Berriedale
Badbea Tower
Helmsdale

Muckle Flugga
Herma Ness
Burrafirth
Haroldswick
Baltasound
Unst
Glout
Cullivoe
Uyeasound
Shetland
Islands
Sellafirth
Belmont
Gutcher
Uyea
Yell
South-haa
Mid Yell
Tresta
Collafirth
W Sandwick
Ronas
1475
Ulsta
Otterswick
Hill
Taft
Bigga
Stenness
Ollaberry
Burravoe
Hillswick
Mossbank
Lunna Ness
Esha Ness
Hamnavoe
Muckle Roe
Brae
Lunna
Skaw
St. Magnus Bay
Lunning
Papa Stour
Voe
Laxo
Whalsay
Vementry
Neap
Sandness
Mainlan
Dale
A971
Tresta
Walls
Gruting
Gunnista
Lerwick
Isle of Noss
Scalloway
Kirkabister
SHETLAND
Quarff
Bressay
West Burra
Fladdabister
Foula
Mousa
1373
Northpunds
Scousburgh
Boddam
Quendale
Tolob
Fitful Head
Sumburgh Head

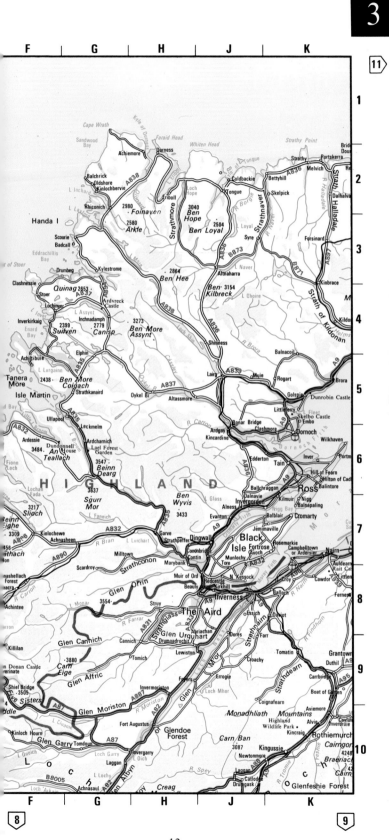

Introduction to Scotland

Scotland, or Caledonia as it was called by the Romans, is a country of dramatic, contrasting scenery within comparatively modest dimensions. On three sides, it is surrounded by sea—to the north and west by the Atlantic Ocean and to the east by the North Sea. On her southern border, which extends for 60 miles approximately along the line of the Cheviot Hills, she merges with England. Although the country is only some 274 miles long running from north to south, a maximum of 146 miles in width—the minimum width being a mere 25 miles between the Firths of Clyde and Forth—it has been estimated that the length of Scotland's jagged coastline totals over 2,000 miles.

By comparison with her English neighbour, Scotland is a hilly and mountainous country, being the home of Ben Nevis—the highest peak in the United Kingdom. There are relatively few large cities or towns and a large proportion of Scotland's numerous islands are still completely uninhabited.

Geography

The Lowlands in the south stretch coast to coast and are edged by broad moors and pastoral farmlands, criss-crossed by rivers that wind between the undulating hills of the Border country. To the north are the central Lowlands, with classical Edinburgh, the country's capital and cultural centre. Bustling Glasgow, the great Victorian city, is the centre of the industrial belt which straddles the Clyde.

Fife, Tayside and Grampian to the east are fertile pasturelands, enriched with inky-blue lochs, and a coastline of high cliffs and golden beaches, along which huddled fishing villages and holiday resorts are neatly scattered.

Inland to the west are snow-capped mountains sloping down to a torn stretch of coast that looks out onto the islands of Mull, Muck, pious Iona and the crofting townships on Skye.

The Highlands, which occupy the major part of the Scottish land mass, are remote, romantic and richly beautiful. Here are a myriad mountains and hills piled high with heather. The coast on the west is magnificently rugged and indented, cut through by a thousand sea lochs.

In the far north are the lands of Caithness and Sutherland—flatter than most of the Highlands and where much of the agricultural land is reclaimed peat bog. Eastwards, sailing deep into the North Sea are the islands of Orkney and Shetland, from which the Norsemen finally retreated leaving behind Scandinavian names as a permanent reminder of their occupation. Westwards in the turbulent Atlantic are the numerous Western Isles which comprise the Outer Hebrides. Lined with silvery sands that are washed clean by great ocean rollers, this group of islands is the last stronghold of Gaeldom.

Altogether, there are some 780 islands scattered in a great wake along the west coast of Scotland and shooting out diagonally beyond the north east of Thurso.

Pentland Hills, Midlothian

Climate

The east coasts of Fife, Tayside and Grampian are recorded as having the most sunshine, as well as the highest temperatures in Scotland. But it is possible to visit Scotland during the height of summer and not see the sun for the duration of a two-week holiday.

The Highlands, resplendent in the sharp shadows of a bright summer's day, can often be cloaked in a veil of mist for days on end. In fact, the world-famous Scottish mist can occur throughout the many hilly areas of the country at virtually any time of the year.

The north west coast, passed by the Gulf Stream, frequently enjoys a delightfully mild climate in which numerous sub-tropical gardens flourish. However the west coast also catches the damp westerly airstreams that condense on the high ground, making this side of Scotland much wetter than the east.

In the north of Scotland, the Hebrides, Orkneys and Shetlands, June days can have an average of 18–20 hours daylight, with marvellous, light, long evenings and a good sunshine record of over six hours a day. During summer, the sun hardly goes down over the Shetlands and there is often enough natural light to read by in the dead of night.

The main tourist season lasts from Easter to September, with the peak summer holiday period in July and August. During winter, skiing holidays are popular in the Cairngorm mountains of Grampian; the season lasts from December to March depending on the snowfall.

Scotland in the autumn, with the leaves rusting red, can be truly spectacular, but the days are shorter and there is often a damp, slightly shivering air. The light is no longer sharp. Everything appears flatter—a kind of brooding monochrome that is exhilarating in its own right.

Skiing in the Cairngorms

History

Prehistoric Scotland (3000BC–AD50)
The first people to arrive in Scotland were nomadic, concerned primarily with the catching and gathering of food. But the first to leave any substantial remains were the Neolithic immigrants who arrived about 3000BC. Being farmers they were mainly concerned with raising crops, yet they were also great stone builders, as well as dexterous potters and weavers, and left behind marvellous chambered cairns. The Bronze Age peoples, who began to arrive about 2000BC, made improvements in the arts, modified burial traditions and began to build vast stone circles and fortified villages. They were followed by the Iron Age peoples, in about 500BC, who built the brochs (fortified towers). In the south and east communal life was strong with people tending to live in fortified villages. In the north and west individualism was a stronger drive, with each family living in self-contained duns or brochs.

The Romans (AD50–200)
The Romans occupied Scotland twice. The first period was highlighted by the defeat of the Picts by Julius Agricola at the battle of Mons Graupius cAD82. But the Romans, unable to advance further, finally withdrew in AD100. They made a second attempt to conquer the Picts in AD140. They built the Antonine Wall stretching from the Clyde to the Forth but by AD200 they withdrew a second time.

A series of devastating raids by the Picts across the Lowlands and over Hadrian's Wall resulted in the launching of an expeditionary force by Emperor Severus in AD208. But the Emperor died at York in AD211 and further attempts to occupy the land beyond the wall were abandoned.

Early Christian Scotland (5thC–6thC)

St Ninian, returning to his hometown of Whithorn after a pilgrimage to Rome in AD397, was the first to introduce Christianity to Scotland. He built a small stone church there, but the rest of the country remained largely heathen until the arrival from Ireland of St Columba and his followers in AD563. He established a small religious community on Iona that was to become the cradle of Christianity in Scotland.

The Four Kingdoms (5thC–11thC)

The various peoples who occupied Scotland eventually formed four distinct kingdoms. In the north were the Picts. In the east Lowlands were the Angles who had come from northern England and the Germanic lands. Occupying the south west, modern day Strathclyde, were the Britons, originally a Welsh tribe. Throughout the islands and along the west coast were the Gaels, Celtic Christians who had landed from Ireland early in the 6thC.

The Norse Occupation (9thC–14thC)

The Norse invasion of Scotland began in the early 9thC. They first occupied the Hebrides, Orkneys and Shetlands and then built numerous settlements along the mainland coast. By AD875 they had occupied the whole of modern-day Caithness in the north east, having destroyed the Picts. What was left of the Pictish kingdom was taken over by the Gaelic king, Kenneth MacAlpine (843–860).

The Beginnings of Scotland (9thC–11thC)

MacAlpine and his descendants battled against the Norsemen and their other enemies, the Northumbrians, during the next 150 years. In 1018 Malcolm II defeated the Northumbrians at Coldstream, with the result that Lothian passed into his control. His grandson, Duncan I (1034–1040), who had already inherited the Kingdom of Strathclyde, succeeded to the throne in 1034. Although the Norsemen still occupied the islands and had a foothold along the mainland coast, to all intents and purposes, a united Kingdom of Scotland had been formed.

The English Influence (11thC–13thC)

Following the Norman Conquest of England, Malcolm III (1057–1093) took Margaret, the Anglo-Saxon princess driven from her lands, to be his Royal bride. A devoutly pious woman, later to be canonized, she anglicised the Scottish church, was responsible for instigating an English-speaking court and brought up her sons in the English tradition.

Three of her sons succeeded to the Scottish throne. One, David I (1124–1153) was responsible for the founding of many abbeys and for introducing the Norman barons to Scotland. They came to build cathedrals and monasteries and many of them, who were granted land, began to build great castles. By the accession of Alexander III (1249–1286) their integration was such that the language of the court had become Norman French. This was the so called 'Golden Age', a period of comparative peace and prosperity. The Vikings were driven from the mainland at the Battle of Largs in 1263, and this led to the annexation of both the Western Isles and the Inner Hebrides. Towns, or burghs, began to prosper as trade flourished. But the genius of Alexander was not only his skill in foreign affairs, but his ability to bring to heel the over-ambitious nobles. Unfortunately in 1286 he died a tragic death. His own children were dead, and the only direct heir was a three-year-old grand-daughter. For the next 300 years, there was the constant threat and reality of English invasion and bitter conflict along the border lands.

The Wars of Independence (late 13thC–14thC)

The claim of Alexander's grand-daughter, Princess Margaret, to the Scottish throne was supported by the Scottish nobles and clergy, and by the English king, Edward I. But on her way to Scotland from her home in 1290, the Maid of Norway died.

Altogether there were no less than 12 claimants to the throne. The Scottish nobles, anxious to avoid civil war, asked Edward I to act as arbitrator. This he agreed to do on condition that whoever he appointed must accept him as feudal overlord. Naïvely, the nobles acceded to these terms. The throne passed to John Balliol who subsequently rebelled against the English crown. Edward, claiming total sovereignty, marched north, defeated the Scots, destroyed the Great Seal and removed to London the Stone of Destiny, on which Scottish kings had for centuries been crowned at Scone.

William Wallace (1270–1305)

Declared an outlaw following the killing of an Englishman who had insulted him, Wallace gathered around him a loyal band of patriots and fought a guerilla-style war by attacking English-held castles. Eventually he gathered an army in the north and destroyed an English force sent to subjugate him at Stirling Bridge in 1297. Edward retaliated and totally defeated Wallace at Falkirk in 1298. Having escaped, the hunted Wallace was finally betrayed in 1305 and executed in London. Various parts of his mutilated body were sent to Scotland as a warning against further rebellion.

Robert the Bruce (1274–1329)

As Earl of Carrick, an Anglo-Scottish-Norman, Bruce had supported Wallace but soon deserted him. Following Wallace's death, several Scottish nobles, including Bruce and John Comyn, another claimant to the Scottish throne, met in the church at Dumfries to organise resistance against the English. A quarrel broke

Bronze statue of Robert the Bruce at Bannockburn

out and Bruce stabbed Comyn to death. By this act not only did he make himself an outlaw, but by committing sacrilege, the most abhorred crime in the Middle Ages, he alienated half the Scottish noble families. Having nothing to lose Bruce hurried quickly to Scone and had himself crowned King of the Scots. For the next 7 years, he dedicated himself to the cause for Scottish independence. Edward I died in 1307 and Bruce waged a brilliant guerilla war against the English, as well as the Scottish nobles who were opposed to him. By 1312 only a few castles remained in English hands, the most important of which was Stirling. Most of the internal Scottish opposition had been suppressed by the time he laid siege to Stirling in 1314. Edward II hurried north with a force of 20,000 men. All Bruce could muster were 5,000, but, with great skill and cunning he destroyed the English army at Bannockburn, some 2 miles from Stirling. In 1320, an assembly of churchmen and nobles asserted Scotland's right to full independence from the English crown and addressed it to the Pope in the Declaration of Arbroath. The Pope acknowledged Bruce as King of Scotland, but it was not until 1328 that peace was finally declared between England and Scotland in the Treaty of Northampton.

Flodden and the late Middle Ages (early 14thC–1513)
Following the death of Bruce and the succession of his weak son David II (1329–1371), the Borders, despite the peace treaty of 1328, were plunged into a century-and-a-half of intermittent warfare with the English. There was bitter internal political intrigue and murderous anarchy, particularly amongst the nobles dispossessed by Bruce, which the monarch contained with great difficulty. But it was also the period which saw the rise of the merchant class, the growth of prosperous burghs and the founding of the first universities at St Andrews 1412, Glasgow 1451, and Aberdeen 1495. This was the period that witnessed the long line of Stuart kings who succeeded David II in 1371. Literary and artistic life flourished, particularly in the reign of James IV (1488–1513). However England's war in France prompted James IV into helping the French by reviving the Auld Alliance and attacking the English. But the Scottish army was disastrously defeated at Flodden in 1513, and the King, together with many of his nobles and countless subjects, was slain.

The Alliance with France (1513–1542)
The difficulties both Scotland and France suffered under the invading English had gradually hardened into an alliance. Scottish soldiers fought alongside the French during the Hundred Years War. The Reformation was under way in England, but James V (1513–1542), staunchly Catholic, refused to follow suit in breaking up the monasteries. He further committed himself to Catholic France by 2 French marriages, the second to Mary of Guise who bore him a daughter, the future Mary Queen of Scots. The Scottish nobles, resenting the French connection and with their eye on the wealth of the monasteries, refused to support the King when Henry VIII invaded Scotland. The Scottish army was defeated at Solway Moss in 1542 and James V, lying ill at Falkland Palace, died soon after news reached him.

Mary Queen of Scots (1542–1587)
Queen at 6 days old, Mary's early years were spent under close guard by her mother, acting Regent of Scotland. A marriage between Henry VIII's son and the young Mary was turned down, and following a series of devastating Border raids conducted by the Earl of Hertford together with his defeat of the Scottish army at Pinkie in 1547, the Scots sent 5-year-old Mary to a safe refuge in France. There, at 15, she married the Dauphin, who became King in 1559. But by the age of 18, Mary was a widow and in 1561 she returned to Scotland to assume her throne and begin her turbulent reign.
In 1560 the Scottish parliament had denounced the Catholic faith and established Protestantism. Mary, a Catholic queen, sought religious toleration—a stance that antagonised the Protestant nobles, especially John Knox. Then she married the Catholic Lord Darnley in 1563. Mary gave Darnley a son, the future James VI of Scotland. But the ambitious and impossible Darnley sought Royal status for himself. This Mary refused. And in February 1567 Darnley was murdered. Mary, suspected of complicity, impetuously married the Protestant Earl of Bothwell, one of the known murderers, in May of the same year. Having offended everyone by her conduct, rebellion broke out. She was forced to flee and in June 1567 was defeated at Carberry Hill. After capture, escape and final defeat at Langside in

Ross & Cromarty

1568, Mary abdicated the throne and fled for safety to England. But Queen Elizabeth, aware of Mary's hereditary claim to the English throne, imprisoned her as a dangerous rival. After 19 years incarceration, Mary was executed in 1587, dying—as it is recorded—with the dignity of a queen.

The Reformation (16thC–18thC)

There were many reasons for the Reformation in Scotland. Among them was the degree of corruption in the hierarchy of the clergy—a state which had reached saturation point. Another was the appeal of the ideas of Calvin, the French theologian. Many Scots who travelled in Europe were impressed with the clarity of his theology in comparison with the more emotional pronouncements of Luther. In John Knox (1505–1572), the Scots found a powerful orator who could articulate their feelings, particularly against the Catholic clergy, who strongly supported the alliance with France. They were further aided by many Scottish nobles who, aware of the advantages that the dissolution of the monasteries had brought their counterparts in England, eagerly joined the Protestant cause. James VI, who succeeded to the throne as a minor, became the first Protestant monarch of Scotland, and as heir to the English throne was anxious not to offend Protestant sensibilities. He supported the Scottish Reformed Kirk and within a century of the death of John Knox, a democratic Presbyterian church had been established in Scotland.

The Union of Crowns (1603)

Queen Elizabeth I of England died in 1603 and James VI (1567–1625) of Scotland journeyed south to become James I of England. He returned only once to Scotland. But the Union of Crowns did not immediately unite the two countries. Squabbles broke out within the church. There were two factions. One, represented by the Lowland Scots, was epitomised by the Covenanters, who believed in a purer Reformation, with little formal worship and equality of ministers. They were supporters of Parliament. The other side, represented by the Highlanders, sought a more formal liturgy and a hierarchy with bishops. They were largely Royalist and Jacobite. Consequently when the Civil War broke out in England, the Scots, who initially remained aloof, entered the fray when the English Parliamentarians appealed to the Lowland Presbyterians for help following a series of early defeats.

The Covenants (1638 and 1643)

James I had managed to introduce a hierarchy of bishops within the Presbyterian church. But when Charles I (1625-1649) attempted to introduce a new Prayer Book, it pushed the religious sensibilities of the Presbyterians to the limit and in 1638 the National Covenant was signed. It was agreed that the principles of the Reformation should be strictly adhered to and the appointed bishops dismissed. For their agreement to side with the Parliamentarians in the Civil War, a second Solemn League and Covenant was signed in 1643.

The Commonwealth (1651–1660)

The alliance with the Parliamentarians was conditional on Presbyterianism being introduced in England. Cromwell was unable to carry out this part of the agreement and thereby angered the Scots. Things worsened following Cromwell's execution of Charles I, not only King of England but King of the Scots, in 1649. Rebelling against the Commonwealth, the Scots proclaimed Charles II King, on condition of his signing both covenants, and they raised an army to invade England. Cromwell defeated the rebel force at the Battle of Dunbar in 1650. A second attempted invasion was defeated at Worcester in 1651. Scotland with England was ruled as a single Commonwealth under a military occupation that lasted until 1660.

The Restoration (1660)

Peace appeared to have been achieved with the Restoration of the Stuart monarchy under Charles II. But with the annulment of all church legislation since 1633, and the re-establishment of episcopacy, bitterness increased and resulted in the rebellion of the Covenanters in 1666. Although defeated, they rebelled again in 1679. Early successes spurred them on to greater efforts but, lacking sufficient support, they were eventually defeated by Monmouth's troops at the famous Battle of Bothwell Bridge in June 1679. Years of cruel suppression of the Covenanters followed until 1688 when William of Orange (1688–1694) succeeded the deposed James II (1685–1688). He agreed to the abolition of the bishops, and at the same time the largely Jacobite Highlanders were asked to take the oath of allegiance to William and Mary. Most were unwilling, but by the last day of 1691 all but the MacDonalds of Glen Coe had signed. The result was the infamous massacre of Glen Coe led by the Campbells of Glenlyon. Then came the Act of Settlement in 1701 which effectively barred the son of James II, the Old Pretender, from the throne. The Scottish Parliament retaliated by the passing of the Acts of Independence in 1704 which declared their right to choose their own monarch and to abstain from England's foreign wars. But in 1707 the Scottish Parliament surprisingly relented and agreed, under the Treaty of Union, that the Scottish and English Parliaments should merge and that the two nations would become one under the United Kingdom of Britain.

The Jacobites (18thC)

During the first half of the 18thC, there were two ill-fated attempts by Jacobite sympathisers to restore the Stuarts to the Scottish throne. The main support for the uprisings came from the Highlanders who were by no means united in this cause. Following the accession of the Protestant Hanoverian George I (1714–1727) on the death of Queen Anne in 1714, the Highlanders rebelled. Led by the Earl of Mar, the Jacobites tried by force to win the crown for James VIII and III, son of James II, and known as the Old Pretender. But their hopes were dashed at the Battle of Sheriffmuir in 1715. General Wade was despatched to Scotland to bring the Highlanders under control through the construction of a network of military roads.

Clan gravestone on Culloden battlefield

But in 1745 the Jacobites, led by the Young Pretender Prince Charles Edward Stuart, rose once again. The Jacobites marched south and were quickly successful, soundly defeating a Hanoverian force at Prestonpans near Edinburgh in September 1745. The Prince and his force advanced as far as Derby but then withdrew. Having failed to capture the strategically important Stirling Castle, Bonnie Prince Charlie and his supporters were forced to retreat further. On 16 April 1746, a tired, half-starving Highland army were decisively and brutally beaten by the Duke of Cumberland (3rd son of George II) and his highly efficient troops at the Battle of Culloden. Some 1,200 Highlanders were slain, whilst the Prince, after many adventures, managed to escape to France and then to Rome where he died in 1788.

The Highland Clearances (1780–1860)

Culloden was effectively the end of a way of life for the Highlanders. They were disarmed, their dress banned by the Act of Proscription in 1747 and in many other ways they were made to feel like second-class citizens. But worse was to come. The attractions of the cultural centres of the Lowlands as well as London required more money. Sheep farmers anxious to utilize the rich grazing lands in the Highlands persuaded the clan chiefs to rent out their lands, but first the crofters had to be removed. Known as the Highland Clearances, the evictions that took place from 1780–1860 depopulated the Highlands. Many left for the miseries of the big Victorian cities, others eked out a sparse living along the barren, rocky coast, while thousands emigrated to the New World. The conditions of the crofters were such that, in Skye in 1882, many crofters resisted the process of eviction by the local sheriff's officers. An absurdly nervous government at Westminster sent up a man o'war to sort out the problem. A commission of inquiry was eventually set up which resulted in the Crofters Holding Act of 1886—giving the crofters security of tenure, grants for improvements and fair rents. But for most it was far too late.

Scotland in the 20thC

Although Scotland has ceased to exist as an independent nation since 1707, the 20thC has seen a revival of national feeling that has expressed itself in the changing fortunes of the Scottish National Party. For the time being, the devolution issue has been resolved, but there still remains a considerable body of opinion that favours the establishment of a separate Scottish legislature to decide purely domestic affairs. Of course, the Scottish legal system which retained its independence with the Treaty of Union, continues to evolve and the makers of law at Westminster are obliged to observe its particular requirements.

North Sea oil rig

In recent years, the single most important industrial development in Scotland has been the discovery of North Sea oil. It has brought a second industrial revolution to the country, with all the attendant benefits and problems. The fact that the oil is drilled out of Scottish waters has been much publicised by nationalist groups, but the exploitation of this vital natural resource has been carried out by an international community and the economic advantages have had a far-reaching effect on the United Kingdom as a whole.

Famous people

Probably the most famous literary Scot is gentle Robert Burns, Scotland's national poet and creator of the nostalgic 'Auld Lang Syne'. Lyrical and compassionate, much of Burns' work is written in dialect and difficult for the Anglo-Saxon to understand. Of no less a stature is Sir Walter Scott who, writing from his home at Abbotsford, put down the story of the border lands with a fiery passion and raised Rob Roy from a cattle thief to a dashing, Hollywood style hero. Patriot and incurable romantic, Scott had a genius for depicting colourful and dramatic incidents in history and for catapulting the ordinary and everyday into something stirring and significant. The works of Robert Louis Stevenson make easier but equally exciting reading and his novels 'Kidnapped' and 'Treasure Island' have entertained young people for almost a century. Also born in Scotland was J. M. Barrie, author of the ever-youthful and immortal 'Peter Pan'.

Many of Scotland's memorable figures emerge larger than life from the pages of history. William Wallace, the 'people's hero' who struggled to free Scotland from English rule and who died a traitor's death—hung, drawn and quartered in 1305. Robert Bruce, outlawed for killing a rival, but who dedicated himself to the liberation and unification of the Scottish kingdom—he ultimately defeated the English at the Battle of Bannockburn against all odds with his army outnumbered 5 to 1. The 16thC is dominated by two equally charismatic, if totally contrasting characters—Mary Queen of Scots whose stormy, intrigue-ridden life ended on the executioner's block in 1587; and John Knox, the zealous Protestant reformer and preacher whose impassioned speeches led to the lasting establishment of a democratic Presbyterian Kirk. Adding drama to the 18thC is Bonnie Prince Charlie, on whom the Jacobites pinned their last hopes: a dashing dreamer whose actions brought defeat to the Highlands and whose own life ended in tragic failure; Prince Charles Edward died a penniless drunk in Rome but has become one of the great romantic figures of Scottish history.

In art, design, philosophy, politics, science, medicine, industry, commerce, architecture, engineering, exploration and technical invention, Scotland has also produced many men of genius whose names are household currency. Alexander Graham Bell—born in Edinburgh—he invented the telephone in 1876. Charles Mackintosh who investigated the by-products of tar and produced the water-proofing process that bears his name. Charles Rennie Mackintosh, distinguished designer, painter and architect, who pioneered many new styles (1868–1928). Robert Adam, the pre-eminent 18thC designer and architect—he established a still-popular fashion based on classical forms. Adam Smith, born in Kirkcaldy and educated at the universities of Glasgow and Oxford, as a philosopher and economist his ideas were particularly influential in the late 18th–19thC. James Watt of steam-engine fame. John Logie Baird, inventor of the first practicable television system. David Livingstone, the great explorer of the African continent. James Ramsay MacDonald, Britain's first Labour Prime Minister. Sir Henry Campbell-Bannerman, who was leader of the Liberal Party and became Prime Minister in 1905. Sir Alexander Fleming, born in 1881 at Lochfield, Ayrshire, he discovered penicillin for which he shared a Nobel Prize in 1945. John MacAdam, the famous road engineer whose name is synonomous with his widely adopted road construction system. Thomas Telford, brilliant bridge, road, canal and docks engineer. Sir James Young Simpson who pioneered the use of chloroform as an anaesthetic, bringing pain relief to surgery.

Other sons of Scotland have achieved great renown overseas. Samuel Greig, born in Inverkeithing, he entered Russian naval service during the reign of Catherine the Great and created a navy manned largely by Scottish officers. Andrew Carnegie, son of a Dunfermline linen weaver, he emigrated to America where he built up an iron and steel empire. In his lifetime, he gave away more than 350 million dollars—most of it to Dumfermline.

The language

The original language of Scotland was Celtic, but spoken with two quite distinct dialects. The tribes of the north spoke a Pictish version, while in the Lowlands, the Britons spoke a Welsh version. During the 6thC the Christian missionaries arrived from Ireland bringing with them their own Gaelic language. The Norsemen, whose invasion and occupation of Scotland began in the early 9thC added their own language to a mixture that eventually was to become one Scottish language of which the Gaelic input was the most dominant. What was left of the Pictish kingdom, virtually destroyed by the Norse, was taken over by the Gaelic king. Nothing was left of its language, save a few place names. Norse, spoken in parts of the outer islands up to the late 18thC, finally disappeared but left as a strong reminder the names of many places. After Culloden, English predominated throughout the country and today, it is only the Western Isles that are a stronghold of Gaelic.

It is thought that place names beginning with Pit or Pet, such as Pitsligo, Pettycur or Pittenweem may be Pictish in origin. Names like Wick, Lybster or Brough of Birsay are Norse in origin. Wick, or Vick, means bay; Lybster means farmstead, while 'brough' signifies a fortified place. The more common Gaelic root words found in place names are: 'aber' of Aberdeen or Aberdour meaning the mouth or confluence of a river; the 'inch' of Inchgarvie or Inchmahome Priory means island—the ruins of the priory actually stand on an island in Lake of Mentieth; 'ross' means peninsula or forest; 'inver' is another word meaning the mouth of a river; 'strath' as in Strathblane, Strathaven or Strathpeffer means a broad valley. Clan is the Gaelic word for children and Mac is Gaelic for son.

The clan

For centuries, the Highland crofters would down tools and follow their clan chiefs into battle in return for rent-free land. The clan system was the underlying social structure in the Highlands. It was a mediaeval tribal system which flourished or died by the sword. The clan chief, no more than a kilted gangster in the mind of an 18thC Lowlander, was a weird amalgam of Renaissance man and daring cattle rustler, whose authority within the clan was absolute, even to his power of hanging any clansman that stole from him.

March of clansmen at a Highland gathering

Dating back to the 6thC and the arrival of the Celts from Ireland, the word clan comes from the Gaelic 'clann' meaning children, hence kinship. Identified mostly by a badge worn in their bonnets, many of the clans were formed by Irish, Norman, as well as Norse settlers. Loyalty to the clan chief often overrode that shown to the king. Although, in principle, the king was the chief of chiefs, the monarch sometimes had to exercise his power ruthlessly as when James I executed the powerful Albany family in 1425. The clan system was at its peak in the 16thC.

Wild and independent, clan feuds were frequent and generally bloody, especially during the three centuries following the death of Alexander III in 1286. However the last clan battle was at Mulroy, near Roy Bridge, in 1688 when the MacDonalds of Keppoch fought and defeated the Mackintoshes in an argument over the ownership of their lands. For the most part, the clans supported the Jacobite cause and achieved a certain unity during the uprisings of 1715 and 1745. But Culloden was the beginning of the end. Seen as a gang of savages by the 18thC southerners, it was only afterwards, encouraged by the romantic pen of Sir Walter Scott, that they were incarnated as something noble and heroic. There is, perhaps, a certain irony in the fact that it was the descendents of these same clan chiefs who were largely responsible for the heartless eviction of their clansmen during the Highland Clearances (1780–1860).

Highland dress

The Highland way of life was brought to an end with the Jacobite defeat at Culloden. The English, determined to bring the Highlanders to heel, passed the Act of Proscription in 1747 which not only disarmed the Highlanders but banned their Highland dress. Although the act was repealed in 1782, it was not until the state visit of George IV attired in Highland dress in 1822, that the fashion for tartan, carried on to this day, began in earnest.

The Scots were not the only nation to wear some form of kilt, but it is the Scottish kilt that is the most memorable. It traditionally consisted of a tartan cloth 5 feet by 16 feet. To dress, the Highlander would spread the cloth on the ground, pleat it, then, lying across it, would wrap it round his body, the upper portion pulled over his shoulder, and the whole belted at the waist. By the 18thC this cloth had been superseded by the kilt that is more akin to the modern version. While the traditional belted cloth was extremely warm, particularly in the snowy mountains where, re-arranged, it became a sleeping bag, it was also a little cumbersome. Before battle, Highlanders would unwrap the tartan cloth and fight instead in their long shirts.

It is commonly thought that particular tartans identified individual clans, but various districts also had their own different ways of making the tartans' patterns and colours. This diversity added richness and also confusion, for up to the 18thC there is little evidence to show that there was any uniformity in the wearing of a particular tartan by any one clan.

The proscribing of the tartan after Culloden created further problems. The knowledge and expertise involved in the making of tartans had been handed on generation by generation. The Highland Society formed in London in 1778, made efforts to collect original tartans, but to little effect. By the time of the Romantic revival of the early 19thC, traditional knowledge was, at best, secondhand. Nevertheless, the demand for tartans was enormous, not just within the British Isles, but overseas, especially in North America. Numerous pattern books were published and new tartans designed, each clearly identified with a particular clan, rather than a district. Today there are over 250 different tartans, divided into dress tartans and hunting tartans.

Music and dance

There are numerous festivals held annually in Scotland, the more important being those at Perth in May, Stirling in late May to early June, and the most celebrated of them all—the Edinburgh International Festival, held during the last weeks of August and first week of September. Of the various artistic performances which take place regularly, the two most memorable spectacles are the traditional Highland dances and the skirl of the bagpipes.

Highland dances, modernised like the clan tartans, are Celtic in origin. Characteristic of these dances are wild swirling movements, with high, often jerky leaps as the dancers rotate around their swords, which are stuck in or laid on the ground. It is thought that the dances may have some relationship to ritualistic sun worship or possibly a choreography aping the pattern of the Celtic High Cross. Many of these dances became increasingly more formalised from the late 16thC onwards. This was due primarily to the dancing masters who organised the Royal entertainment at court, particularly during the reign of Mary Queen of Scots.

The bagpipes, the traditional accompaniment to the Highland dances, were found in one form or another in both Ancient Egypt and Greece, in addition to Scotland and Ireland. Used for entertainment, as well as to accompany Highlanders into battle, they were originally introduced to the British Isles by the Romans.

Architectural styles

Early Christian (5thC–12thC)
In the 4thC and 5thC Scotland came under the influence of the Picts, but they continued to use Iron Age structures such as wheel-houses, crannogs and brochs. Most new buildings were insubstantial affairs, constructed mainly of wattle and daub.

cross slab,
Ruthwell Church

cross slab,
Whithorn

Christianity was first introduced to Scotland by St Ninian. Returning to his home town of Whithorn after a pilgrimage to Rome in AD397, he founded a small stone church over which a priory was later built. All that remains of this earlier structure are some grave slabs.

Beehive cells. Circular in plan with a corbelled roof, they were built of dry stone walls. They were either simple chapels or, where near a monastery, the cells of monks. Remains are found at Aileach in the Garvelloch Islands. Many were grouped within a circular rampart known as a cashel.

Round towers. Dating from the period of Viking raids, these served as bell towers, as well as a place of refuge for the clergy in times of danger. They are tall slender round towers, tapering slightly inwards, with a conical top. Built of hewn stone and with a highly raised entrance, the ground was reached by a ladder. Although Irish in origin, fine examples are found at Abernethy, Brechin and in the Orkneys at Egilsay.

Round tower,
Brechin

Sculptured stones & crosses. A characteristic of early Christian Scotland, the stone slabs have a carved cross in relief, with rope, foliage or animal carvings. The crosses generally consist of a circle surrounding the intersection of shaft and arms. These are found largely in the west, and are Celtic in origin. Others have sculptured scenes of biblical themes. The latter type are of Pictish origin and found mainly in the east.

Kildalton cross, Islay

8ᵗʰC cross-slab,
Meremonno

Norse period (9thC–14thC)
In the 9thC the Viking invasion began. By AD875 the whole of Caithness had been conquered. The most typical Viking structure was the stone longhouse, usually 100 feet long and over 20 feet wide and, rather like the great Saxon halls, open to the roof with a central fire. Remains are found at Jarlshof and Birsay, amongst other places. The most important monument of the Norse period is the cathedral at Kirkwall, even though the style is Romanesque.

Romanesque (11thC–12thC)
Until the 15thC, when a strong national style developed, mediaeval architecture in Scotland followed a similar pattern to that in England. The great religious orders of the Benedictines, Cistercians and Augustinians were encouraged to settle in the 12thC and gradually superseded the Celtic monastic

St Rule, St Andrews
11thC

Kelso Abbey

foundations. To conform with the religious orthodoxy of Western Europe, they utilized the standard plan of church and living quarters grouped around a cloister. Of interest are the abbeys of Iona 13thC, Sweetheart 13thC, Jedburgh 12thC, and Kelso 12thC.

Characteristic features: Bold architecture reflected in very long church plans, ponderous cylindrical piers and flat buttresses. Windows are small and deeply splayed. Rib and panel vaulting introduced. Elaborately carved mouldings.

Abbeys, churches & cathedrals. The cruciform plan, with side aisles of English and Continental architecture, was the chief model. The main roofs were timbered and the aisles vaulted. Good examples are the 12thC abbeys at Kelso and Dunfermline. Also of interest in this style is the cathedral of St Andrews, which was one of the longest religious buildings in Britain, being 14 bays in length. Bell towers were generally square and apses polygonal.

Romanesque
work nave
Dunfermline
c1150

Parish churches. The average parish church consisted of an aisle-less, 2-chamber structure, rather richly decorated—elaborately carved capitals, grotesque masques for corbels and round arches complete with chevron moulding. Of particular interest is Leuchars parish church 1185, in Fife.

details,
Leuchars church
1185

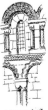

blind arcading,
Leuchars church 1185

Castles. The typical Norman castle of the 11thC and 12thC was the motte and bailey. It consisted of a raised earthwork mound, the motte, which was ringed with a timber wall enclosing a courtyard, the bailey. Of interest are the earthwork remains of the Mote or Urr. Many castles began to be rebuilt of stone in the 12thC, but of these the only surviving Norman keep is at Castle Sween.

Gothic (12thC–16thC)
The transition from Romanesque to Gothic architecture occurred much later in Scotland than in England. It is seen most clearly in the choir at Jedburgh Abbey, where you have a mixture of Gothic pointed arches and Romanesque round arches. The Gothic transformation was complete with the construction of the choir in Glasgow Cathedral 13thC. Also of interest are the 13thC cathedrals of Elgin, Dunblane and Aberdeen.

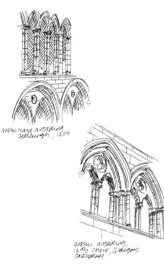

gothic nave arcading, Jedburgh, 1200

gothic arcading, 12thC choir, Glasgow Cathedral.

Characteristic features: Pointed arches, replacement of massive Norman pillars by groups of slender shafts, windows increased in size, and the introduction of diagonally set angle buttresses. Window tracery was geometric in form. Later on, curvilinear or flowing lines were introduced. Vaulting utilised an increasing number of intermediate ribs. Carving was generally more naturalistic.

French influence. Owing to strong ties with France in the late 13thC, Scottish architecture began to move away from the English influence and to borrow freely from the French Flamboyant style. The result, seen particularly in the design of window tracery and carved ornamentation, was a proliferation of curvilinear forms in structures and tracery, as well as the lavish use of openwork. Good examples are found at Melrose Abbey and Sweetheart Abbey. Examples of other late Gothic buildings include (the albeit over-enthusiastically restored) St Giles Cathedral 15thC, Edinburgh, and Holy Rude 1414, Stirling.

St Giles Cathedral, Edinburgh, 1385–1416

Doune Castle, 14thC.

Castles. The castles of the 13thC and early 14thC were stone versions of the motte and bailey type. When defence of the curtain wall became more important, projecting towers were added and the wall was reinforced by a plinth, as well as by archer slits and battlements. The keep was brought forward and attached to the curtain wall as a gatehouse dwelling. Good examples at 14thC Tantallon Castle, Lothian, and Doune Castle, Central.

Fortified hall houses. Also typical of the period was the fortified hall house. It consisted of a large hall on the first floor, built above a vaulted ground storey. Of interest is 14thC Rait Castle, Highland.

Tower houses. The great symbol of feudal Scotland. They were built mainly between the 14thC and 17thC, were rectangular in plan with the rooms stacked vertically, and reached by one or more turnpike staircases. Walls were thick and floors barrel-vaulted. Of interest are Threave Castle 1369–90, Dumfries & Galloway, and Borthwick Castle

Borthwick Castle

1430, Midlothian. Many had wings added later. French influence was particularly strong in the late 14thC and early 15thC. This resulted in the appearance of the long gallery and the corbelled angle turret or bartizan.

The effect of gunpowder. Royal palaces such as those at Dunfermline, Edinburgh and Stirling were radically remodelled to cater for the development of gunpowder. Arrow slits were replaced by gunloops, while high curtain walls and towers were superseded by gun platforms and embrasures. New walls were kept low, but much thicker.

The Renaissance (15thC–17thC)
The first indication of the Renaissance in Scotland was the application of Italianate details to many mediaeval castles and palaces, as in the great halls of the castles at Edinburgh and Stirling.

Characteristic features: Renaissance ideas were reflected in the formality of planning and symmetry of façades, but mediaeval angle towers and corbelled turrets were still used. Classical forms were used for painted ceilings, plasterwork and woodwork.

Churches. Although much ecclesiastical work of the period consisted of modifications

Chapel Royal, Stirling Castle 1594

Craigievar Castle, 1626

to existing Gothic buildings, some religious buildings, like the Chapel Royal, Stirling Castle, with its Classical doorway and flanking columns, were more affected by Renaissance fashions.

Castles. Traditional Scottish forms were so popular that when new façades in the Classical style were added to the Royal palaces of Stirling 1540–42, and Falkland 1537–41, they made little or no impression. It was in the late 16thC that Renaissance styling became of greater importance—as seen at Crichton Castle, where the north side, added 1585, was modelled on an Italian Renaissance palace in Ferrara. Also of interest: Huntly Castle 1602.

Crichton Castle Italianate façade added 1581–91

The Reformation (16thC–18thC)
The Reformation brought a radical transformation of church architecture. Characteristic was the unique centrally planned church at Burntisland. Built in 1592 and square in plan, it has a central floor space for the long communion table of the reformed rite.

Burntisland church, 1592

Burntisland Church

The addition of a transeptal aisle, sometimes with a laird's loft and burial place, resulted in the typical Scottish T-shaped church plan as at Pitsligo 1634 and Anstruther Easter 1634. Both these churches are traditional in construction, with harled walls and moulded masonry doorways. The Renaissance influence grew stronger from the mid 17thC. Typical is the 1633 Tron Kirk, Edinburgh, which shows the influence of the Netherlands Renaissance.

Scottish Baronial (16thC–17thC)
This was the heyday of Scottish tower houses in which mediaeval defensive features were regenerated for decorative purposes. Characteristic is the decorative exuberance of corbelled upper floors, machicolated parapets and pepper-pot turrets. Symbolic of the castellated romanticism is the angle turret, a feature borrowed originally from France by the mediaeval builders. Of interest are Claypotts Castle 1569–88, Craigievar Castle 1626 and Glamis Castle, late 17thC.

Heriot's Hospital, Edinburgh 1628–59

Palladian Renaissance (16thC–18thC)
Scotland's first major Classical building was Heriot's Hospital 1628–50, Edinburgh. Designed by William Wallace, it has a Renaissance plan with a huge central courtyard, but retains the traditional corner towers crowned by corbelled turrets. It was not until the late 17thC that a gentler style emerged, characterised by the use of pilasters, pedimented centre block and projecting wings. The father of the Classical school in Scotland was Sir William Bruce, who was responsible for the additions to the Palace of Holyrood 1671–8, as well as the design of Hopetoun House 1699–1703 and Kinross House 1686–91.

Palace of Holyrood 1671–78 by W. Bruce.

The dominant figure of the 18thC was William Adam, a pupil of Bruce, and the father of architects John and Robert. He built a series of remarkable country houses. Of particular interest is Duffhouse 1730, Banff, and the marvellous east front at Hopetoun House, added 1721–60.

Neo-Classicism (18thC–early 19thC)
Characterised by vast frontages of excessive regularity and punctuated at key points by pedimented porticos, and crowned by domes or cupolas. Of interest are buildings in the New Town, Edinburgh, including Charlotte Square 1791, and the University of Edinburgh 1789–94, both by Robert Adam. Much inspiration was derived from classical Roman architecture.

Gothic Revival (18thC–early 19thC)
The revival of Gothic architecture stemmed from the ideas of a romantic movement in the late 18thC. Of interest are:
Culzean Castle 1771–92, and Melville Castle 1786, both characterised by battlemented parapets, round corner towers, pointed arches and less formal planning.

culzean castle, 1780

Commercial & industrial buildings
(18thC–early 19thC)
The rich mineral resources of Scotland were reflected in the development of numerous industrial buildings, such as New Lanark Mills and village 1785. Founded by Richard Arkwright and David Dale, and later managed by Robert Owen, this small industrial town is one of the finest monuments of the Industrial Revolution. Also of interest are the mills at Blantyre 1785, and the Stanley Cotton Mills and village 1785.

Canals & bridges (early 19thC)
Numerous canals were built during this period, including the famous Caledonian Canal 1814–22. Designed by Thomas Telford, it incorporates the remarkable Neptune's Staircase, a series of 8 locks devised to climb the steep ascent to Loch Lochy. Many bridges were also improved. Of particular interest is Kelso Bridge. Built in 1803 by John Rennie, it was the prototype for Waterloo Bridge. Another of the finest suspension bridges of the period was built by Sir Samuel Brown across the Tweed at Hutton in 1820.

Victorian period (1837–1901)
A time when traditional forms gave way to

adapted, historical styles and when new materials were used in construction. Architects grouped themselves under the banners of the Greek Revival and the Gothic Revival, and the battle of styles began in earnest. In the late Victorian period, the typical materials used were iron and glass for railway stations, exhibition halls, warehouses and bridges. Good examples are: Glasgow Stock Exchange 1877; Royal Scottish Museum 1861, Edinburgh; Anchor Mills 1871–83, Paisley; the Caledonian Road Church 1867, Glasgow; the Custom House 1840, Glasgow.

Hill House

The Vernacular tradition
(late 19thC–early 20thC)
The Vernacular tradition of stepped gables, roughcast rendering and asymmetrical composition had a simplicity and austerity that made it possible for architects to re-use its forms without being modish. Good examples are Melsetter House 1898–1902, Holy Island, by William Lethaby, and several buildings by Charles Rennie Mackintosh such as Windy Hill 1899, Kilmacolm, and Hill House 1902–04, Helensborough.

20th Century
It was not until the late 19thC and early 20thC that Scottish architecture began to produce something truly original once more. The great architect of this period was Charles Rennie Mackintosh whose Glasgow School of Art 1897–1909 is the masterpiece of modern Scottish architecture. But the

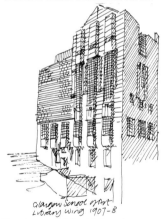
Glasgow School of Art Library wing 1907–8

flowering was brief and belonged to one man. Elsewhere things were much the same as in England. In the early 20thC, Renaissance and Georgian styles were reserved for civic architecture, while the Gothic style was predominant for churches and educational buildings. Steel-framed construction produced other, fresher alternatives. But it was mainly the profusion of new materials and the development of more sophisticated mechanical servicing that encouraged the proliferation of all kinds of modern architectural styles. In fact, almost anything could be done and nearly everything was done.

Caledonian Road Church, Glasgow.

Scottish Lowlands and Border Country

1

Borders, Dumfries and Galloway—a rich rolling blanket of hills and lush farmland stretching coast to coast along the boundary with England. Here is a land of ice-cold lochs and famous fishing rivers snaking across the landscape. The Baroque outline of the west coast begins with the pastoral landscape of the Solway Firth breaking out eventually into a bold, vigorous coastline further north. This was the hunting ground of Viking raiders, and it was here that St Ninian first introduced Christianity to Scotland, when he built a church at Whithorn in the 5thC. By the 12thC Christianity was firmly entrenched in the great abbeys at Sweetheart, Glenluce and Crossraguel.

The south west was the setting for Scotland's struggle for independence in the late 13th and early 14thC, when Wallace and then the great Scottish hero Robert the Bruce took up the banner against the English. It was also a land torn by anarchy as the powerful families fought each other—the grim reminders of this strife being the castles at Caerlaverock and Threave. It was through here that Mary Queen of Scots wound her triumphal way in 1563, but it was also through here that she made her escape some 5 years later. In these lands, the 17thC Covenanters suffered, the churchyards marked by the graves of their martyrs. But this is also the land of gentle Robert Burns, Scotland's national poet.

Eastwards the tales become more blood curdling. The Borders, a land fought over since Roman times, still ring to the sound of the marauding border raiders of the middle ages; the silent stone built tower houses, a permanent testament to the bygone terror. It is here you find the famous border abbeys of Kelso, Melrose, Jedburgh and Dryburgh, pious skeletons in a chilling stillness. This is the country of Sir Walter Scott who had the imagination to set the border story down on paper from his study at Abbotsford.

St Monance

North west to Strathclyde is the bustling city of Glasgow, catapulted by the Industrial Revolution into one of Britain's finest Victorian cities. The River Clyde was once a little salmon river, but by the late 19thC Clydeside had become the greatest ship building centre in the world. This industrial waterway pours itself out into the wide waters of the Firth of Clyde. Contained by the islands of Islay and Jura, this is the pleasure ground of Glasgow and the south west. Here the coast is dotted with resorts and the spacious waters are a haven for yachting. To the east is Lothian where Edinburgh, the capital of Scotland for the last 500 years, is wrapped in an eiderdown of hills. Proudly she stands on her crags, and still casts one of the most stirring silhouettes of any city in Europe. Two towns in one, the cultural centre of Scotland, home of the great Edinburgh Festival, and full of poignant reminders of Scotland's independent history.

There are remnants of prehistoric Britain in the large Iron Age hill fort at Traprain Law, which was a major tribal centre for the Votadini, who once occupied the eastern Lowlands. At Cramond the Romans built a fort. Other remains include the great Roman frontier wall, the Antonine Wall, built during the 2ndC, and lying between Dunbarton and Bridgeness.

Further north you come to the fertile farmlands of Fife and southern Central. This was the land of the fierce Picts who forced the Romans to withdraw behind their wall. There are magnificent Royal residences at Dunfermline and Stirling; a string of picture postcard fishing villages such as Crail or St Monance enrich the East Neuk—the rocky coastline south of St Andrews; small inland villages with Royal connections, like delightful Ceres where Falkland Palace was the Renaissance hunting lodge of Stuart kings. It was near Stirling that Robert the Bruce won Scotland's independence at the Battle of Bannockburn, while in St Andrews, where Scotland's first university was founded, another kind of battle still takes place—the occasional Open—for here is the historical home of golf.

Ceres

The coast

Aberdour Fife   1 L 3
Fife. Pop 4,200. EC Wed. Aberdour, on the Firth of Forth, can offer silver sands backed by trees and an attractive old town. 12thC St Fillan's church is worth a visit; also Aberdour Castle.

Aberdour Castle, Fife

Ailsa Craig Strathclyde   1 E 7
Ayr. Set 10 miles off the Ayrshire coast, at the mouth of the Firth of Clyde, this remarkable 1,110-foot-high rock rises from the waves in the shape of an onion—in fact a well-known strain of onion is named after it! It carries a powerful lighthouse, nicknamed 'Paddy's Milestone', after the thousands of Irish immigrants who sailed this way to reach once-prosperous Clydeside.

Annan Dumfries & Galloway   1 L 9
Dumfries. Pop 6,100. EC Wed. MD Fri. This Victorian red stone market town, a fishing and boating port, stands on the eastern shore of the Annan Estuary. Of interest: Georgian Moat House, now a museum, and Annan Academy where Thomas Carlyle taught.

Anstruther Fife   1 N 2
Fife. Once the major herring port of Scotland until the herring abandoned their traditional winter habitat in the Firth of Forth. A network of narrow streets squeeze past the bent-backed houses to a large harbour—now almost as busy with lobster boats and tourists as in the heyday of the herring fishing fleets.

Ardrishaig Strathclyde   1 F 3
Argyll. Pop 900. Canal village of tall, windswept houses owing its prosperity to the Crinan Canal, which was built in 1801 to connect Loch Fyne with the Sound of Jura and the Atlantic Ocean beyond.

Ayr Strathclyde   1 G 6
Ayr. Pop 47,900. EC Wed. MD Tue. The centre of the Robert Burns 'Industry' and country. The cottage where Burns was born in 1759 is at Alloway, 2 miles south. Also of interest: 13thC Auld Brig o'Ayr, the Auld Kirk, and Loudoun Hall. An attractive resort with 2 miles of safe sandy beaches and a fishing harbour.

Brig o'Doon, Alloway

Ballantrae Strathclyde   1 F 8
Ayr. Pop 300. Full of smugglers' swagger in cob-webbed corners, it consists of a tiny harbour built into the muddy estuary of the River Stinchar. A straggle of stone built houses peters out along the shore to the north. Dominating the whole ensemble are the ruins of 15thC Ardstinchar Castle.

Bass Rock Lothian   1 N 3
East Lothian. Set 2 miles offshore from North Berwick, at the mouth of the Firth of Forth, this sheer rock carries a lighthouse to warn navigators, and a dense colony of nesting gannets that dive from a great height to grab fish. Boats from North Berwick harbour take you round the rock.

Burntisland Fife   1 L 3
Fife. Pop 5,700. One of the ghost ports of the Forth, yet in recent memory it was a flourishing place sending coal to southern England, and before that the terminus of the Firth of Forth rail ferry, the first in the world. Yet not all is decay. Outstanding is the parish church of St Columba, built in 1592 as a copy of the old North Church in Amsterdam, and in very recent times the first steps towards the renaissance of the town centre have been undertaken. Surprisingly there is an outdoor Olympic-size heated sea-water swimming pool, and all the trappings of the seaside, including a small sandy beach to the west of the deserted docks.

Burntisland Church

Cairnryan Dumfries & Galloway   1 F 9
Wigtown. Pop 200. EC Wed. This town of whitewashed cottages on the shore of Loch Ryan was an important wartime port, and parts of the Mulberry Harbour used in the Normandy landings were assembled here. East of the harbour is the unusual Dutch-style Lochryan House (1701).

Campbeltown, Argyll

Campbeltown Strathclyde   1 D 6
Argyll. Pop 6,000. EC Wed. The capital of Kintyre, and possibly the site of Dalriada the capital of the ancient Kingdom of Strathclyde. An attractive seaside holiday town which seems to have avoided the more vulgar excesses of its southern competitors. Of interest: the fine Celtic cross at the quay-head. Davaar Island has a painted crucifixion scene in the cave. Good fishing. Shingle beach.

Connel Ferry Strathclyde   1 E 1
Argyll. Pop 200. EC Wed. Delightfully situated on the south side of Loch Etive. Two notable features are the Falls of Lora, and the cantilever road and rail bridge which spans the loch.

Cowal Strathclyde   1 F 3
Argyll. Pop 7,400. The Cowal Peninsula lies in south Argyll, between Loch Long and Loch Fyne. Four other sea-ways run deep into its forested hills, namely Loch Goil, the Holy Loch, Loch Striven, and the Kyles of Bute. Most of its magnificent scenery can be explored along coastal roads, though many steep loch-sides are roadless, and indeed pathless, for stretches of many miles. Dunoon, the only town, is usually approached by car ferry from Gourock on the Clyde. Shingle beaches, often weedy, but safe for bathing.

Crail Fife   1 N   2
Fife. Pop 1,100. Once the centre for
Scotland's trade with Europe in the 16thC.
It's a picture postcard fishing port of stone
built houses, with stepped gables and
pantiled roofs, lining a picturesque street
which runs down to a pint-sized harbour. Of
particular interest—an 8thC Pictish cross
slab in St Mary's Church, and the 16thC
Tolbooth Tower.

Cramond, Midlothian

Cramond Lothian   1 L   3
Midlothian. Right at the mouth of the River
Almond, this large village is held back from
the riverside by a long terrace of
whitewashed houses which border the quay.
Almost a suburb of Edinburgh it's a
favourite place for an evening walk along the
causeway to Cramond Island if the tide is
right, or to watch the sailing boats and
shipping in the Forth. Unsafe for bathing.

Creetown Dumfries & Galloway   1 H   9
Kirkcudbright. Pop 900. EC Thur. A
welcoming little place identified as the
Porton ferry in Scott's novel 'Guy
Mannering'. The well displayed rock and
gem museum is the best of its type in
Britain. Four miles south is Carsluith Castle,
a roofless 16thC tower; a little further south
are a few safe sandy beaches.

Crinan Strathclyde   1 D   2
Argyll. An enclosed harbour nestles at the
foot of the cliffs forming the western basin
of the Crinan Canal. Locks lead west to the
sea and eastwards for 8½ miles to the sheer
beauty of Ardrishaig on Loch Fyne. What a
delightful spot this is, with puffers, as the
small coasters are known, moving slowly
through the canal with the cruising yachts
and the Loch Fyne herring fleet.

Culross Fife   1 K   3
Fife. Pop 500. Frozen history, but not dead
history. Once a busy port and Royal burgh,
the cobbled streets and tiny houses with
their pantiled roofs and crow-stepped gables
still form the most complete example of a
16th and 17thC burgh, thanks to valiant
work by the National Trust for Scotland.
Stepping sharply down a ridge of land beside
the Forth, the lower town and upper town
are connected by steep, narrow streets.
Culross Palace is a handsome merchant's
mansion with a central court, built
1597-1611. Other buildings of interest
include the Tolbooth (1626) with 18thC
tower; the Abbey, now in ruins, founded for
Cistercians in 1215. The Abbey church has a
fine choir and beautiful central tower. The
Back Causeway contains a group of restored
17thC houses. Also of interest is the Study
(1633), a merchant's house and now the
information centre; Butcher's House (1664)
complete with trade symbols, and Snuff
Cottage (1670).

mercat cross, Culross

Dirleton Lothian   1 M   3
East Lothian. Pop 400. This village has
everything. Set around a wide green and
17thC church. It also has one of the loveliest
ruined castles in Scotland. Attractive walks
down to the beach.

Drummore Dumfries & Galloway   1 F   10
Wigtown. Pop 300. A wash of gabled houses
brushed tightly across a ridge of green. At its
foot, a small harbour and pencil line of
sandy beach fronting Luce Bay. Of interest
nearby is a wall of cliffs, 300-foot-high and
crowned by a bone white lighthouse.

Dumbarton Strathclyde   1 H   4
Dunbarton. Pop 25,600. EC Wed. A jumble
of industrial sheds, shipping yards and
terraced housing brought abruptly alive by
the twin peaks of Dumbarton Rock, a
240-foot-high rock rising sharply from the
waters of the Clyde. This prominent
landmark to every traveller by road, rail, or
ship down the Clyde has been nicknamed by
generations of sailors as 'The Maiden's
Breasts'. It was originally a plug of molten
basalt at the heart of an ancient volcano.
The harbour town grew up in the shadow of
a mediaeval stronghold built round the
higher of the two peaks—'Wallace's Seat'. All
that remains of the castle are the 18thC and
17thC fortifications, the latter now a
museum. A shipbuilding centre since the
16thC (the Cutty Sark was built here), today
the town also makes its living from blending
and bottling whisky.

Dunbar Lothian   1 N   3
East Lothian. Pop 4,600. EC Wed. A narrow
steep-sided gash in the cliffs forms the
dramatic gateway to Dunbar's harbour.
Around the harbour is a picturesque
collection of old warehouses, and further
inland the old Town with its quaint Town
House of 1620. South of Dunbar are the
White Sands; good bathing.

Dunbar

Dunoon Strathclyde   1 F   3
Argyll. Pop 9,000. EC Wed. A holiday town
on the Firth of Clyde with two fine bays
with safe swimming, and ruins of a castle.
Mary Campbell, Burns's sweetheart
'Highland Mary' was born here. There is a
statue of her on Castle Hill.
The town has always been popular with
Glaswegians as the Clyde ferries call here
regularly. In August, however, bursting
point is reached with the Cowal Games, the
largest of all Highland Gatherings with its
spectacular 'march of a thousand pipers'.

Dunure Strathclyde   1 G   7
Ayr. Pop 500. Tiny, heart-warming harbour
lined with sturdy stone houses on the edge
of a sandy bay, the whole pressganged
together by the shadow of steep cliffs. On
the cliffs above are the ruins of a 15thC
castle, once a Kennedy stronghold. It was
here that Gilbert Kennedy, 4th Earl of
Cassillis, roasted alive Alan Stewart,
Commendator of Crossraguel.

Elie Fife   1 M   2
Fife. Pop 900. Self-effacing village of stone
built houses arranged with quiet dignity
around a sheltered 16thC harbour. The
village was later absorbed by its younger
neighbour, Earlsferry. Many charming
17thC houses including an L-plan house in
South Street; it has a staircase tower and is
known as the 'castle'. Fine sandy beach.

Eyemouth Borders   1 P   4
Berwick. Pop 2,500. EC Thur. A busy fishing
town with cobbled streets, narrow 'pends' or
archways leading to small courtyards. To the

east of the harbour is Gunsgreen. Now a boarding house, the Georgian Gunsgreen House became a centre of smuggling in the 18thC because of its many secret passages. A popular seaside centre with good sandy beaches.

Garlieston Dumfries & Galloway   **1** H 10
Wigtown. Pop 500. EC Wed. Once one of the many little thriving Solway ports, the small harbour is now used by boating and fishing enthusiasts. Approximately 1 mile to the north east is the ruin of Eggerness Castle, and 3 miles south are the remains of Cruggleston Castle, with nearby a 12thC church in the Romanesque style used as a potato factor. The beach is mud and shingle.

Girvan Strathclyde   **1** F 7
Ayr. Pop 2,700. EC Wed. With a foot in the industrial camp as well as one in the tourist, Girvan is managing well. Terraces of red and grey stone houses flank wide roads leading down to the harbour which bustles with activity. Some very dramatic coastline at nearby Kennedy's Pass. There is a good beach and plenty of the traditional amenities.

Glenluce Dumfries & Galloway   **1** F 9
Wigtown. Pop 700. EC Wed. The 12thC abbey ruins, north of the village, hold much of interest including an almost intact chapter house of 1470. The village itself faces a wide expanse of saltings, mud and shingle. Unfortunately the sands to the west are occupied by a firing range.

Helensburgh Strathclyde   **1** G 3
Dunbarton. Pop 14,000. EC Wed. A superior suburb of Glasgow, it is also a popular holiday town on the edge of Gare Loch. Laid out in the 18thC on a rectangular grid that still survives. John Logie Baird the television pioneer was a native of the town.

Kippford

Kippford Dumfries & Galloway   **1** J 9
Kirkcudbright. Pop 200. Stone houses built on a hillside overlook a pebble beach and Rough-Firth. Although the Solway Firth dries out at low water the harbour is a safe anchorage, which probably accounts for its popularity with smugglers of old. Ten miles along the coast to the east is the village of Kirkbean where John Paul Jones, sea captain and privateer, was born.

Kirkcaldy Fife   **1** L 3
Fife. Pop 51,300. EC Wed. Sprawling industrial seaside town with invigorating mile-long esplanade skirting the Firth of Forth. Birthplace of the famous architect, Robert Adam 1728–92. Of particular interest are a fine group of 17thC merchants' houses in Sailors' Walk, near the harbour. On a dominating site is Ravenscraig Castle, a 15thC fortress complete with massive walls and armed to the teeth with gun loops. It is reputedly the first of Britain's castles built to withstand cannon fire and firearms.

Kirkcudbright Harbour

Kirkcudbright Dumfries & Galloway   **1** J 10
Kirkcudbright. Pop 2,500. EC Thur. A gorgeous 18thC souvenir lying on the River Dee with a picturesque little harbour dominated by McLellan's Castle built in 1582. Visit the Hornel Museum in 18thC Broughton House, home of the artist, the late E. A. Hornel. The town has a flourishing artists' colony. Sandy beaches.

Largs Strathclyde   **1** F 4
Ayr. Pop 9,800. EC Wed. Snack bars in little seaside houses and a large seafront amusement arcade rather spoil this old fashioned Victorian resort. Even so the 2-mile long 'prom' has superb views of Ailsa Craig, and the town itself is hemmed in by green hills. Popular with yachtsmen. Shingle beach, but very safe bathing.

Leven Fife   **1** M 2
Fife. Pop 9,500. A busy sea port up until the 19thC when the harbour was silted up, it thrived first on hand-loom weaving, then coal mining and finally engineering. But more recently the town's popularity as a holiday resort, with its good beaches and golf courses, is such that tourism could soon become the main industry.

Musselburgh Lothian   **1** M 3
Midlothian. Pop 17,000. EC Thur. Sometimes called 'Honest Toun' (whether by its inhabitants or the surrounding villages is not known!). A fishing and manufacturing town at the mouth of the River Esk, famous for its golf course. The 16thC Tolbooth and the bridge, which rests on Roman foundations, are well worth seeing. Above the town, Inveresk has some good Georgian houses. Sand and shingle beach. Sea is polluted and unfit for bathing.

Newburgh Fife   **1** L 1
Fife. Pop 2,100. Mini harbour town spread-eagled along the banks of the Tay. An ancient Royal burgh, its reedy mudbanks are not only a magnificent wild life habitat but also a main source of supply for roof thatching. 18thC Mugdrum House has a fine 13-foot-high Celtic stone pillar.

North Berwick Lothian   **1** N 3
East Lothian. Pop 4,400. EC Thur. The harbour is a delight, and bustles with sailing craft and inshore fishermen's boats. Small shops and restaurants abound in the busy, narrow, sheltered High Street, and behind it all the Napoleonic watchtower on the 613-foot North Berwick Law still maintains a watchful eye. By the tower is an archway formed from the jawbones of a whale. Either side of the harbour are good bathing beaches.

North Berwick, East Lothian

Oban Strathclyde   **1** E 1
Argyll. Pop 6,900. EC Thur. MD Tue. An old fashioned Victorian seaside town, but in the nicest way. The chief glory of the place is in its setting, overlooking the Firth of Lorn. Ferries leave here for Mull and other islands.

'McCaig's Folly', overlooking the town, is an unfinished replica of the Colosseum in Rome built by a banker John Stuart McCaig in 1890 as a memorial to his family. Fine views from Pulpit Hill.
See also the Free Church in Rockfield by Augustus Pugin, and St Columba's Roman Catholic Cathedral by Sir Giles Scott. Shingle and rock shore.

Pittenweem Fife   1 N 2
Fife. Pop 1,500. A painter's paradise of stone built houses brushed in vigorous strokes around a sheltered harbour. Of interest is the 12thC priory; Kellie Lodge, a handsome town house built during the port's 16thC prime; also a group of houses called The Gyles.

Portpatrick Dumfries & Galloway   1 E 9
Wigtown. Pop 1,100. EC Wed. Until about 1860 this used to be one of the main ports for Ireland, but its harbour was too badly exposed to winter gales, and the service was transferred to Stranraer. Set at the foot of low cliffs, terraces of brightly painted cottages make a brave sight from seaward. Attractive sandy bays and good sailing facilities.

Portpatrick

Port William Dumfries & Galloway   1 G 10
Wigtown. Pop 500. EC Wed. A small fishing village built on a sandy coast at the foot of low hills. The tiny harbour dries out at low water. Of interest—the remains of Chapel Finian 5 miles north west, a small chapel or oratory dating from the 10th or 11thC in a contemporary Irish style.

Prestonpans Lothian   1 M 3
East Lothian. Pop 3,500. A struggling industrial community in the shadows of a power station. The town's prosperity dates back to the 12thC, when monks from Newbattle Abbey began to extract salt from seawater, an industry that was continued well into the 19thC. It was here Bonnie Prince Charlie won his resounding victory over the English in 1745. Of particular interest is Prestongrange Mining Museum. This austere stone building houses a heroic symbol of the closed collieries, a giant beam pumping engine. The last of its type in Scotland—it was in operation from 1874 to 1954.

Prestwick Strathclyde   1 G 6
Ayr. Pop 13,400. Where Ayr ends, Prestwick begins. Famous as the Heathrow of Scotland, it is nevertheless one of the more established seaside resorts, with a long promenade-backed sandy beach. There is also a large seawater bathing lake.

Rothesay Strathclyde   1 F 4
Bute. Pop 6,300. EC Wed. Former capital of the Isle of Bute, it is the great Clyde pleasure resort for Glasgow and the surrounding industrial belt. A clothed cap conviviality pervades the mob of buildings which surround the bustling harbour, filled with small boats. Of particular interest is the 13thC curtain wall castle, a magnificent ruin caught amongst streets of terraced cottages. There are many Neolithic and Bronze Age sites including standing stones at St Ninian's Point; some notable Iron Age forts at Castle Cree and Loch Fad. Also worth a visit are the ruins of St Blanes, a 12thC church with handsome Norman arch dividing the nave from the chancel. Sandy beaches stretch out northwards.

St Abb's Borders   1 O 4
Berwick. Pop 200. Lively mix of houses and terraces brushed in workmanlike fashion on the leeward side of a huge rocky headland. Around the fishing harbour is a gawkish row of net houses for the storage of fishing tackle. Of interest nearby is the 19thC lighthouse 400 feet up on the top of St Abb's Head; Fast Castle, the 14thC stronghold, now a wave-battered skeleton on a rocky crag above the sea. It was immortalised as Wolf's Crag in Scott's 'The Bride of Lammermoor'.

St Andrews

St Andrews Fife   1 M 1
Fife. Pop 13,200. EC Thur. Old grey town wrapped comfortably in its 17thC and 18thC gentility, the buildings reflecting the once-prosperous trade between Fife and the Low Countries. Besides being the birthplace of golf (the Royal and Ancient Club was founded in 1754), it is also the seat of Scotland's oldest university, established 1410. The University Library (1612) houses the hall where the Scottish Parliament met in 1645. St Mary's College (1538) is the theological faculty. The cathedral, founded in 1160, was once the largest in Scotland, being a noble 350 feet in length. It was destroyed during the Reformation and is now a pious skeleton. There remains a well-preserved precinct wall with projecting towers and an imposing entrance gateway. St Rule's (1070–93) is a Romanesque church that looks curiously ungainly with its tall square tower. Holy Trinity, the stately town church, was built in 1412.

St Andrews Castle

Other places of interest are: the 13thC castle, a fierce ruin on a rocky plinth beside the sea; the Pends, fine vaulted 14thC gatehouse, one of the principal entrances to the priory precinct; 16thC St Leonard's Chapel; Dean's Court, a town mansion also 16thC. The attractive harbour was rebuilt in the 17thC with stone quarried from the cathedral. There is also a 2-mile stretch of one of the best and safest beaches in Scotland.

St Monance Fife   1 M 2
Fife. Pop 1,300. The epitome of the small Fife seaside town, with colour-washed houses standing shoulder to shoulder, clambering down to a grey stone harbour. Within spitting distance of the sea spray is a handsome church—a robust barn of a building, with a lofty central tower crowned by an octagonal steeple. Built c1362, its origins date back to the 7thC.

Southerness Dumfries & Galloway   1 J 10
Kirkcudbright. A tiny hamlet full of vigorous do-it-yourself charm, pinioned by a disused

lighthouse on a sandy point of land facing out across the Solway Firth. On a fine day, you can see as far as the Lake District. Although the Solway Firth has few safe places to swim, here are safe sandy beaches with few rocks.
lighthouse, Southerness-on-Solway

Stranraer Dumfries & Galloway   **1 F 9**
Wigtown. Pop 9,900. EC Wed. MD Fri.
Scotland's port for Ireland and very busy
too, but in the older part of the town there
is peace in the narrow attractive winding
streets. A market town with a fine 16thC
castle which was doing its job repressing the
peasantry well into the 19thC, though
latterly as the town gaol!
At Coreswall Point there are magnificent
views to Ireland, Arran, and the Mull of
Kintyre. Good sandy bathing beaches near
the harbour.

Tarbert Strathclyde   **1 E 4**
Argyll. Idyllic fishing village washed up
against an encircling wall of steep cliffs,
north of the Kintyre peninsula. Interesting
14thC castle. Good shingle beaches.

Troon Strathclyde   **1 G 6**
Ayr. Pop 11,900. EC Wed. Described as the
St Andrews of the west because of its many
fine golf courses, including the old course
where several 'Opens' have been held. Built
on a nose of land snootily pointing out to
sea, it is a relaxing place hemmed in by
crescents of sandy beach. A busy harbour
runs the length of the promontory.

Whithorn   **1 H 10**
& Isle of Whithorn Dumf. & Gall.
Wigtown. Pop 1,000. Whithorn is another of
the quiet little dignified towns of this area,
with a broad main street. It has secured its
niche in history as the place where
Christianity first came to Scotland. The
12th–15thC priory of St Ninian is
approached through a delightful 17thC
archway or 'pend' which contains a museum
of 5th and 7thC carved stones.

Isle of Whithorn

The Isle of Whithorn, 3 miles south east, is
no longer an island but ruins of a 13thC
chapel mark the spot where St Ninian
landed in AD395. There are also the remains
of an Iron Age fort and a 17thC tower.

Wigtown Dumfries & Galloway   **1 G 9**
Wigtown. Pop 1,100. EC Wed. An elegant
town with a wide main street fringed with
stone houses and a Victorian French Gothic
town hall.
The church dates from 1853, built close to
the ruins of a very much older foundation.
In the churchyard there is a stone
commemorating the Wigtown Martyrs of
1685, two women Covenanters who, for their
beliefs, were tied to stakes in the estuary and
left to drown.

Islands

Arran Strathclyde   **1 E 5**
Bute. Pop 3,600. An attractive and unspoilt
island of nearly 200 square miles in the Firth
of Clyde. Mountainous, particularly in the
north where Goat Fell gives marvellous
views. In the south it is pastoral, with sandy
shores. Coasts of rock and sand. Of interest:
the castle at Brodrick Bay and the scattered
prehistoric standing stones.

Islay Strathclyde   **1 B 4**
Argyll. Pop 3,800. When the Lord made
time, he made plenty of it, and life on Islay
moves at a gentle tempo. The delightfully
named Port Ellen is an attractive little town
with a safe sandy beach at Kilnaughton Bay.
Whisky drinkers will want to make the
pilgrimage to nearby Glen Laphroaig.
In the north steep, thickly wooded slopes
plunge down to the picturesque hamlet of

Port Askaig where the ferries for Jura and
the mainland berth. Kilarrow church at
Bowmore is circular, it is said, so that the
devil would have no corners in which to
hide.

Jura, Colonsay and   **1 C 3**
Oronsay Strathclyde
Argyll. Pop 300. Jura is a lonely, sparsely-
populated island with one road and only one
real village. It is dominated by the Paps of
Jura, three peaks over 2,000 feet high. In the
north the road peters out at Killchianaig, but
the energetic may feel like the 8-mile walk
up the track to the very northern tip where
the whirlpool of Corryvrecken can be seen
and heard.

Keills, Jura

The small islands of Colonsay and Oronsay
lie 8 miles to the west. They are separated
by a narrow strait which can be crossed on
foot at low water. Colonsay House at Kiloran
has sub-tropical gardens; Oronsay has the
remains of a 14thC priory.

Inland towns & villages

Abbey St Bathans Borders   **1 O 4**
Berwick. A pleasant little village in the
Lammermuir Hills, on the Whiteadder
Water. The church incorporates part of an
important 12thC abbey. On Cockburn Law
nearby is Edin's Hall Broch (defensive tower)
one of the very few Iron Age brochs in
lowland Scotland.

Ancrum Borders   **1 N 6**
Roxburgh. Pop 300. Stern-faced village with
green and 16thC market. Stranded beside the
River Ale, it is surrounded by the blood-
stained border country—full of faint echoes
of the warring English and Scottish armies.

Auchtermuchty Fife   **1 L 1**
Fife. Pop 1,500. Market centre for the rich
farming land around. The town's prosperity
was based on the linen factories, distilleries
and saw-mills, many of which have long
since gone. Dotted among the peaceful side-
streets of the old town are many fine
thatched cottages. The 18thC Town House
and Tolbooth are also of interest.

Bannockburn Central   **1 J 3**
Stirling. A small mining village today, but in
1314 it was the site of one of the classic
battles of history. Robert the Bruce with a
lightly equipped army of 5,500 soundly
defeated the forces of King Edward II of
England numbering some 20,000.
The effects of this cunningly conceived and
bravely fought battle were to last for 200
years until the Battle of Flodden in 1513
when the English got their revenge, and
defeated King James IV. A bronze statue of
Bruce marks the battle site.

Bannockburn, Stirling

Barr Strathclyde   1 F 8
Ayr. Pop 200. Virgilian scene belying a
roguish past. This secluded village of whitewashed houses shelters at the foot of green
hills in a dogleg of the River Stinchar. In
bygone days, it straddled a smugglers'
shortcut from the coast to the Stinchar Glens
beyond.

Blantyre Strathclyde   1 J 4
Lanark. Pop 18,000. EC Wed. Model
industrial town founded by David Dale. The
first mill was built in 1785, a second in
1791. David Livingstone, the great
missionary-explorer of Africa, was born here
in 1813 in a cottage in Shuttle Row.
Mementos from his travels and illustrations
of his life's work can still be seen there. The
town also gave its name to Blantyre in
Zimbabwe.

Bowden Borders   1 N 6
Roxburgh. Pop 200. Quiet village nestling at
the foot of the Eilden Hills. Of interest:
16thC Mercat Cross and one of Scotland's
earliest churches. Built 1128, it has a fine
17thC laird's loft and lovely barrel-vaulted
ceiling.

Broughton Borders   1 L 5
Peebles. Pop 1,100. EC Wed. Small
Tweeddale village noted for its colourful
gardens. The restored vault in the ruined
church is thought to be the cell of 7thC St
Llolan. Numerous hill forts on the
surrounding hills.

Castle Douglas, Kirkcudbright

Castle Douglas Dumf. & Gall.   1 J 9
*Kirkcudbright. Pop 3,300. EC Thur. MD
Mon, Tue, Thur.* A modern town regarded as
the commercial capital of Kirkcudbright. It
is, however, a well built place and fortunate
in having Carlingwark Loch and on its
shores a civic park. Set in rich farmland,
Castle Douglas holds weekly cattle markets.
On an island in the River Dee, west of the
town, is the ruined 14thC Threave Castle. It
belonged to the Black Douglases and over
the castle doorway projects the 'gallows
knob' from which the Douglases hanged
their enemies. Replaced in 1640 by Threave
House which has stupendous gardens.

Ceres Fife   1 M 2
Fife. Pop 700. A cottagey place with a
mediaeval hump-backed bridge. The church
above the village contains the fine tombs of
the Earls of Crawford. The fat, happy,
bibulous old gentleman whose image is
carved into a 16thC wall was the last provost
of Ceres in1578.

Clackmannan Central   1 K 3
Clackmannan. Pop 2,500. In the picturesque
square of this ancient county town are the
Tolbooth with its 17thC bell tower, the old
town cross, and the mysterious stone of
Mannan, of unknown antiquity. The old
Clackmannan Tower on King's Seat Hill is
worth a visit.

Coldstream Borders   1 O 5
Berwick. Pop 1,500. A well built small town
in a delightful setting on the Tweed. Once a
refuge for eloping couples. The 5-arched
bridge across the Tweed here was built by
Smeaton, designer of the first successful
Eddystone Lighthouse. Contrary to popular

belief the Coldstream Guards were not raised
here, but this was the place where their
depot was originally set up in 1650.

Cumbernauld Strathclyde   1 J 3
Dunbarton. Pop 38,300. EC Wed. A
completely new town designed and built in
the 1950s to house Glasgow's overspill.
Cumbernauld New Town is an outstanding
example of community architecture. The
buildings are grouped together in a variety of
layouts to form neighbourhoods safely away
from main roads.

Dalkeith Lothian   1 L 4
Midlothian. Pop 9,500. EC Wed. An
industrial and market town whose centre has
been well restored and rebuilt, although the
town was originally granted its charter in
1144. One mile south are the remains of the
12thC Newbattle Abbey, now an educational
college.

Dalmeny Lothian   1 L 3
West Lothian. Pop 500. A delightful
anachronism. It is a village of single storey
housing clustered round a green, that seems
more the epitome of pastoral England than
rural Scotland. Also of interest: picturesque
12thC Norman church.

Denholm Borders   1 N 6
Roxburgh. Pop 600. The unexpectedness of
finding yet another Scottish village with a
spacious green is exhilarating. Once a busy
stocking-weaving centre, 2 mills still survive.

Dollar Central   1 K 2
Clackmannan. Pop 2,300. EC Tue, Thur, Sat.
Sometimes referred to as the 'classic burgh',
it is a small well built town famous for its
academy designed by William Playfair and
founded in 1818.
About a mile to the north is 15thC Castle
Campbell, or Castle Gloom as it used to be
called. It has a wonderful setting over deep
gorges and superb views.

Dumfries Dumfries & Galloway   1 K 8
Dumfries. Pop 29,400. EC Thur. MD Wed.
This grey stone and stucco walled gateway to
Galloway straddles the broad River Nith as
it winds its way through the surrounding
pastoral tranquillity. The river is crossed by
no less than 5 bridges. Old Bridge, built in
1431, is thought to be the second oldest in
Scotland. At one end of the bridge is Old

Bridge House, a 17thC single storey house
with period furnished rooms. The
Midsteeple 1707, an unpretentious building,
is the Tolbooth which was used as a
courthouse and prison until 1867.
Dumfries's most famous resident was Robert
Burns. 18thC Burns House is where the poet
spent the last years of his life until his death
in 1796. It is now a museum with the
interior preserved in period style. Globe Inn,
much frequented by the poet, has the chair
where he often sat. In the churchyard of St
Michael's is the mausoleum where Burns
and his family are buried. Also of interest:
Burgh Museum which is a mid 18thC
windmill and houses amongst other artifacts
an 1836 camera obscura.

Dundonald Strathclyde   1 G 5
Ayr. Pop 2,300. Picturesque village hovering
in the shadows of a large rocky hill, which
stands out like a great boil on the flat coastal
plain. Down one side of the hill are the ruins
of Dundonald Castle, a 13thC fortress, once
the bastion of the Stuarts.

Dunfermline Palace

Dunfermline 1 K 3

Fife. Pop 53,400. EC Wed. MD Sun. Cloaked in a dark grey aura of matter-of-factness, this flourishing textile town was once the capital of Scotland. It is here that 7 kings, 1 empress, a queen, and 4 princes were born—and as many royals are buried. But despite such blue-blooded beginnings, this historic place charmingly shrugs off its Royal connections.

Dunfermline Abbey, one of the first Anglo-Norman establishments in Scotland, was founded in 1070. Robert Bruce was buried here in 1329. The Abbey church, begun in 1150, is now a stunted relic with only its magnificent Romanesque nave surviving. The ponderous cylindrical piers, decorated with chevron moulding, carrying octagonal scalloped capitals reminiscent of the work at Durham Cathedral. The Gothic Revival choir was added in 1817–22. Catholics make an annual pilgrimage to the tomb of St Margaret in the Lady Chapel at the east end of the choir. To the south is the refectory, all that remains of a 13thC monastery.

Fire almost destroyed Dunfermline in 1624 and few other historic buildings have survived. Another fire in 1976 inflicted substantial damage on the town centre and reduced St Paul's Church of Scotland to ashes. Andrew Carnegie, the linen-weaver's son who became America's iron and steel king, was born in Dunfermline in 1835. Today his birthplace in St Margaret Street is a museum. Pittencrief Park, with its beautiful gardens, was given to the town by Carnegie in 1903.

Duns Borders 1 O 4

Berwick. Pop 1,800. EC Wed. Pleasing little Duns is the county and market town. In the burgh chambers is a small museum commemorating the former world racing driver Jim Clark, killed in 1968, who was a native of Duns.

East Kilbride Strathclyde 1 J 4

Lanark. Pop 67,800. EC Wed. Scotland's first New Town, it was founded in 1947 and absorbed an existing village with an 800-year history. Now one of the most successful community developments in Britain, with a sound industrial portfolio, good housing and excellent amenities. Of interest historically is 13thC Mains Castle.

East Linton Lothian 1 N 3

East Lothian. Pop 900. EC Wed. Sprightly village full of old world bonhomie. Built on the banks of the River Tyne, it is a tiny island in the sea of agricultural East Lothian. Of particular interest is the parish kirk, built 1733 and incorporating a 13thC chancel. Nearby is Preston Mill, a mediaeval flour mill. Recently restored, it is the only survivor of a once typical site along the banks of the Tyne and is the oldest working water mill in Scotland. The scene from the 14thC bridge over the river is lovely and was much admired by Scottish artists of the 19thC.

Ecclefechan Dumfries & Galloway 1 L 8

Dumfries. Pop 800. EC Thur. A large quiet village of distinctive character with a burn flowing through its centre. Thomas Carlyle's birthplace, the 'Arched House', is a good example of its period (1790).

Edinburgh Lothian 1 L 3

Midlothian. Pop 453,400. Majestic and striking as befits a first city, Edinburgh stands high on a blanket of hills with sweeping views out to the waters of the Firth of Forth, or across to southern Scotland, and to the Highlands beyond. Its focal point is a huge volcanic rock that sits on the townscape like a giant paperweight. Crowning the precipitous rock like some battered coronet is the castle, an undulating leviathan of stone walls, gables and towers—each century's offerings seemingly glued together inseparably. Around it the city has grown, two towns in one, Old Town and New Town, side by side but discreetly divided by handsome Princes Street. Here is a city to match any Hollywood metaphor; it was described by Robert Louis Stevenson as 'this profusion of eccentricities, this dream of masonry and living rock, not a drop scene in a theatre, but a city in the world of everyday reality'.

A fortress city in AD452, it was occupied first by the Picts, then by the Romans and then, the Angles. The sound, if not the spelling, of Edinburgh probably comes from a 7thC Northumbrian, King Edwin, who rebuilt the castle. In his honour, the town was subsequently named Edwinesburg. By the 11thC the castle was a Royal refuge. Holyrood Abbey was founded in 1128 and in 1329 King Robert the Bruce granted the city a charter. It was from the 1450s that Edinburgh unobtrusively replaced Perth as Scotland's capital. Under James IV (1488–1513), who was an enthusiastic patron of the arts and education, the Royal College of Surgeons was granted a charter and the first printing press, the basis of one of the city's oldest industries, was set up. Scotland's first first post-Reformation university—the University of Edinburgh—was established in 1583 under James VI, son of Mary Queen of Scots. During the 17thC, it was an Edinburgh mob that spearheaded a rebellion which led to Presbyterianism becoming the national religion. The city was occupied by Oliver Cromwell in 1650, but following the Union of Parliaments in 1707, the capital gradually began to flourish once more as a cultural centre.

For the first 300 years of Edinburgh's reign as capital of Scotland, the city only consisted of the Old Town. A mediaeval huddle, Old Town is worn jauntily like a hat, down the side of Castle Rock, its bent-backed houses leap-frogging over each other like some ritualistic reel. The 18thC New Town, disdainfully aloof like some heroic piper, thoughtfully stalks the sloping ground beyond in a slow march of terraced crescents and squares. The New Town belongs to the golden age of Edinburgh when the city became a literary haven for the likes of Dr Johnson, Boswell, Burns, the philosopher David Hume, and others. Of course, Sir Walter Scott is still the city's most celebrated literary offspring.

The 19thC brought the Industrial Revolution: the railway was built beside Castle Rock in 1836, new roads were constructed and towards the end of the century, the expanding industries had made the city prosperous. Although Edinburgh is not primarily an industrial town, its long-standing industries such as brewing,

Old village, Edinburgh

Edinburgh New Town panorama

distilling and printing are very much in evidence today, as are its associations with the worlds of banking and insurance. Electronics and nucleonics are two of the city's more recent industrial enterprises. It was only in the 20thC that the Palace of Holyroodhouse once again became a Royal residence.

Districts

The heart of historic Edinburgh is Old Town, side-stepping eastwards from Castle Rock along the Royal Mile to the Palace of Holyroodhouse. Rich in antiquity and Royal association, this area was until 2 centuries ago all of old Edinburgh. Characteristic are the 'lands' or tenements, sometimes up to 14 storeys high, crowded in a warren of wynds, closes and courts. Well worth a visit are: 17thC Brodie's Close where the town councillor-cum-burglar Deacon Brodie lived—he was Robert Louis Stevenson's model for 'Dr Jekyll and Mr Hyde'; Gladstone's Land, abutting James Court, is a handsome 6-storey tenement built 1620 and now owned by the National Trust for Scotland; Mylne's Court is an interesting 17thC complex that has been converted into student accommodation; White Horse Close, an original 17thC coaching terminus, stands at the bottom of Canongate; Riddle's Court, late 16thC, has fine crowstepped gables and a turreted staircase tower.
Other places of interest: John Knox House 1490 is complete with timbered galleries, and remains one of the most fascinating examples of late mediaeval Edinburgh—John Knox lived here between 1561–72; Huntly House 1517, now a museum of local history; Acheson House 1633, now the Scottish Craft Centre; Outlook Tower, Castlehill, with a Camera obscura. See also the Canongate Tolbooth with its corbelled turrets, spire and bracketed clock, once the civic centre of Canongate when it was a separate burgh from the city. Near St Giles Cathedral are: Mercat Cross—a public gathering place for trade, festivity, Royal proclamations and, sometimes, execution; the Parliament House that was used until 1707; a heart-shaped design embedded in the cobblestones and marking the site of the Old Tolbooth—this spot is known as 'The Heart of Midlothian' and has been immortalised in Sir Walter Scott's novel of the same name.
The Georgian New Town, with its gracious squares and crescents, dates back to 1767 when the city was granted permission to extend its limits. Situated on a flat table-top of land parallel to the Old Town, this wonderfully preserved Georgian development was laid out to the plan of a 23-year-old architect, James Craig. Particularly magnificent is Charlotte Square which was

designed by Robert Adam in 1791. The house at No 7 is open to the public and is fully furnished in the style of the period. It is also the present-day residence of the Moderator of the General Assembly for the Church of Scotland. Opulent St Andrew Square 1769 is, aptly, where many financial institutions have their headquarters. Especially handsome is No 35 with its Ionic portico, bold entablature and crowning attic storey. Register House, designed by Robert Adam 1774–89, stands at the end of Princes Street; Scottish public records dating from the 13thC are kept here. Fine examples of Georgian architecture can also be seen in Moray Place and Ainslie Place.
The grandeur of Edinburgh is gently counterbalanced by the rustic areas which lie within the city boundaries. Hidden in a sharp saddle of land, through which winds the River Leith, is Dean Village. Once the grain milling centre, it is now a picturesque jumble of houses and mills. Cramond Village, a whitewashed hamlet, sits beside a tiny harbour which is usually well sprinkled with yachts and sailing boats. Other villages of interest are: Duddingston, a charming cob-webbed entity on the banks of a loch; and Davidson's Mains village with sharp, no nonsense aura.

Castles & palaces

Dominating Edinburgh is the sprawling castle which crowns the huge rock 443 feet above sea level. In prehistoric times the rock was fortified, but the oldest part of the present castle still in use is St Margaret's Chapel 1076. Nearby is Mons Meg, the 15thC cannon that fired the Royal salute in the past. The Old Palace and Old Parliament Hall are also 15thC, although much of the castle was remodelled in the late middle ages. Just before the drawbridge is the Half-Moon Battery from which the 'one o'clock gun' is fired daily except Sun. The castle is approached by a large sloping parade ground, Castle Esplanade. This is where the Festival military tattoo takes place and where 300 witches were burned at the stake between the 15th and early 18thC.

Edinburgh Castle

At the far end of the Royal Mile is the Palace of Holyroodhouse, set against the backdrop of Arthur's Seat—a volcanic rock that rises some 822 feet up from Holyrood Park. At its summit, there is a superb panoramic view of the city, the rural surroundings, the Pentland Hills and the Firth of Forth. The Palace itself was originally a guest house of the Abbey of Holyrood and was transformed into a Royal residence by James IV in the early 16thC. Here Mary Queen of Scots spent 6 years of her reign, but the present-day Palace was largely rebuilt by Sir William Bruce in the 17thC following its destruction during the Cromwellian occupation. The last Stuart to reside at Holyrood was Bonnie Prince Charlie, who briefly held court there before he was defeated at Culloden. The Palace is now the official Royal residence in Edinburgh of HM The Queen. The ruined Abbey, State and historical apartments are usually only closed to the public during State visits.

St Giles Cathedral, Edinburgh.

Churches

St Giles Cathedral (not strictly speaking a cathedral in the proper sense of the word) is the High Kirk of Edinburgh and thereby of Scotland. Endowed with numerous memorials, it has endured a succession of enthusiastic over-restorations and alterations through the years. Although little remains of the original building, its square central tower c1495 still raises unspoiled the famous Crown of St Giles. At the junction of High Street and the 'Bridges' is Tron Church 1637. It is so named because of the weighing beam, the tron, by which merchants' weights were checked and which traditionally stood outside the church. Also of interest: Canongate Church 1688, with aisled Latin Cross plan and attractive façade; Greyfriars Church 1612 is now a much altered historic site but stands where the National Covenant was signed in 1638.

Streets

Princes Street could be called the handsomest honky-tonk strip in Britain. A spacious street, one mile in length, it is divided from the steep slopes of Castle Rock by a landscaped valley of gardens. It was completed in 1805 as part of Craig's plan for the New Town and today is Edinburgh's most popular shopping thoroughfare. Of its

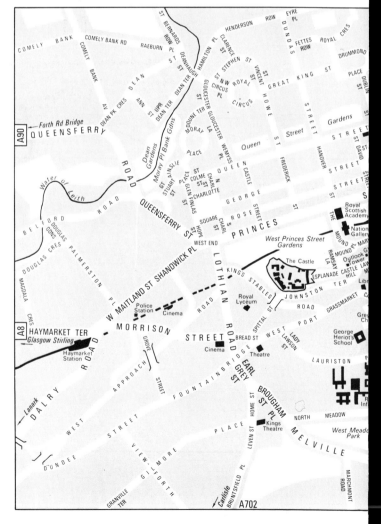

monuments, the most conspicuous is the 200-foot-high Gothic spire and canopied arches of the Scott Monument built 1844. George Street is the most elegant street in New Town, a brilliant piece of perspective planning teminated by Charlotte Square in the west and St Andrew Square in the east. Ann Street, an extension of New Town, is a small scale almost toy town street, built by the Edinburgh painter Raeburn for his wife as a birthday present. The famous Royal Mile is the backbone of Old Town and is made up of the Esplanade, Castle Hill, Lawnmarket, Parliament Square, High Street and Canongate.

charlotte Square, Edinburgh

Interesting buildings
Heriot's Hospital 1628–50 by William Wallace is an ambitious, Renaissance courtyard plan, complete with mediaeval angle towers, crowned by corbelled turrets. St Cecilia's Hall 1761–3 is a handsome elliptically-planned concert room by Robert Milne. It also houses a world-famous collection of harpsichords and clavichords. There are several fine examples of Neo-Classical architecture including the Register House 1774 and the University of Edinburgh 1789–94—both buildings by Robert Adam. The barrel-vaulted Old University Library was built in 1815–28. W. H. Playfair was responsible for the Royal College of Surgeons 1829. Of Victorian Edinburgh typical are: Donaldson's Hospital 1854, again by W. H. Playfair; the Royal

Scottish Museum 1861 by Captain Fowke; North Bridge 1897, a magnificent feat of cast iron construction. Forsyth's Stores 1907 is an austere early 20thC building by J. J. Burnet.

Galleries & museums
The National Gallery of Scotland, Princes Street, has a fine collection of Scottish artists' work, as well as European and English paintings from the Renaissance to Cézanne, including some superb Constables and Rembrandts. The Scottish National Portrait Gallery, Queen Street, has portraits of famous Scots from the mid 16thC to 20thC. The Royal Scottish Museum, Chambers Street, houses the national collections of natural history, decorative arts, archaeology, geology, technology and science. The Museum of Childhood, Hynford's Close, has a fascinating collection of historical toys, books, costumes and dolls. The Edinburgh Wax Museum, 142 High

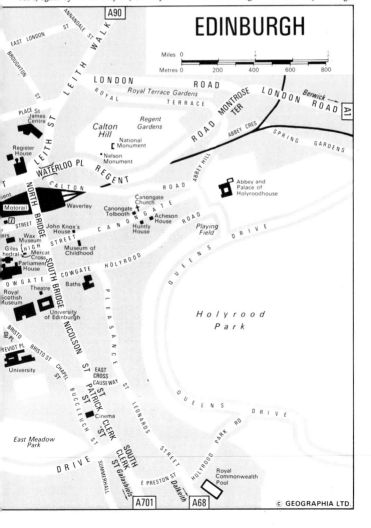

Street, has over 150 wax figures depicting the major characters in Scottish history. Also worth a visit are: the Crown Room in Edinburgh Castle where the most important Scottish regalia are displayed; the Great Hall, also on Castle Rock, houses some interesting weaponry and armour; Canongate Tolbooth, now a city museum containing a collection of Highland dress.

Shopping
The city centre has an impressive range of shops and stores offering everything from traditional Scottish products—whisky, haggis, woollen and tartan goods—to antiques and high fashion. Princes Street, the Royal Mile and George Street are essential stops on the spree circuit. There are pedestrian shopping precincts at Rose Street and St James Centre.

Sport
Angling, bowling, golf, pony-trekking, skiing and yachting are just some of the sports that are well catered for in Edinburgh. On the Pentland Hills, south of the city, is Hillend Ski Centre which is the largest artificial ski slope in Britain. At the Meadowbank Sports Centre, opened in 1970, there are facilities for over 30 sports and temporary membership is available to visitors. Safe beach swimming can be enjoyed round the city's coastline, or indoor swimming at the Royal Commonwealth Pool. Of course, Edinburgh is well known for her golf courses (both public and private), where clubs and balls may be easily and cheaply hired.

Entertainment
Set in parkland of great natural beauty, Edinburgh Zoo, Corstorphine Hill, is world famous for its Antarctic penguins, the largest colony in captivity. There is also an excellent children's farm, as well as a vast collection of birds, reptiles, mammals and fish. The Royal Botanic Garden, Inverleith Road, has a wide range of exotic plants, a superb rock garden, and exhibits from the Scottish National Gallery of Modern Art are also displayed. During the *3rd week of Jun* there is the Royal Highland Show at Ingliston.
Apart from the International Festival, held annually for *3 weeks Aug–Sept*, the city has a vital and varied cultural life. There are 4 fine theatres (King's, Royal Lyceum, Church Hill and Leith); several cinemas catering for both specialist and general contemporary tastes; the Scottish National and Scottish Chamber Orchestras appear often at the Usher Hall (*Sep–Apr*), and the Edinburgh Proms take place *every Jun*.
Light evening entertainment in the form of cabaret, dinner dancing and Scottish spectacles can be found at some of the major hotels, particularly in season. Restaurants are located throughout the city with a reasonable cross-section concentrated between the East and West End of Princes Street through to Queen Street. Pubs are as plentiful as they are popular—there being some 500 in the city, approximately 1 to every 900 in the resident population.

Ednam Borders   1 O 5
Roxburgh. A small village with unusual musical connections. The birthplace (1790) of James Thomson who wrote 'Rule Britannia' and Henry Lyte who wrote 'Abide with Me' and other popular hymns.

Falkirk Central   1 K 4
Stirling. Pop 37,600. EC Wed. MD Tue. An industrial town in sight of the Highlands on the River Carron. To the east and west of the town are sections of the Roman Antonine Wall which once stretched from the Forth to the Clyde. The parish church has a tower (1734) by William Adam, and in the churchyard are monuments to the dead of the two battles of Falkirk, 1298 and 1746. Callendar House south east of the town centre has been evolving for 400 years. In the nearby town on Carron were made the carronades which were the first guns fired by HMS 'Victory' at Trafalgar.

Falkland Palace, Fife

Falkland Fife   1 L 2
Fife. A small town of picturesque old houses and cobbled streets. The 16thC Falkland Palace was a favourite residence of Scottish kings. The Royal Tennis Court, dating from 1539, is the oldest in Scotland.

Fintry Central   1 H 3
Stirling. Pop 2,000. EC Wed. A tiny village on the Endrick Water with the Fintry Hills to the north and the extensive Campsie Fells to the south. 3 miles east, the Loup of Fintry is a fine waterfall.

Galashiels Borders   1 M 5
Selkirk. Pop 12,600. EC Wed. A modern town with a few old gems, notably the Mercat Cross (1695), Old Gala House with 17thC ceiling paintings, and an impressive war memorial comprising a fine statue of a mounted border 'riever' or mosstrooper.

Gifford Lothian   1 N 4
East Lothian. Pop 700. EC Wed. Founded in 1708, it is a model village complete with Mercat Cross, becalmed in a sea of green woodland. The 18thC houses are joined by an avenue of lime trees leading to the entrance gates of Yester House. Begun by James Smith (1699–1729) in a style reminiscent of Hopetoun, the house was radically altered by William Adam in 1745. The church (1708–10) contains a plaque commemorating the birth of the Rev John Witherspoon, a signatory of the American Declaration of Independence.

Glasgow Strathclyde   1 H 4
Lanark. Pop 816,300. Centre of a vast, sprawling industrial complex, the city began life as a makeshift hamlet of huts huddled round a 6thC church, built by St Mungo on the banks of a little salmon river—the Clyde. It was called Gleschow, meaning 'beloved green place' in Celtic. The cathedral was founded in 1136; the university, the second oldest in Scotland, was established in the 15thC; and in 1454 the flourishing mediaeval city wedged between the cathedral and the river was made a Royal burgh. The city's commercial prosperity dates from the 17thC when the lucrative tobacco, sugar and cotton trade with the New World flourished. The River Clyde, Glasgow's gateway to the Americas, was dredged, deepened and widened in the 18thC to make it navigable to the city's heart.
By the 19thC, Glasgow was the greatest shipbuilding centre in the world. From the 1820s onwards, it grew in leaps and bounds westwards along a steep ridge of land running parallel with the river. The hillside became encased in an undulating grid of streets and squares. Gradually the individualism, expressed in one-off set pieces characteristic of the 18thC and early 19thC, gave way to a remarkably coherent series of terraced squares and crescents of epic proportions—making Glasgow one of the finest of Victorian cities. But the price paid

for such rapid industrialisation, the tremendous social problems manifest in the squalor of some of the worst of 19thC slums, was high. Today the city is still the commercial and industrial capital of the West of Scotland. The most notorious of the slums have been cleared but the new buildings lack that sparkling clench-fisted Glaswegian character of the 19thC. Ironically, this character was partially destroyed when the slums were cleared for it wasn't the architecture that had failed, only the bureaucrats, who designated such areas as working class ghettos.

Districts
Little remains of mediaeval Glasgow, which stood on the wedge of land squeezed between the cathedral and the River Clyde. Its business centre was The Cross, a space formed by the junction of several streets—the tall, square Tolbooth Steeple, 1626, in the middle. Opposite is Trongate, an arch astride a footpath, complete with tower and steeple salvaged from 17thC St Mary's Church—destroyed by fire in 1793. The centre of 20thC Glasgow is George Square, a tree-lined piazza planned in 1781 and pinned down by more than a dozen statues including an 80-foot-high Doric column built in 1837 to carry a statue of Sir Walter Scott. Buildings of interest: the monumental neo-Baroque City Chambers 1883–88 which take up the east side and the Merchants' House 1874, on the west. To the south of the square, in a huddle of narrow streets, is the old Merchant City. Of interest here is the elegant Trades House, 85 Glassford Street, built by Robert Adam in 1794. An elegant Ionic portico stands on a rusticated ground storey flanked by domed towers. Hutcheson's Hospital, 158 Ingram Street, is a handsome Italianate building designed by David Hamilton in 1805. Nearby is Stirling's Library, originally an 18thC private residence, it became the Royal Exchange in 1827 when the Corinthian portico was added.

Stirlings Library, Glasgow

To the north west is Kelvingrove, Victorian Glasgow at its best. Built around a steep saddle of land, landscaped by Paxton in 1850 and lined along its edge with handsome terraces.
Last but not least are the banks of the River Clyde. From Clyde Walkway on the north bank you can see: the Suspension Bridge of 1871 with its pylons in the form of triumphal arches; the old clipper ship, C. V. Carrick, a contemporary of the Cutty Sark, moored by Victoria bridge; 17thC Merchants' Steeple; the Gothic Revival St Andrew's R.C. Cathedral of 1816; the church, built 1739, in nearby St Andrew's Square is a typical copy of London's St Martin-in-the-Fields.

Cathedrals & churches
Glasgow Cathedral is a perfect example of pre-Reformation Gothic architecture. Begun in 1238, it has a magnificent choir and handsome nave with shallow projecting transepts. On a windy hill to the east is the Necropolis, a cemetery with a spiky skyline of Victoriana consisting of pillars, temples and obelisks, dominated by an 1825 Doric column carrying the statue of John Knox. Other churches of interest: Lansdowne Church built by J. Honeyman in 1863; St George's Tron Church by William Stark 1807; Caledonian Road Church, a temple and tower atop a storey-high base, designed

George Square, Glasgow

by Alexander Thomson in 1857; a similar design is to be found at the United Presbyterian Church, St Vincent Street, 1858, but on a more highly articulated ground storey; Queen's Cross Church 1897 is an amalgam of Art Nouveau and Gothic Revival by the brilliant Charles Rennie Mackintosh.

Interesting buildings
Victorian Glasgow was extremely eclectic architecturally. Good examples of the Greek Revival style are Royal College of Physicians 1845, by W. H. Playfair and the Custom House 1840, by G. L. Taylor. The Queen's Room 1857, by Charles Wilson, is a handsome temple used now as a Christian Science church. The Gothic style is seen at its most exotic in the Stock Exchange 1877, by J. Burnet. The new Victorian materials and techniques with glass, wrought and cast iron were also ably demonstrated in the buildings of the time. Typical are: Gardener's Stores 1856, by J. Baird; the Buck's Head, Argyle Street, an amalgam of glass and cast iron; and the Egyptian Halls of 1873, in Union Street, which has a masonry framework. Both are by Alexander Thomson. The Templeton Carpet Factory 1889, Glasgow Green, by William Leiper, is a Venetian Gothic building complete with battlemented parapet.
The great genius of Scottish architecture is Charles Rennie Mackintosh whose major buildings are in Glasgow. In the Scotland Street School 1904–6, he punctuated a 3-storey central block with flanking staircase towers in projecting glazed bays. His most famous building—Glasgow School of Art 1897–9—is a magnificent Art Nouveau building of taut stone and glass; the handsome library, with its gabled facade, was added later in 1907–9.

Streets & shopping
The Oxford Street of Glasgow is Sauchiehall (meaning 'willow meadow') Street. This with Buchanan Street and Argyle Street is the main shopping centre. Here you will find the department stores, boutiques and general shops. All three streets are partly pedestrianised, but the most exhilarating is undoubtedly Buchanan Street. Of particular interest is the spatially elegant Argyll Arcade 1828, the Venetian Gothic-style Stock Exchange 1877, and the picturesque Dutch gabled Buchanan Street Bank building 1896. In Glasgow Green is The Barrows, the city's famous street market, formed by the junction of London Road and Kent Street. The market is *open weekends.* Some parts of the city have *EC Tue.*

Buchanan Street, Glasgow

Art Galleries, Glasgow

Galleries & museums

The Art Gallery and Museum, Kelvingrove Park, a palatial sandstone building with glazed central court, has one of the best municipal collections in Britain; superb Flemish, Dutch and French paintings, drawings, prints, also ceramics, silver, costumes and armour, as well as a natural history section. Provand's Lordship c1471, in the High Street, is Glasgow's oldest house and now a museum of 17th-18thC furniture and household articles. Pollok House, a handsome house designed by William Adam in 1752, has paintings by William Blake and a notable collection of Spanish paintings, including works by El Greco. The Museum of Transport, Albert Drive, has a magnificent collection of trams, cars, ship models, bicycles, horse-drawn carriages and 7 steam locos. The People's Palace, Glasgow Green, built 1898 with a huge glazed Winter Garden, has a lively illustrated history of the city. But the oldest museum in Glasgow is the Hunterian Museum, University of Glasgow, Gilmorehill, opened in 1807, it has a fascinating collection of manuscripts, early printed books, as well as some fine archaeological and geological exhibits. 400-year-old Haggs Castle, St Andrew's Drive, is now a children's museum with practical demonstrations and exhibits showing how everyday life has changed over the centuries.

Parks & gardens

There are over 70 public parks within the city. The most famous is Glasgow Green. Abutting the north bank of the River Clyde, it was acquired in 1662. Of interest are the Winter Gardens attached to the People's Palace. Kelvingrove Park is an 85-acre park laid out by Sir Joseph Paxton in 1852. On the south side of the city is the 148-acre Queen's Park, Victoria Road, established 1857–94. Also of interest: Rouken Glen, Thornliebank, with a spectacular waterfall,

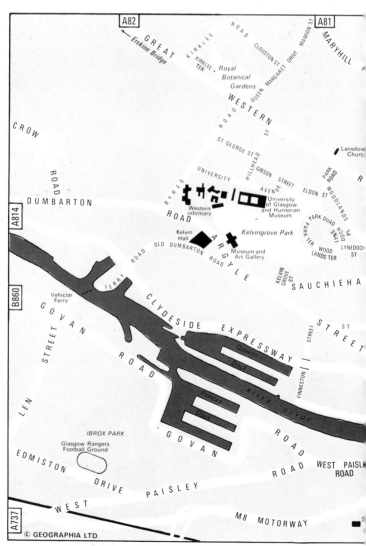

© GEOGRAPHIA LTD.

Kibble Palace / Glasgow

walled garden, nature trail and boating facilities; Victoria Park, Victoria Park Drive, with its famous Fossil Grove flower gardens and yachting pond. In Great Western Road are the Botanic Gardens. Founded in 1817, the gardens' 42 acres are crammed with natural attractions, including the celebrated Kibble Palace glasshouse with its fabulous tree ferns, exotic plants and white marble Victorian statues.

Sport

For both spectator and participant, football is Glasgow's favourite sport. Celtic and Rangers, Scotland's most famous rival teams, have their grounds within the city, at Parkhead and Ibrox Park respectively. Rugby is also popular and there are several clubs with good facilities. Golf, rowing, bowling and yachting are also well catered for.

Usually visitors are welcome at the multi-purpose sports centres, of which there are an increasing number.

Entertainment

As Scotland's commercial and industrial capital, Glasgow offers a good choice of leisure activities. The city now has 6 theatres where productions ranging from serious drama to pantomime, pop and musicals are performed. The Theatre Royal, Hope Street, is Scotland's only opera house and has been completely restored to its full Victorian splendour. The Scottish National Orchestra gives concerts at the City Hall, Candleriggs, every *Sat night in winter*, while the Kelvin Hall is the venue for the proms in *Jun.* Cinemas are still thriving in Glasgow, as are the many public houses, some of which provide meals and live entertainment. In the city centre and Byres Road, West End, there is a fair number of restaurants where traditional home cooking, as well as international cuisines, can be sampled. More night life can be found at the city's discos and dance halls—Tiffany's, Sauchiehall Street and the Plaza, Eglinton Toll. Outdoors, apart from the many parks and nature trails, there is Calderpark Zoological Gardens, situated 6 miles from the centre

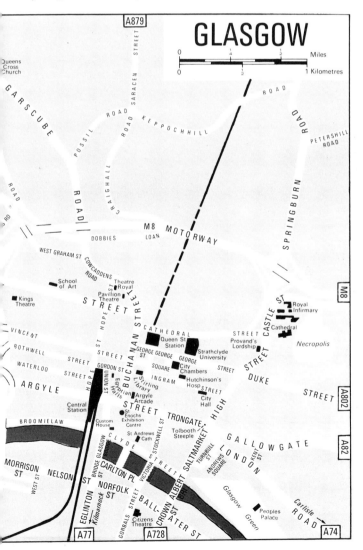

GLASGOW

University of Glasgow

between Mount Vernon and Uddingston. Here you may see white rhinos, black panthers and iguanas among many species. Departing from Stobcross Quay, you can also cruise down the Clyde in 'P.S. Waverley' —the last sea-going paddle-steamer in the world.

Glenrothes Fife   **1** L   2
Fife. Pop 27,300. The second of Scotland's New Towns, it was founded in 1948 to accommodate miners and their families from the depressed Lanarkshire coalfields. There is a multiplicity of architectural styles in the 9 residential sectors. Of particular interest are the strikingly different church designs, reflecting the various religions within the community.

Gordon Borders   **1** N   5
Berwick. Once associated with the 'Gay Gordons' who moved to Aberdeenshire in the 14thC. The nearby turreted Greenknowe Tower dates from 1581 and retains its 'yett' (a sort of iron gateway).

Gretna Dumfries & Galloway   **1** M   9
Dumfries. Pop 1,900. EC Wed. Until 1856 it was possible in Scotland to contract an immediate binding marriage by making a solemn statement before witnesses. Since then the law has been tightened up but it is still possible to get married in Scotland without parental consent. Gretna Green was ideally situated for this 'trade'. The Toll Inn for instance performed no less than 1,300 of these marriages in 6 years, and well over 1,000 were joined in wedlock in front of the anvil in the village smithy.

Haddington Lothian   **1** N   3
East Lothian. Pop 6,500. EC Thur. MD Fri. Caught in a bend of the River Tyne, the heart of this handsome town is a triangle of land punctuated by the high steepled Town House, around which the 3 principal streets pinwheel. One of the most attractive small towns in Scotland, it is a living museum of 17th-19thC architectural history with over 129 listed buildings. The Town House, which was designed by William Adam in 1748, is an urbane stone building articulated with pilasters, pedimented gables and Palladian style windows. The steeple was added in 1830.
Other buildings of interest: 17thC Haddington House; 18thC Kinloch House; sumptuously decorated Carlyle House also of the 18thC; Poldrate Mill, an 18thC 3-storeyed corn mill with an undershot water wheel; Mitchells Close, recently restored, includes 3 craft workshops with forestairs, pantiled roofs and crowstepped gables. The period feel of the place comes across best in some fine grouping of buildings: St Anne's Place, an elegant classical space set off by an 18thC manse; the High Street with its

Haddington Town Hall

market cross; Court Street where smart 18thC town mansions neatly counterbalance the 19thC austerity of the Corn Exchange and County Buildings; St Mary's Church, a barn of a building, constructed in the 14th and 15thC. The River is crossed by 2 16thC bridges, Abbey and Nungate.

Hawick Borders   **1** M   6
Roxburgh. Pop 16,300. EC Tue. Pronounced 'Hoyck'. Hawick knitwear is exported all over the world. This Victorian town has suffered and triumphed through the centuries in bloody tit-for-tat raids with the English. Reputed to have the oldest livestock market in Britain. The Common Riding celebration is held in early *Jun.*

Innerleithen Borders   **1** M   5
Peebles. Pop 2,200. EC Tue. Gentle town, full of quiet pleasantries, built at the junction of Leithen Water with the River Tweed. Originally only a handful of houses, before its fortunes were established with the setting up of the first of many wool mills in 1790. Set amongst rolling hills, the town was catapulted into popularity as a watering place following its depiction in Scott's 'St Ronan's Well' in 1824. Also of interest: Traquair House, the oldest continuously inhabited house in Scotland. St Ronan's Games including the Cleikum Ceremony are held annually in *Jul.*

Inveraray, Argyll

Inveraray Strathclyde   **1** F   2
Argyll. Pop 400. EC Wed (winter). By the harbour at the head of Loch Fyne, a staccato line of whitewalled houses dramatically relieved by a tall dark tower, and laid out like a neat tartan pattern in the flat valley bottom. The old village, burnt by Montrose in 1664, was demolished in 1743 by the Duke of Argyll who had decided to rebuild his castle and to replan the town. Roger Morris, with the assistance of William Adam, drew up the plans. Following their deaths, work was continued by Robert Milne and John Adam. Milne designed the Town House in 1753 and the Palladian church in 1794. The Neo-Gothic castle, a bizarre, but beautiful baronial extravaganza compared with the classical austerity of the town, has a lavishly decorated interior by John Adam. It also contains a collection of paintings, furniture, tapestries and Scottish weapons.

Jedburgh Borders   **1** N   6
Roxburgh. Pop 4,000. EC Thur. An ancient Royal burgh and county town. Mary Queen of Scots' House, a charming example of a 16thC dwelling house, is now a museum. See also the castle, built as a county jail in 1823, which replaces an earlier structure destroyed in 1409 by order of the Scots parliament as the English were getting more use out of it than the Scots! The substantial ruins of Jedburgh Abbey are well worth visiting.

Kelso Borders   1 O 5
Roxburgh. Pop 5,200. EC Wed. MD Fri.
Sparkling country town spreadeagled across a
magnificent setting at the junction of the
rivers Tweed and Teviot. For centuries the
flashpoint in the bloody border wars between
the Scots and English. Its 12thC abbey,
perhaps the greatest in the Borders, was
destroyed by the Earl of Hertford in 1545.
The centre of the town is a spacious cobbled
'grand place' bordered by fine buildings.
The 5-arched bridge built by John Rennie
across the River Tweed in 1803 was a model
for London Bridge. Buildings of interest:
Ednam House, an elegant Georgian mansion
built in 1761 and now a hotel; Cross Keys
Hotel, famous 18thC coaching inn; the
Town House, an 1816 Palladian style
building. A mile NW is Floors Castle.

Kilconquhar Fife   1 M 4
Fife. Tiny village of whitewashed cottages,
with red tiled roofs, wrapped picturesquely
round a crooked street. The church,
complete with 80-foot-high tower, stands
rather aristocratically like a stag at bay on a
convenient patch of ground above the
village. The churchyard slopes down gently
into beautiful Loch Kilconquhar.

Kinross Tayside   1 L 2
Kinross. Pop 3,000. EC Thur. The small
town of Kinross is a popular base for
fishermen on nearby Loch Leven. The
17thC Tolbooth has fine decorations by
Robert Adam, and the town cross still has
attached the old jougs or iron collar for
wrongdoers.

Kirkliston Lothian   1 L 3
West Lothian. Now by-passed by the M9
motorway, peace has returned to this
centuries-old village noted for its 12thC
church. Two miles west are the remains of
Niddry Castle where Mary Queen of Scots
stayed in 1568.

Kirkoswald Strathclyde   1 G 7
Ayr. A small farming village lying some 4
miles west of Maybole. Noted for its Robert
Burns associations through 'Souter Johnnie'
and 'Tam o'Shanter'. Nearby is the great
Robert Adam mansion—Culzean Castle.

Ladykirk Borders   1 O 5
Berwick. Attractive Tweedside village
encircling a stone built kirk, erected in 1500
by James IV in gratitude for having escaped
from drowning in the River Tweed.

Langholm Dumfries & Galloway   1 M 8
Dumfries. Pop 2,300. EC Wed. The chief
town of Eskdale, its good stone houses and
woollen mills sit well by the river.

Lauder Borders   1 N 5
Berwick. Pop 600. Resting quietly along a
bank of the Leader Water, it is a tiny Royal
burgh with curious 17thC Tolbooth—now
the Town Hall, with forestair and cellar gaol
below. The church, a Greek cross in plan
and surmounted by an octagonal steeple, was
designed by Sir William Bruce in 1673. He
also remodelled and extended nearby
Thirlestane Castle, which has a fine
Restoration style drawing room.

Linlithgow Lothian   1 K 3
West Lothian. Pop 5,700. EC Wed. Small and
peaceful town, still a Royal burgh, which lies
in the shadow of the Royal Palace
overlooking Linlithgow Loch. Of interest are
some fine 17thC houses including West Port

Linlithgow Palace

House. The striking church of St Michael,
begun 1242, was largely rebuilt following a
fire in 1424, in an elegant Scottish decorated
style.

Lochmaben Dumfries & Galloway   1 L 8
Dumfries. Pop 1,300. Washed in along the
western ridge, bordering a flat loch-filled
valley, this quiet and still town was once the
stamping ground of the powerful Celtic-
Norman Bruce family. The ruined 14thC
castle was originally an impregnable fortress
covering some 16 acres.

Lockerbie Dumfries & Galloway   1 L 8
Dumfries. Pop 3,000. EC Tue. MD Thur. A
quiet redstone town in Annandale where in
1593 the last great border family feuds ended
in a bloody battle between the Johnstones
and the Maxwells. There were few Maxwells
left.

Maybole Strathclyde   1 G 7
Ayr. Pop 5,100. EC Wed. Once the
stronghold of the Cassillis Kennedys, and
with a history dating back to the foundation
of its first church in 1193, it is still a
growing town, leapfrogging lazily over a
sprawling hill. Of particular interest are the
castle and ancient Tolbooth.

melrose abbey

Melrose Borders   1 N 5
Roxburgh. Pop 2,200. EC Thur. Another
town which grew up beside a 7thC
monastery. The existing monastery ruins
date however mainly from the 15thC,
although there is evidence to suppose Robert
the Bruce's heart is buried in the abbey. The
market cross dates from 1642.
Don't miss Sir Walter Scott's house
'Abbotsford'; Darnick Tower; and 2 miles
west, Dryburgh Abbey where Sir Walter
Scott and Field Marshal Earl Haig are
buried.

Moffat Dumfries & Galloway   1 L 7
Dumfries. Pop 2,000. EC Wed. Handsome
town cradled in a deep saddle of land betwen
rugged mountains. Centre of the
surrounding sheep-farming district, it has a
spacious tree-lined main street. Marking the
centre is the Colvin fountain crowned by a
huge bronze ram. In 1633 its chalybeate
springs were discovered and by the 18thC
the town had developed as a fashionable spa.
Air Chief Marshal Lord Dowding, Fighter
Command chief in World War II, was born
here, and John MacAdam the roadmaker is
buried here. Of interest: Moffat House, now
a hotel, designed by John Adam for the Earl
of Hopetoun in 1762; the Grey Mare's Tail,
a 200-foot waterfall lies to the north east.

Morebattle Borders   1 O 6
Roxburgh. Peaceful huddle of houses, its
back nestling at the edge of the Cheviots, its
front basking on the banks of Kale Water.
Of interest is Corbet Tower, burnt by the
English in 1544 and restored in 19thC.

Moscow Strathclyde   1 H 5
Ayr. The name is authentic and it even sits
on the Volga, a local burn. A small hamlet
some 5 miles north of Galston on the
Glasgow road.

New Abbey Dumfries & Galloway   1 K 9
Kirkcudbright. EC Thur. This village is
overlooked by the red sandstone ruins of the
Cistercian abbey founded in 1273 by
Devorguilla, mother of the King, John
Balliol. When her husband, also John Balliol,
died she kept his embalmed heart in a silver-
and-ivory casket by her side for 21 years
until her death. She and the casket were
buried beside Balliol in front of the abbey
altar. Since then the church has been called
'Sweetheart Abbey'.

Newcastleton Borders   **1** M   8
Roxburgh. Pop 900. Model village planned in grand manner on a flat valley bottom. Consists of a central street with main square and smaller flanking squares. Built beside Liddel Water, it was founded in 1793 by the Duke of Buccleuch as a handloom-weaving village.

New Lanark Strathclyde   **1** K   5
Lanark. Pioneering industrial town founded by the philanthropist David Dale in 1783 when the first cotton spinning mill was built. With rows of terraced tenements grouped around the mill, the town was conceived as a radical experiment in community living. Dale's son-in-law Robert Owen, who began to manage the town from 1800 onwards, has been accorded most of the praise by history for developing this scheme. See also the 90-foot waterfall at Cora Linn.

New Luce Dumfries & Galloway   **1** F   9
Wigtown. Tiny village that nestles serenely in the saddle of land at the junction of two rivers. Five miles south is Glenluce Abbey.

River Cree, Newton Stewart

Newton Stewart Dumf. & Gall.   **1** G   9
Wigtown. Pop 2,000. Handsome market town along the banks of the River Cree and surrounded by a rolling blanket of greenery.

Oldhamstocks Lothian   **1** O   4
East Lothian. A single line of pantiled cottages, wide grass verges and bone white church stare peacefully out across a wooded valley. A touch of melodrama is added by a ruined castle dominating the high ground beyond.

Ormiston Lothian   **1** M   4
East Lothian. Pop 2,000. This attractive model village was the work of John Cockburn, the 18thC agricultural pioneer, who in 1735 planned the village as a combined manufacturing and agricultural centre. As scale was of paramount importance to him, he decreed that houses in the main street should not be less than 2 storeys high.

Paisley Strathclyde   **1** H   4
Renfrew. Pop 95,400. EC Tue. MD Mon. A major thread producing centre for the world, this textile giant began life as a handful of houses thrown with polite disdain around the walls of the 12thC abbey—by the banks of the River White Cart. Destroyed by the English in 1307, it was rebuilt in 1450 to be destroyed yet again, following the Reformation. Of particular interest: the abbey church 12th–15thC; the Thomas Coats Memorial Baptist Church 1894; the shawls and plaids in Paisley Museum; Anchor Mills 1871–83, brick-built industrial shed on a heroic scale.

Peebles Borders   **1** L   5
Peebles. Pop 6,100. EC Wed. MD Fri. Delightful old town sparkling in the pastoral setting along the broad banks of the River Tweed. There is a handsome High Street. This was the birthplace of the Chambers brothers, founders of the famous Scottish publishing firm, and the home of the writer John Buchan. Of interest: the ruins of 13thC Cross Kirk standing on high ground on the right bank of Eddleston Water; the remains of St Andrew's Church, founded 1195; mediaeval Neidpath Castle, 1 mile west of the town; 15thC Tweed Bridge.

Peebles High St

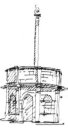

Cross, Preston

Preston Lothian   **1** M   3
East Lothian. Inland, just east of Prestonpans, the village is a haven of handsome gentility. Worth a visit are: Preston Tower, a 15thC fortified house; Northfield House, late 16thC tower house; Hamilton House, a harled courtyard house built 1628; fine 17thC Mercat Cross complete with unicorn, chamber and criers' platform.

Romanno Bridge Borders   **1** L   5
Peebles. A tiny village on the Lyne Water. Three miles south are the ruins of Drochil Castle, left unfinished in 1581 after its owner, Regent Morton, had been executed.

Ruthwell Dumfries & Galloway   **1** L   9
Dumfries. In a specially constructed apse the church holds the beautiful 8thC Ruthwell Cross, one of the most notable carved stone runic crosses in Europe. Dr Henry Duncan, founder of the savings bank movement, was minister here. In a cottage which can still be seen, the first savings bank was opened in 1810.

St Boswells Borders   **1** N   6
Roxburgh. Pop 1,000. Appealing village built along the River Tweed with an attractive tree-lined green. Of interest nearby is Mertoun House, 2 miles north east, and the village church of Bowden built in 1128 by the monks of Kelso, 2 miles west.

Selkirk Borders   **1** M   6
Selkirk. Pop 5,700. EC Thur, Sat. A town which made its contribution to the years of border bloodshed, but now concentrates on its tweedmills on the banks of the River Ettrick.
Sir Walter Scott was Sheriff of the county for 33 years; his statue stands in the triangular market place. Nearby is a statue of Mungo Park, the African explorer born in 1771. Of interest: The 'Common Riding Ceremony'; the Ironmongery and Countryside Museum in 17thC Halliwell's Close.

Skirling Borders   **1** K   5
Peebles. A delightful village with a green. Curious ironwork at Skirling House.

Stenton Lothian   **1** N   3
East Lothian. Pop 100. Blush coloured stone village of age-old pantiled cottages meandering round a village green. Some cottages have external stairs. Of particular interest: 16thC Rood Well housed in a miniature rotunda; an old tower converted into a dovecot; reconstructed here, a weighing beam for measuring bales of wool at the Stenton fairs.

Stirling Central   **1** J   3
Stirling. Pop 29,800. EC Wed. MD Thur. Well-mannered university town busily minding its own business in the shadows of its formidable castle, perched like some prehistoric monster on a skyscraper high rock. Scotland's major stronghold for

Stirling Castle

centuries, Stirling was first occupied by the Romans, then the legendary King Arthur, and from the 12thC the sprawling castle was the favourite residence of the Scottish kings. Stirling Castle, like many Scottish Royal palaces, was largely transformed in the late middle ages, partly by the development of gunpowder but also by the influence of Renaissance architecture. In fact the Royal Palace, built by James V 1538–1542, was one of the earliest attempts to absorb Renaissance ideas. The Great Hall was built in 1503 and the Chapel Royal in 1594. Most of the other buildings were added during the 16th and 17thC. The fine Gothic Church of the Holy Rude (1450–1540) is where Mary Queen of Scots was hurriedly crowned in 1543. The church, which replaced an earlier one destroyed by fire, was originally intended to have a second tower above the cross, but this was never carried out.

Other buildings of interest: Mar's Wark, a handsome Renaissance palace built for the Earl of Mar in 1570; Argyll's Lodging 1632, now a youth hostel, is a typical town house of the period; The Guildhall, also known as Cowane's Hospital, built 1639–49 as an almshouse by John Cowane, a merchant who made a fortune in trade with the Netherlands; the Tolbooth, with its stone tower, characteristic crowstepped gables and fine ashlar façade—formerly the town hall and jail, it was designed by Sir William Bruce in 1702. Nearby is the Mercat Cross flanked by cannon. The town holds a well known spring festival.

Stobo Borders   1 L 5
Peebles. Another pretty village in the Tweed Valley. The tower, nave and chancel of Stobo church are Norman. A barrel-vaulted porch protects a 13thC doorway. Across the river is Dawyck House where Carl von Linne (Linnaeus), the great Swedish naturalist, visited his pupil Sir James Nasmyth, who introduced many species of trees, including the larch, into Scotland.

Stow Borders   1 M 5
Midlothian. Pop 1,400. EC Thur. A charming little village on the Edinburgh-Galashiels road, with a fine packhorse bridge of 1655.

Symington Strathclyde   1 G 5
Ayr. Pop 1,200. A cluster of 2-storey gabled houses standing unselfconsciously on high ground, with magnificent views across Ayrshire and the Firth of Clyde. The village grew up round the 12thC Norman church, remarkable for its particularly fine roof. Also of interest are the ruins of Craigie Castle, a 13thC hall house extended in the 15thC.

Tweedsmuir Borders   1 L 6
Peebles. Picturesque village full of quiet contemplation and set in the pastoral landscape along the banks of the River Tweed. This is the land about which John Buchan wrote, as well as the country of the martyrs of Covenanting days whose graves lie in the churchyard.

Walkerburn Borders   1 M 5
Peebles. Pop 800. Tiny mill village founded by Henry Ballantyne in 1854. Of particular interest is the Scottish Museum of Wool Textiles which illustrates the history of spinning and weaving.

West Linton Borders   1 L 4
Peebles. Pop 700. Rugged Tweedale village straddling the old drovers road across the Pentland hills and once their market centre. Famous for its stone carving tradition. A good example is the 17thC village well.

Regional features

Model fish boats
Many of the more old fashioned fishmongers in this region have model trawlers on display in their shops. A thoughtful reminder of the men who still have to hunt the fish, and the dangers they have to face even in this technological age

Northfield doo'cots Lothian   1 N 3
Preston, East Lothian. Beehive shaped stone doo'cots or dovecots like the one at Northfield House held anything from 600 to 1,000 brace of pigeon, bred all the year round to provide fresh young 'squab' which were a delicacy in mediaeval times when all meat had to be salted to last the winter. There are 62 doo'cots remaining in East Lothian, and many more over the rest of the Lowlands.

Doo'cot, East Lothian

Tower houses
The great symbol of feudal Scotland, it was the simplest and most utilitarian type of fortified domestic dwelling. Built mainly between the 14th and 17thC, the standard plan was a simple rectangle with all the rooms stacked vertically and reached by one or more turnpike stairs. A by-product of politically unstable times, the tower house was the most economical way of providing security with a certain degree of comfort. Its defensive aspects, which were primarily passive, depended on thick walls and barrel-vaulted floors. In some of the earlier examples there was often an open parapet corbelled outwards. Gun loops were introduced later with the development of fire-arms. Wings were sometimes added to the principal block, while others had additional buildings within the barmkin to form a courtyard. By the late 16thC the defensive nature of the tower house gradually gave way to purely domestic requirements.

Famous people

Adam Family   1 L 3
Kirkcaldy, Fife. Famous family of 18thC Scottish architects starting with William Adam (1689–1748), who trained his four sons, John, James, Robert and William. The father, himself trained by Sir William Bruce, was responsible for the completion of Hopetoun House. Of the sons the most illustrious is Robert Adam, who was born at Kirkcaldy in 1728 and died in London in 1792. He and his brother James designed many fine buildings both in England and Scotland, particularly in the Lowlands. They also revolutionised the art of interior decoration at the time. Among Robert Adam's most notable works are Charlotte Square in Edinburgh and Culzean Castle, Ayr.

James Boswell (1740–95)   1 H 6
Auchinleck House, Strathclyde. 3 miles W of Auchinleck. Friend and biographer of Dr Johnson, James Boswell was the son of a Scottish judge, who built the family home here in 1760. Reluctant student of law, Boswell first became friends with Samuel Johnson during a trip to London in 1763. Following extensive travels in Europe when he met Voltaire and Rousseau, Boswell wrote several essays and journals and in between, practised at the bar in Edinburgh. His 'Journal of a Tour of the Hebrides', published in 1785, was based on a tour of Scotland with Johnson in 1773. Boswell's brilliance as a biographer is celebrated in his 'Life of Samuel Johnson', published 1791.

Burns cottage, Alloway

Robert Burns (1759–96)　　　**1 K** 8
*Burns House, Burns St, Dumfries &
Galloway.* Scotland's most famous bard,
author of 'Auld Lang Syne' and many other
verses. Written in dialect, much of his work
is difficult for the Anglo-Saxon to
understand. Many places of pilgrimage have
been preserved, including his birthplace at
Burns Cottage, Alloway, near Ayr, which is
now a museum. The Bachelors Club, a
debating society founded by Burns and his
friends, used to meet in a little 17thC house
at Tarbolton in Ayrshire which is now
maintained by the National Trust for
Scotland. From 1791 until his death Burns
lived in Dumfries, and his house in Burns'
Street is now a museum.

Thomas Carlyle (1795–1881)　　**1 L** 8
*The Arched House, Ecclefechan, Dumfries &
Galloway.* Birthplace of the historian, critic
and essayist. The cottage is maintained as a
museum.

Andrew Carnegie (1835–1919)　　**1 K** 3
Dunfermline, Fife. The great philanthropist
and millionaire industrialist was born here in
a cottage which is preserved as a museum to
him. During his life he donated to the world
nearly 3,000 libraries and gave Dunfermline
Pittencrieff Park.

John Paul Jones (1747–92)　　**1 K** 9
*Arbigland, Dumfries & Galloway. N of
Southerness.* Honoured by the Americans as a
founder of their navy, but regarded nearer
home as a pirate. John Paul Jones, the son of
a gardener, was born here and at one time
imprisoned in the Tolbooth at
Kirkcudbright. Her served first on slavers
and was later commissioned in the navy of
the New World. He is said to have been the
first to hoist the Union flag over a battleship
during the American War of Independence.
After further adventures in European waters,
he became an admiral in Catherine the
Great's Russian navy. He eventually
returned to France where he died. Kirkbean
church has a memorial font presented by the
US Navy in 1945.

John Knox (1505–72)　　　**1 L** 4
*John Knox House, High St, Edinburgh,
Lothian.* A radical Protestant, Knox was the
leader of the Reformation in Scotland and
fanned the movement by his fiery sermons
preached from the pulpit of St Andrews
University chapel. He was educated at
Haddington School, then Glasgow University
and in 1547, he was captured by the French
after the capitulation of St Andrews castle
and spent 19 months in the galleys. In 1558
he wrote his famous tract, 'The Blast of the
Trumpet Against the Monstrous Regiment
of Women'—a work that greatly offended
Elizabeth I of England. The tidal wave of
self-righteousness that he set in motion
encouraged the destruction of the Scottish
monasteries.
His house now contains a Knox museum.

John Knox's House, Edinburgh

David Livingstone (1813–87)　　**1 J** 4
Shuttle Row, Blantyre, Strathclyde. A
museum and national memorial has been
made of the birthplace of the missionary-
explorer of 'Dr Livingstone, I presume'
fame.

Rob Roy MacGregor (1671–1734)　**1 F** 2
Shira, Strathclyde. Hollywood style hero
catapulted amongst the folk lore greats by
the romantic pen of Sir Walter Scott, who
sketched him as a latter day Robin Hood. In
reality he was a free-booting, colourful cattle-
thief. He was present at the battle of
Sheriffmuir (1715), which was the first
attempt by Jacobites to restore the Stuarts to
the Scottish throne. He gave himself up in
1722, was imprisoned in London, then
pardoned 5 years later. For 10 years Rob
Roy lived in a cottage, now roofless, 5 miles
up in the glen of Shira.

Mary Queen of Scots (1542–87)　**1 L** 4
Queen of Scotland at 6 days old, at 16 she
married the Dauphin, at 17 she was Queen
of France and at 18 a widow. Mary returned
to Scotland in 1561 to begin her tragic
tumultuous 6-year reign. Mary is associated
with many places in Scotland, principally
Holyroodhouse. But she was imprisoned
twice in Loch Leven Castle near Kinross;
Falkland Palace was her place of relaxation;
and she spent her honeymoon with the Earl
of Bothwell at Borthwick Castle in
Midlothian. At Craigmillar Castle, 3 miles
south of Edinburgh on the old Dalkeith
Road, stayed many of Mary's French
entourage and the district is still known as
Little France.

Mungo Park (1771–1806)　　　**1 M** 6
Selkirk. The explorer was born near here and
there is a statue to him in the High Street
and a museum with some relics of his
expeditions to the River Niger and to
Sumatra.

Sir Walter Scott (1771–1832)　　**1 N** 5
*Abbotsford House, Borders. 3 miles W of
Melrose.* An ordinary house set in an
extraordinary landscape which helped to
shape much of Anglo-Scottish history. Scott's
genius and romanticism gave him the vision
to set the border story down on paper in his
study at Abbotsford which has been
preserved as he left it. Scott is buried in
Dryburgh Abbey.

Cathedrals, abbeys & churches

Ceres Church Fife　　　　　**1 M** 2
Ceres, Fife. In the late 18thC, oblong hall
churches with handsome galleries for the
excess congregation appeared. Here the
gallery is supported on cool white Grecian
columns above which runs a simple plaster
frieze. The irreverent may be assailed by
doubts that they have really come to the
theatre.

Crossraguel Abbey Strathclyde　　**1 G** 7
Ayr. 2 miles SW of Maybole. Romantic ruins
of a great monastic complex founded in 1244
by the Earl of Carrick for the Clunaic order.
The extensive ruins evoke an idyllic picture
of mediaeval monastic life, enhanced by
16thC turreted gatehouse, dovecot, dignified
chapter house with groin vaulting springing
from a central pillar, and bare bones of a
church with fine late Gothic choir.

Dalmeny Church Lothian　　　**1 L** 3
Dalmeny, nr Edinburgh, West Lothian. One of
the finest specimens of a 12thC Romanesque
church in Britain. The ribbing vaulting is
exceptionally fine.

Dryburgh Abbey Borders　　　**1 N** 6
Berwick. Nestling among trees in a horseshoe
bend of the River Tweed, it is perhaps the
best preserved of the famous group of border

Dryburgh Abbey, Berwick

Kelso Abbey, Roxburgh

monasteries. Founded in 1150, remains include fine chapter house with beautiful articulated entrance portal. The tombs of Sir Walter Scott and Field-Marshal Earl Haig are contained in the north transept of the ruined abbey church.

Dunfermline Abbey Church Fife   **1 L 3**
Dunfermline, Fife. This massive and soulful Norman church is built on the remains of a Benedictine abbey founded by Queen Margaret. Notice the carved columns of the nave with that peculiarly Norman zig-zag pattern and topped off with bold cushion capitals. Before the high altar lies buried Robert the Bruce, his grave being marked by a modern brass.

Dunfermline Abbey

Durisdeer Church Dumf. & Gall.   **1 K 7**
Dumfries. An elegant late 17thC church, built by the Duke of Queensberry and still containing its original box pews. In the north wing is the elaborate, but very beautiful, black and white marble monument to the second Duke and Duchess of Queensberry.

Glenluce Abbey Dumf. & Gall.   **1 F 9**
Glenluce, Wigtown. 2 miles NW of Glenluce. Founded by Roland Earl of Galloway in 1192 for the Cistercian order, its skeletal remains stand on wooded banks of the river. Of particular interest is the magnificent vaulted chapter house c1470, and the remains of an unusual cloister arcade.

Hamilton Parish Church   **1 J 4**
Strathclyde
Lanark. Centrally planned churches, like this one, are rare in Scotland. Designed by William Adam in 1732, it is a cross in formation with one arm given over to portico and vestry, leaving the traditional T-plan for the main body of the church.

Jedburgh Abbey Borders   **1 N 6**
Jedburgh, Roxburgh. Red sandstone shell standing in saintly disdain beside the Jed Water. Founded in 1138 for monks from Beauvais. Transitional in style it stands out from the traditional Norman-Romanesque work by combining pointed arches with round ones, as well as by the overall delicacy of detail and refinement of proportions. Of particular interest are the early 12thC choir arcades.

Jedburgh Abbey

Kelso Abbey Borders   **1 O 5**
Roxburgh. Only the ruins of the west end of this famous border abbey remain. Founded by King David I in 1128 for monks from Picardy, it was destroyed by the English in 1545. Of particular interest is the church which has a Rhenish plan with east and west transepts—unique in a period when the English and Continental cruciform plan with side aisles was more generally adopted.

Leuchars Church Fife   **1 M 1**
Leuchars, Fife. An ungainly agglomeration of boxes, including heavy 17thC tower and belfry. But the original Norman church, the chancel and apse built by Saier de Quincy c1185, is a sculptural delight with rich chevron moulding and fine arcading.

Lyne Church Borders   **1 L 5**
Lyne, Peebles. A small church built in 1645 to meet the simple needs of Reformed worship. Like the new religion it's sturdy and compact without frills. The church contains the original barrel-shaped pulpit and canopied pews which are now rarely seen in buildings of this period.

Melrose Abbey Borders   **1 N 5**
Melrose, Roxburgh. There were buildings here in the distant past, but nothing to compare with the simple delicate grandeur of the 15thC abbey, much of which survives today. The window tracery of the south transept is formed into curvilinear and flamelike forms, and the great east window is of a very high order. One of Scotland's great religious houses: what a pity it was so ravaged in 1544.

St Columba's Parish Church Fife   **1 L 3**
Burntisland, Fife. Built 1592, this was the first church to be built in Scotland after the Reformation. Based on a church in Amsterdam, it is a passionate but discreet amalgam of Dutch Classicism and the proud self-reliance of the Scottish Vernacular. Square in plan, it is crowned by a square drum tower surmounted by an octagonal top. Spacious galleried interior with central floor space.

St Monance Church Fife   **1 N 2**
Between Elie and Crail, Fife. The old kirk of St Monance has been a place of worship for 600 years. It is built so close to the sea that in stormy weather spray is flung right into the church door. Interesting octagonal steeple incorporating belfry windows. The interior is lit by beautiful decorated windows.

St. Monance

Sweetheart Abbey Dumf. & Gall.   **1 K 9**
Kirkcudbright. Typical of the Scottish monasteries that were built to replace the earlier Celtic settlements is Sweetheart Abbey 1273. A Cistercian foundation, it was planned on the European pattern round a church, with living quarters grouped around a cloister. What remains is a roofless skeleton, a gargantuan central tower and well preserved precinct wall.

Torphichen Preceptory

Torpichen Preceptory Lothian   1 K   3
West Lothian. 2¼ miles N of Bathgate.
Wistful sanctuary sheltering in an upland
valley. Founded in 1153 for the Knights
Hospitallers of the Order of St John of
Jerusalem, it became their major Scottish
seat.

Castles & ruins

Caerlaverock Castle Dumf. & Gall.   1 K   9
Dumfries. 7 miles SSE of Dumfries.
Impressive 13thC castle, now a snarling
sandstone ruin built on a curve of land near
the Solway Firth. A great triangle in plan
complete with round corner towers, it is
entered through a monumental double-
towered gatehouse—accessible only from the
north. Inside are 15thC guest houses and
handsome Renaissance buildings c1638. The
castle is surrounded by a moat.

Caerlaverock Castle

Cardoness Castle Dumf. & Gall.   1 H   9
Cardoness, Kirkcudbright. 15thC tower house
standing haughtily atop a rocky hill. Four
storeys high with handsome fireplaces in the
principal rooms. *Closed winter except Sun.*

Castle Sween Strathclyde   1 D   3
Knapdale, Argyll, 8 miles SW of Lochgilphead.
This is the earliest stone castle in Scotland.
The broad flat buttresses and the round
arched entrance are characteristic of Norman
work. There are no windows, and all the
living quarters were built of wood with the
courtyard being partially roofed in.

Cessford Castle Borders   1 O   5
Berwick. 2½ miles S of Morebattle. Ruined
14thC stronghold, once considered the third
strongest fortress in Scotland. It originally
belonged to the Kers, one of the more
formidable of the border mafia.

Crichton Castle Lothian   1 M   4
Crichton, Midlothian. Brooding ruin standing
stubbornly on a bare dumpy hill. The
original was a 14thC standard tower house to
which elaborate additions were made
between the 15th-17thC, transforming the
whole into a handsome quadrangular
mansion. Of particular interest is the arcaded
range, an avant-garde Italianate façade
reminiscent of the Palazzo dei Diamanti,
Ferrera, which was added c1590 by the Earl
of Bothwell following his extensive travels in
Italy. *Closed Fri in winter.*

Dirleton Castle, East Lothian

Dirleton Castle Lothian   1 M   3
Dirleton, East Lothian. This castle of warm
red and grey stone is set on a rock outcrop
overlooking a rich arable plain. It dates
partly from the 13thC but there is a 3-storey
Renaissance portion still standing and
an 11thC dovecot.

Drochil Castle Borders   1 L   5
Peebles. 3 miles NW of Lyne. Intended more
as a palace than a castle, it was begun by
Regent Morton in 1578 but was still
incomplete at the time of his execution in
1581. Of interest for its foreign architectural
influences in a period when most architecture
in Scotland was stubbornly Scottish.

Drumlanrig Castle Dumf. & Gall.   1 K   7
Dumfries. 3¼ miles NNW of Thornhill. A
17thC castle in pink stone with 4 tall corner
towers capped by cupola-topped turrets. The
front façade is an arcaded terrace and is
reached by a Baroque flight of steps. James
Smith designed the castle for the 1st Duke of
Queensberry, who was so horrified by the
cost that he only stayed in it for one day.
Marvellous collection of Louis XIV
furniture, silver, paintings and relics of
Bonnie Prince Charlie. *Closed winter.*

Dunstaffnage Castle Strathclyde   1 E   1
Argyll. 3 miles NNE of Oban. A 13thC castle
of enclosure, but with a few frills in the way
of extra flanking towers. It was burnt down
in 1685, but partially restored and lived in
until 1810 when it was again burnt down.
Once home of the Scottish Kings. It is said
that the Stone of Destiny, or Stone of Scone,
was kept there until removed to Scone.

Floors Castle Borders   1 O   5
Kelso, Roxburgh. Crenellated leviathan with
angle towers, corbelled corner turrets and
domes. It was designed by Sir John
Vanbrugh and William Adam in 1721 and
later re-modelled by W. H. Playfair
(1838–49) in a heavy Tudor-Jacobean style.
Closed winter, Fri & Sat in summer.

Floors Castle, Roxburgh

Hermitage Castle Borders   1 M   7
Roxburgh. Chillingly aggressive castle, ready
to pounce. The bleak exterior is wrapped
round a central courtyard. The upper
openings once gave access to a wooden
gangway that projected out over the enemy.
Two great flying arches connecting the
projecting towers add grimness of scale to
the drama.

Linlithgow Palace Lothian   1 K   3
Linlithgow, West Lothian. Magnificent ruins
of one of the great fortified palaces of
Scotland. Bristling with gun-ports and
corbelled parapets, it stands on a finger of
land poking out into Linlithgow Loch. The
oldest part remaining is an angle tower
added by Edward I in 1302. The palace's
present form and character belong to the

Linlithgow Palace, West Lothian

early 15thC when James I began to enrich and extend the old palace on more spacious and convenient lines. Its heart is a great quadrangle with round towers articulating the angles. The most interesting work belongs to the reign of James V, particularly the 16thC east and south façades of the quadrangle.

Mote of Urr　　　　　　　　**1 K　9**
Kirkcudbright. Circular mound and trench are all that remain of this early 12thC castle.

Neidpath Castle Borders　　　**1 L　5**
Nr Peebles. Set on a bluff overlooking the River Tweed, this castle was once a stronghold of the Frasers, but eventually came into the hands of the Dukes of Queensberry. The walls of the oldest part are 11-foot thick, but even that didn't prevent Cromwell's artillery smashing it into submission during the Civil War.

Neidpath Castle

Peel Tower Borders　　　　　**1 N　4**
Cranshaws, Berwick. 15thC tower house and one of the best examples in the Border Country. Peel, derived from the Latin word 'palus' meaning palisade, was the name given to a tower house in this region. The tower here is depicted in Scott's 'The Bride of Lammermoor.'

Rothesay Castle Strathclyde　　**1 E　4**
Bute. Like clenched teeth and a brutish scowl, this is a magnificent 13thC curtain wall castle with drum towers and circular central courtyard. The entrance is reached through a high tower projecting into the encircling moat. It replaced a circular fortress built in 1098.

Roxburgh Castle Borders　　　**1 O　3**
Roxburgh. 2 miles NE of Roxburgh. The windswept remains stand on a huge mound. This 12thC castle was one of the most formidable in the border lands. At its foot was a walled town. Having changed hands many times, it was finally destroyed by the Scots in 1460.

Tantallon Castle Lothian　　　**1 N　3**
East Lothian. 3 miles E of North Berwick. Perched precariously on the edge of the cliff above the Firth of Forth and opposite the Bass Rock, the ruins of Tantallon are so substantial as to make one believe they have beaten time as well as old foes. The frontal curtain wall and imposing central gatehouse date from the 14thC.

Tantallon Castle

Threave Castle Dumfries & Galloway **1 J　9**
Kirkcudbright. 1½ miles W of Castle Douglas. The 14thC home of the Black Douglases, so called for their merciless pillaging of the countryside. The castle looks hard and pitiless as it rises out of the waters of the River Dee, and in the old days this was enhanced by the Douglas habit of hanging their enemies from a gallows knob over the main entrance. There is now a wildfowl refuge on the estate.

Turnberry Castle Strathclyde　**1 G　7**
Turnberry, Ayr. The remains of this ancient castle, the childhood home of Robert the Bruce, stand behind the duned-back sandy beach on a windswept promontory of land.

Unusual buildings

The Forth Bridges　　　　　**1 L　3**
The great rail bridge built 1893–90 was the wonder of its age. Designed by Sir John Fowler and Sir Benjamin Baker it is of steel construction on the cantilever principle. Over a mile long it cost over £3,000,000, a phenomenal figure at the time.

Forth Rail Bridge

By contrast the Road Suspension Bridge, opened in 1964, seems to soar effortlessly over the water with a spectacular centre span of 3,300 feet. Even so the two bridges provide an effective counterbalance.

Forth Road Bridge

Home Farm Strathclyde　　　**1 G　7**
Culzean Castle, Maybole, Ayr. Magnificent counterbalance to the castle, it is a quadrangle of farm buildings and diagonal entrances articulated by handsome turreted archways. Designed by Robert Adam, the buildings were sensitively rehabilitated and extended in 1974 by the Boys Jarvis Partnership to form the administrative centre of Scotland's first country park.

Andrew Melville Hall Fife　　**1 M　1**
St Andrews University, St Andrews, Fife. Amalgam of Adamesque grandeur with shipyard functionalism. Hostel designed by James Stirling in 1964. Originally planned with 8 long wings climbing down the side of a hill, but only 2 were built, enclosing a garden valley and linked by central communal facilities. A key feature is the encircling glazed promenade deck, as on an ocean liner. Also of note are the faceted façades of the bedroom wings, giving each room sharp views over the surrounding countryside.

Nuffield Transplantation Surgery Unit Lothian　　　**1 L　4**
Edinburgh, Midlothian. The unit is part of the Western General Hospital in Edinburgh. A reinforced concrete structure designed for a specific medical purpose. In meeting its special requirements (filtered ventilation, and windows guarded against direct rays of the sun), a building of impressive architectural merit has been created.
Proof that concrete buildings need not be monolithic slabs. Curved and flat surfaces, light and shade, and a strong outline combine to make this a most satisfying structure.

The Pineapple Central　　　**1 J　3**
Airth, Stirling. Standing in a 14-acre walled garden, here is a delightfully bizarre, 45-foot-high pineapple-shaped garden retreat built in 1761.

Maam Steading Strathclyde　　**1 F　2**
Inveraray, Argyll. Splendid crescent of farm buildings designed in 1790 by Robert Milne for the 5th Duke of Argyll. Originally intended as a huge circular court of buildings, only the north side was completed. Handsome Gothic style barn and cow-byres terminated with castellated walling.

Tithe Barn Borders　　　　　**1 P　4**
Foulders, Berwick. Two-storeyed tithe barn, complete with external stair and crowstepped gables. One of the few examples left in Scotland; tithe barns were used for storing the tithes, a tax paid to the minister.

Union Bridge Borders   **1** P   5
Hutton, Berwick. Built acrtoss the River
Tweed by Captain Sir Samuel Brown in
1821, it was the first suspension bridge of
any note to be constructed in Britain.

The Watchtower Fife   **1** L   2
Kinross. At one end of the spacious Kinross
Park is an old churchyard with a squat
watchtower. It was erected to guard against
the 'Resurrectionists' who illegally exhumed
bodies and sold them for anatomical
research, notably in Edinburgh. There are
several other examples of such care for the
departed 'loved one' dotted round the region.

the watchtower, Kinross

Houses & gardens

Achamore Strathclyde   **1** D   5
Isle of Gigha, Argyll. $\frac{1}{4}$ *mile from Ardminish
by ferry from mainland.* With the climatic
benefit of the Gulf Stream this outstanding
garden, built up by Colonel Sir Brian
Horlick, boasts tender and exotic plants.
Shrubs from the Himalayas, Andes and
Caucasus flourish here. *Closed winter.*

The Binns Lothian   **1** K   3
Nr Linlithgow, West Lothian. The historic
home of the Dalyells, among them General
Tom Dalyell who raised the Royal Scots
Greys there in 1681. Fine plaster ceilings
put in between 1612 and 1630. The front
has a castellated parapet and 2 towers. *Closed
winter.*

Brodick Castle Strathclyde   **1** E   5
Isle of Arran. A large baronial mansion
dating back in parts to the 14thC though the
major part was designed by Gillespie
Graham in 1845. There is a magnificent
collection of treasures including paintings by
Clouet, Watteau, and Turner. Also silver,
china and other objects d'art. Lovely
gardens. *Closed winter.*

Culross Palace Fife   **1** K   3
Culross, Fife. A very fine late 16thC town
mansion built around an open yard for Sir
George Bruce. Many of the panelled rooms
are painted all over with religious scenes.
Attractive gardens. *Closed winter.*

Culross Palace, Fife

Culzean Strathclyde   **1** G   7
Maybole, Ayr. Pronounced 'Culeen'. One of
a series of 'Adam castles' that sprang up in
the late 18thC. Designed by Robert Adam
for the 10th Earl of Cassilis between

Culzean Castle, Ayr

1777–90, it is an eclectic building of
Wagnerian dimensions. Built high above the
sea on ragged cliffs, the crenellated
exuberance of Gothic towers and battlements
is counterbalanced by Georgian elegance. Of
particular interest: the lovely round drawing
room with its own circular carpet; elegant
stucco ceilings; handsome oval staircase. The
gardens and exotic woodlands became
Scotland's first country park.

Dawyck House Borders   **1** L   5
Peebles. SW of Stobo. Garden showpiece of
the Borders. A 19thC castellated mansion
with an impressive collection of trees and
shrubs, including a magnificent avenue of
silver firs, an avenue of limes, lovely
rhododendrons. Also has the first horse-
chestnuts ever planted in Scotland (1650)
and Scotland's first larches (1725). *Closed
winter.*

Falkland Palace Fife   **1** L   2
Falkland, Fife. Owned by HM The Queen,
Falkland was the hunting palace of the
Stuart Kings from the mid 15thC until the
death of King James VI of Scotland (James I
of England) in 1625. The south wing, the
only one in tolerable preservation, presents
an elegant ornamental façade with attractive
mullioned windows. See: the 17thC Flemish
tapestries; the old Royal Tennis Court.
Gardens restored to their original plan.
Closed winter.

Glenarn Strathclyde   **1** G   3
Rhu, Dunbarton. A wonderful springtime
garden with magnolias, daffodils, primulas
and rhododendrons. *Closed winter.*

Hopetoun House, west front

Hopetoun House Lothian   **1** L   3
South Queensferry, West Lothian. Designed
by Sir William Bruce 1699–1703 for the 1st
Earl of Hopetoun, this is probably the most
extravagant and grand of all his houses. It
consists of a centrally planned block with
projecting corner pavilions and storey-high,
convex screen walls that link flanking
ancillary wings. The house was considerably
enlarged by William Adam, who added the
monumental east front between 1721–60.
Elegant furniture and a fine collection of
paintings including works by Reubens,
Titian, Van Dyck, Canaletto and
Gainsborough. The grounds are laid out in
the style of Versailles. *Closed winter.*

Inveraray Castle Strathclyde   **1** F   2
Inveraray, Argyll. Grey, massive and square,
relieved only by a round tower at each
corner. It could be ugly, but somehow Roger
Morris, who designed the house in 1746, just
gets away with it. Inside the great hall,
armoury, state rooms, tapestries and portraits
are very well worth inspection. *Closed winter.*

Inveraray Castle, Argyll

Kellie Castle Fife   **1** N   1
Nr Pittenweem, Fife. It now consists of two
16thC towers united by a 17thC range.
Good plaster work and painted panelling. A
fine example of the domestic architecture of
the lowland counties of Scotland. *Closed
winter.*

Kinross House Tayside   **1** L   5
Loch Leven, Kinross. Dignified country house
by Sir William Bruce. Built 1686–91, it is a

Kinross House

handsome Renaissance palazzo raised above a rusticated ground storey, with a recessed central block entered via a portico. The 17thC gardens have a superb parterre, statuary and topiary. The herbaceous borders are magnificent. *Irregular opening.*

Lauriston Castle Lothian   **1** L   3
Davidson's Mains, Edinburgh, Midlothian.
Built around a turreted and corbelled 16thC tower it is now a country mansion of great charm, standing in grounds overlooking the Firth of Forth. Fine furniture, Flemish tapestries and Blue John ware.

Mellerstain Borders   **1** N   5
Gordon, Berwick. 6 miles NW of Kelso. One of the most attractive mansions in Scotland and another joint effort by the Adam brothers. William built the wings in 1725 and Robert the main block 40 years later. Terraced gardens in Italianate style. The interior decorations and ceiling by Robert are very fine. Beautiful library. Old master paintings and antique furniture on view. *Closed winter.*

Mertoun House Borders   **1** N   6
Roxburgh. 2 miles NE of St Boswells. Fine Renaissance style house with delicately articulated façade. Built by Sir William Bruce 1703–9. Worthwhile collection of pictures.

Palace of Holyroodhouse, Midlothian

Palace of Holyroodhouse Lothian   **1** L   3
Edinburgh, Midlothian. HM The Queen's official residence in Scotland. The palace originated as a guest house of the Abbey of Holyrood, now a picturesque ruin. As seen today the palace is mainly the work of King Charles II who began rebuilding in 1671. The portraits of 111 Scottish Kings were painted in 2 years by a hack artist, one James de Witt, completing in 1684.

Traquair House Borders   **1** M   5
Innerleithen, Peebles. Dating back to the 10thC, Traquair is one of the oldest inhabited homes in Scotland, although most of it was rebuilt in the 17thC. A gaunt grey place with little turrets and small windows. The house contains silver, glass, tapestries and embroideries from the 12thC and relics of Mary Queen of Scots. Beer is brewed to a 200-year-old recipe and sold to visitors. *Closed winter.*

Windy Hill Strathclyde   **1** G   4
Kilmalcolm, Renfrew. Cool, stuccoed and relaxed—an amalgam of Scottish Baronial and traditional Vernacular architectural styles. L-shaped in plan, with a semi-circular staircase tower and projecting polygonal bay. Designed by C. R. Mackintosh 1899–1901. *Private house.*

Traditional dwellings

Clay Houses
During the 18th and 19thC many houses in south west Scotland, especially Dumfries and Galloway, were made of clay. They were usually built in layers on a stone foundation which acted as a damp-proof course. In parts of the Borders region small stones were mixed with clay to form a very hard durable material. A characteristic of the south east during the 19thC was cat and clay work, in which the walls were constructed of bunches of straw mixed with soft clay and packed into a wooden framework of upright and cross spars. Most houses were roofed in pantiles.

Cruck Houses
In the late 18thC many people still lived in cruck-formed turf houses, particularly in parts of Stirlingshire, now Central region. A cruck-frame was a primitive form of timber-framing, employing curved tree-trunks joined at their apex and planned in one or more bays. The external walls were made of turf layers or by carving away the surrounding ground, which left only the solid walls.

Dalriadic Houses
A feature of the Strathclyde region, as well as the islands of Islay and Jura, is a version of the black house known as the Dalriadic type. The black house owes its name to the fact that originally it had no chimney and the smoke from the central peat fire usually blackened the timbers as it percolated out through the roof. Unlike the black houses of Skye and the Hebrides, the Dalriadic has gable ends. However, the thatch, as with the Skye type, is carried over the walls, front and back, to form overhanging eaves.

Dalriadic House

Because the gable walls of the Dalriadic type were the easiest on which to build a fireplace and chimney, it became a prototype for much cottage building throughout the Highlands. An upper storey was often provided by the addition of dormer windows in the roof.

The Longhouse
The typical farmhouse was the longhouse—consisting of living quarters built under the same roof as the stable and byre. It was rare to find a solid cross wall dividing the domestic quarters from the byre. Usually, there was only a light partition of wattle and daub. This consisted of a foundation of timber stakes woven with branches and reeds to form a basket weave, which was then covered with a mixture of clay, dung and horsehair. In the early 19thC both cattle and dwellers entered the house by the same entrance. Later the byre was built as a separate dwelling. Good examples are to be found at Auchindrain, Strathclyde.

Shielings
In many parts of Argyll shepherds continued to build shielings, a hut or roughly constructed cottage, until sheep farming was replaced by cattle farming during the late 18thC. The deserted shieling huts are numerous and widespread in the upland pastures.

Tenements
Dating back to 17thC Stirling are the 4-storey tenement buildings, characterised by tall circular staircase towers projecting into the street. The tenements in Edinburgh and Glasgow are similar but often contain a covered passage on the ground floor serving as a pedestrian thoroughfare.

Museums & galleries

Also see under Edinburgh and Glasgow.

Coldstream Museum Borders   1 O 5
Berwick. Illustrated history of the Coldstream
Guards. Exhibits include uniforms and an
edition of the special 'Coldstream Bible'.
Closed winter.

Commendators House Borders   1 N 5
Melrose, Roxburgh. Commendators were
laymen appointed by the crown in the mid
16thC to take over the duties of abbots. The
15thC building contains many relics from
the monastery.

Fire Engine Museum Lothian   1 L 4
McDonald Rd, Edinburgh, Midlothian. Covers
the history of fire fighting. Edinburgh had
the first municipal brigade in the world.

Gladstone Court Museum   1 K 5
Strathclyde
Biggar, Lanark. Recreation of a 19thC
shopping street, gas works, telephone
exchange and a 17thC farmhouse. Veteran
and vintage car run in *Aug. Closed winter.*

Ironmongery Museum Borders   1 M 6
Selkirk. Treasure trove of ironmongery and
household utensils from 4 generations ago,
housed in a row of late 17thC cottages.

Mary Queen of Scots   1 N 6
House Borders
Jedburgh, Roxburgh. Mary stayed here in
1566. Her bedroom, thimblecase and watch
are among the memorabilia. *Closed winter.*

Prestongrange Mining   1 M 3
Museum Lothian
Prestonpans, East Lothian. Fascinating
mining museum which includes a giant beam
pumping engine, in use from 1874-1954. It
is one of the few remaining working Cornish
beam engines. *Closed weekends except by
arrangement.*

Scottish Fisheries Museum

The Scottish Fisheries Museum   1 N 2
Fife
Anstruther, Fife. Everything to do with
fishing, ancient and modern, including an
aquarium and an old fisherman's house.

Scottish Museum of Wool   1 M 5
Textiles Borders
Walkerburn, Peebles. Illustrated history of
spinning and weaving from the cottage
industry to the present day. From Easter to
October demonstrations of hand carding,
spinning and weaving as done a century ago
are given. *Closed winter.*

Souter Johnnie's Cottage   1 G 7
Strathclyde
Kirkoswald, Ayr. The home of John
Davidson, the prototype of Souter Johnnie in
Burn's 'Tam o'Shanter'. A thatched 18thC
cottage with Burns relics. *Closed winter.*

Tweedale Museum Borders   1 K 5
Peebles. Founded in 1857, the museum was
extended in the early 20thC thanks to
Andrew Carnegie. Interesting insight into
local history. *Closed weekends.*

Weavers Cottage Strathclyde   1 G 4
Kilbarchan, Renfrew. Characteristic handloom
weavers cottage of the 18thC. Restored by
the National Trust. *Irregular opening.*

Botanical gardens

Benmore Younger   1 F 3
Botanic Garden Strathclyde
Argyll, 7 miles NW of Dunoon. A garden
given by the late Sir Harry Younger in
public trust. Some rare and beautiful plants,
shrubs and trees. There is also a good
pinetum and a fine avenue of sequoias.
Closed winter.

Crarae Lodge Strathclyde   1 E 2
Minard, Argyll. 11 miles S of Inveraray. A
33-acre forest garden set in a Highland glen
containing a splendid selection of conifers,
eucalyptus and shrubs.

Royal Botanic Garden Lothian   1 L 4
Inverleith Row, Edinburgh, Midlothian.
Started in 1670, there are some superb
collections, notably hardy plants and shrubs
from western China, rock plants and alpines.
The modern palmhouse with its suspended
glass roof houses some fine tropical and sub-
tropical specimens. There are experimental
gardens, conservatories and a charming
woodland garden. *Closed winter.*

Kilmun Arboretum Strathclyde   1 F 3
Nr Holy Loch, Dunoon, Argyll. Established
by the Forestry Commission in 1930, there is
a large collection of conifers and hardwoods
grouped in specimen plots. Look out for the
fine plantings of eucalyptus. 180 acres with
marked routes and woodland walks.

Logan Botanic Garden   1 F 10
Dumfries & Galloway
Port Logan, Wigtown. A sub-tropical paradise
flourishes here, due to the Gulf Stream and
its sheltered position. Huge cabbage palms
reflect in lily ponds; the stunted shapes of
the Australian tree ferns provide an exotic
background for the rhododendrons for which
Logan is also famous. *Closed winter.*

Threave House Dumfries & Galloway 1 J 9
Castle Douglas, Kirkcudbright. A 1,300 acre
estate used by the National Trust for
Scotland as a gardening school. There are
peat, rock and water gardens including a
wildfowl refuge, and in spring great drifts of
daffodils.

Zoos, aquaria & aviaries

Calderpark Zoo Strathclyde   1 H 4
Uddington, Glasgow, Lanark. Set in parkland,
this zoo includes lions, lemurs, chinchillas
and reptiles in its collection. It has an
aquarium and ample picnic sites.

Edinburgh Zoo Lothian   1 L 4
*Corstorphine Hill, Murrayfield, Edinburgh,
Midlothian.* Set in 80 acres of natural
landscape. Famous for its penguins, it also
has one of the finest collections in Europe of
animals, birds, fish and reptiles.

Nature trails & reserves

Aberlady Bay Lothian   1 M 3
East Lothian. Excellent area for wildfowl and
waders, marine biology and botany. Access
from carpark beside A198 just outside
Aberlady village.

Ae Forest Dumfries & Galloway   1 K 8
Dumfries. Start at Forest Office at Ae village,
2½ miles off Ae Bridge on A701. 3½ mile forest
walk with forest and wildlife interest and
good scenery. Information from the
Conservator, Greystone Park, 55 Moffat Rd,
Dumfries.

Barns Ness Lothian   1 O 3
East Lothian. Off A1 SE of Dunbar.
Geological interest and good for coastal birds
and migrants in season. Marine biology and
botanical interest. Guide from information
centres at North Berwick and Dunbar.

Beecraigs Country Park Lothian   1 K 3
West Lothian. 700-acre country park with
walks and trails within minutes of

Linlithgow. Includes a 20-acre pine-clad loch stocked with brown trout and rainbow trout. Also roe deer, badgers, foxes, magnificent wild flowers and over 70 species of birds recorded.

Enterkine Wood Strathclyde   **1 G   6**
Ayr. Scottish Wildlife Trust reserve at Annbank, entrance from road between B744 and B730. Birds, plants and mammals of mixed woodland and stream. Details from Wildlife Trust, 19 Highfield Ave, Prestwick.

Inverinan Strathclyde   **1 E   1**
Argyll. At Loch Awe off B845. Wildlife of managed forest. Forest Centre. 5 walks of 1¼–5 miles. Booklet from Forestry Commission, 21 India St, Glasgow.

Linn Park Strathclyde   **1 H   4**
Cathcart, nr Rutherglen, Glasgow, Lanark. More than 200 acres of pine and deciduous woodland with many varieties of plants and insects as well as riverside life. Also a collection of British ponies and Highland cattle, a children's zoo and a 14thC castle.

Loch Lomond National Nature   **1 G   3**
Reserve Central
Dunbarton/Stirling. Via A809 from Glasgow, B837 to Drymen and then to Balmaha. Woodland scenery, birds and botany. Archaeological interest. Details from Nature Conservancy Council, 12 Hope Terrace, Edinburgh, Midlothian.

South Bute Strathclyde   **1 E   4**
Bute. Three-hour walk. Seashore and hill. Plants and coastal birds. Guide from Bute Museum, Rothesay.

Birdwatching

Aberlady Bay Lothian   **1 M   3**
East Lothian. Magnificent 1400 acre nature reserve where over 200 species of birds have been observed, as well as being the only spot in Britain where all 5 species of tern nest.

Almondell and Calderwood   **1 L   4**
Country Park Lothian
Mid Calder, Midlothian. Made up of two adjoining estates in the wooded valley of the River Almondell, between Mid Calder and East Calder. The country park, abundant in beech and sycamore trees, has over 80 recorded species of migrant and resident birds including the greater spotted woodpecker and the rare kingfisher.

Arran Strathclyde   **1 E   5**
Magnificent wilderness where as many as 2 or 3 pairs of golden eagles hunt. Bird-watchers paradise. With over 50 miles of coastline you can see herons, mallards, eiders, shellduck, mergansers and gannets. Inland you find buzzards, kestrels, harriers, peregrine, sparrow-hawks and possibly even goshawks.

Ayr and Doonfoot Strathclyde   **1 G   6**
Ayr. The sea front at Ayr south to the mouth of the Doon generally produces good birds of passage and in winter a selection of waders and duck may be found. Fulmars, gannets and kittiwakes are seen offshore in summer, while glaucous gulls are regular in winter, especially in Ayr harbour itself.

Bass Rock Lothian   **1 N   3**
East Lothian. Superb seabird island off North Berwick with a huge gannet colony, shags, fulmars and auks. Local boatmen run regular sailings around the Bass in summer and these give superb views of most of the birds. Details are posted at North Berwick Harbour.

Carsethorne and   **1 K   9**
Southerness Dumfries & Galloway
Kirkcudbright. The Solway Firth is quite superb for its numbers and variety of wildfowl and waders in autumn and winter. Carsethorne, reached via the minor road from A710 at Kirkbean, is particularly good for scaup, pintail and huge knot flocks, while Southerness, also easily accessible from A710, has sea duck and purple sandpipers and often grey geese on the fields inland.

Edinburgh Lothian   **1 L   3**
Midlothian. The birdwatcher visiting Edinburgh will find the Forth coast from Seafield (Leith) east to Portobello and Joppa good for waders and winter sea duck and grebes – the duck often in astonishing numbers (scaup and goldeneye especially). In the city itself, Holyrood Park is well worth a visit and Duddingston Loch has a good selection of birds and an impressive winter flock of porchard.

Islay Strathclyde   **1 B   4**
Argyll. A superb island for birds at any season, with a variety of habitats. Golden eagle, peregrine and hen harrier may well be encountered, while eiders, mergansers and black guillemots are certainties. Choughs are found on the Mull of Oa. In winter, look at Loch Indaal for divers and sea duck and barnacle and grey geese. Leaflet from the Islay Tourist Office at Bowmore.

Kilconquhar Loch and   **1 M   2**
Elie Fife
Fife. Off the A917 N of Elie. Good for assorted wildfowl and famous for its August passage of little gulls. Can be viewed from the footpath beside the church. Elie itself is an excellent spot for winter divers and sea duck, shearwaters and skuas.

Kintyre Strathclyde   **1 D   5**
Argyll. The whole of this long peninsula is splendid birdwatching country at any season. Two particularly good areas are the Mull of Kintyre in summer (easily found via signpost from Southend)—good for hen harrier, golden eagle, peregrine and seabirds—and, in winter, the area around Rhunahaorine Point—Greenland whitefronted and grey lag geese, great northern divers, grebes and sea duck; this second area lies opposite Gigha and alongside A83 to Campbeltown.

Fossil hunting

Visit the local museum. Its fossil collection usually states where individual fossils have been found. When visiting quarries always seek permission to enter if they look privately owned or worked. Be careful of falls of rock.
Lower Palaeozoic rocks, Ordovician and Silurian, with fossils may be seen around Girvan, Ayrshire, where there are corals, brachiopods, trilobites, molluscs and crinoids with graptolites in thin bands. Further east at Moffat, Dumfriesshire, Ordovician and Silurian shales have common graptolites. Graptolites and trilobites may also be collected around Barr, Ayrshire. Devonian rocks around Cupar in Fife have yielded fish-remains as have lower carboniferous cementstones in Berwickshire, together with arthropods (insects, etc), plants and molluscs. Coal measures with plants and molluscs occur in the area of Sanquhar, Canonbie and Thornhill in Dumfriesshire and in the coalfields of the central valley of Scotland.

Hills & mountains

Arthur's Seat Lothian   **1 L   4**
Edinburgh, Midlothian. This 800-foot rounded hill, springing up in the grassy King's Park, is the remains of an old volcano. Columns of hard basalt rock are revealed in its sheer inland cliffs nearby, the Salisbury Crags and Samson's Ribs. A motor-drive climbs its flanks, and the easy walk to its summit cairn gives splendid views over the city.

Ben Lomond Central   **1 G   2**
Stirling. The shapely cone of Ben Lomond, 3,192 feet, and the southernmost Highland

mountain, rises gracefully above Loch Lomond's eastern shore.
Tremendous views, far into the Highlands or east across Scotland to the Forth, reward the climber. Ben Lomond means 'the beacon mountain'.

Campsie Fells Central   **1 H   3**
Stirling. Set centrally in the Lowlands, between Dumbarton on the Clyde and Stirling on the Forth, the Campsies are a grim grey mass of basalt rocks and thin sheep pastures, continually seen but seldom visited. They hold the huge Carron Valley reservoir, surrounded by the sprucewoods of Carron Valley Forest.

The Cobbler Strathclyde   **1 G   2**
Argyll. A quaint mountain this, towering over Arrochar. Its twin summits earn it the Gaelic name of An Goblaich—the 'forked one'. Once English tourists arrived, somebody saw a resemblance to a cobbler bent over his last, and everyone has imagined this ever since. You can climb both forks, but it's risky.

Dunbartonshire   **1 G   2**
Highlands Strathclyde
Little-known, the Dunbartonshire Highlands form a broken range of rounded peaks holding deep glens, between Loch Lomond and Loch Long. North of Tarbet, where there is a narrow lowland gap, they get grimly mountainous.
Between Ben Vane and Ben Vorlich, both craggy 3,000-foot-high peaks, lies grey, cold Loch Sloy, a high level hydro-electric power reservoir that feeds a power-house on the Loch Lomond side.

Eildon Hills Borders   **1 N   6**
Roxburgh. According to legend these shapely hills, soaring above Melrose where the plain of the Tweed first meets the western uplands, were cleft into 3 by a wizard, to settle a dispute with the devil. Geologists, more practically minded, insist that they are relics of 3 extinct volcanoes. Either way, they look miraculous.

Eildon Hills, Roxburgh

Moorfoots and Lammermuirs   1 M   4
This twin hill range runs halfway across Scotland south of Edinburgh, dividing the fertile Lothian lands along the Firth of Forth from the equally rich Tweed Valley country of the Borders.
Vast 1,500-foot-high sheep walks, they give sweeping views from their broad summits, which are crossed by excellent roads. Soutra Hill commands a splendid prospect over the Forth to the Highlands.

Ochil Hills Tayside   **1 K   2**
Stirling to Kinross. Often mistaken for the Highlands themselves, this dramatic range can be seen from everywhere in the central Lowlands. Built up of hard brown basalt rock, they rise sheer from the level Clackmannan plain, for 20 miles east of Stirling, tapering down in height towards Kinross. The highest point is Ben Cleuch, 2,363 feet.

Pentland Hills Lothian   **1 L   4**
Midlothian. Uncrossed by any road, the 1,500-foot-high Pentland range stretches for 20 miles south west of Edinburgh. Its grassy slopes, which serve as sheep pastures and water catchments for reservoirs, are crossed by fascinating hill tracks. At the northern end, close to Edinburgh, there is a popular artificial ski-slope. Highest point, Scald Law near Penicuik, 1,898 feet.

Countryside

Dumfriesshire Dumf. & Gall.   **1 K   8**
The county is made up of 3 broad sunny dales, all facing southwards towards the Solway Firth. Its northern boundaries lie high on the sheepwalks of the rolling Lowther Hills, but the southern lowland is rich farming country, broken by forests and the parklands of great mansions. Nithsdale, on the west, runs down past Drumlanrig Castle, historic seat of the Duke of Buccleuch, to Dumfries, the bustling county town.
Annandale runs south past Lockerbie to the English border at Gretna Green. Eskdale, the narrowest, comes down through Langholm with its lovely riverside woodlands. The highest point is Hart Fell, 2,651 feet, which rises close to the Devil's Beef Tub Pass, so named after cattle-raiders, which lies 6 miles north of Moffat.

Fife Peninsula Fife   **1 L   2**
This hilly peninsula between the Firth of Forth and the Firth of Tay was the historical cradle of the Scottish Kingdom where authority and religion flourished, safe from attack from northern Highlander or southern English invader. Easily reached today by the Forth and Tay road and rail bridges, its landscape bespeaks centuries of care. Every fertile acre is fully tilled, or grazed by thriving cattle, and the lower slopes carry plantations of larch or pine. Scattered at random, small steep basalt hills, relics of old volcanoes, rise to rounded moorland summits, hiding little lochs within their folds. The rock-girt, stormy coast holds a string of tiny fishing harbours such as Crail, Pittenweem and Anstruther. The highest point is West Lomond, a steep bell-shaped hill, 1,712 feet in altitude, south west of Auchtermuchty.

Galloway Dumfries & Galloway   **1 G   8**
South west Scotland's Highland province. Its heart is the lonely 'Range of the Awful Hand', so called from its shape when viewed from the north. Now embodied in the Galloway Forest Park, this is a roadless region of 2,500-foot-high granite hills, broken by peat bogs and studded with clear, cold lochs. Glen Trool, the glen of the 'winding loch', namely Loch Trool, runs far into these hills which have all the wild rocky character of the Highlands. It has a 135,000-acre forest park of wild hills, waterfalls and lochs culminating in the highest mainland peak of southern Scotland—the 2,770-foot-high Merrick, so called from Gaelic *tiu meurig,* the finger or highest knuckle of the 'hand'.

Galloway Highlands

Kintyre Strathclyde   **1 D 5**
Argyll. This 50-mile-long, narrow peninsula, only 8 miles across, runs due south from mainland Argyll to end in a bold bluff called the Mull of Kintyre, only 15 miles from Benmore Head on the coast of Northern Ireland.

Kintyre itself is a pleasing blend of small stock-raising farms, heather moors on low hills, and young spruce forests planted by the Forestry Commission. Its only main road, A83 from Lochgilphead, runs first down lovely Loch Fyne on the eastern shore, to Tarbert, a picturesque fishing harbour. Crossing the narrow isthmus to West Loch Tarbert, with the west coast islands of Islay and Jura in view, there follows 10 miles of open Atlantic coast, pounded by great waves blown in from distant America.

Lanarkshire Strathclyde   **1 K 5**
This fine expanse of the upper dale of the Clyde, 800 feet above sea level, deserves exploration from centres such as Biggar or Lanark. The exposed, conical summit of windy Tinto Hill, 2,335 feet, dominates the scene, with larger ranges of the southern uplands, all grassy sheepwalks, rolling away on every hand. On the level valley floor a pattern of shelterbelts and small woods around mansion houses protects the upland farms from the worst snowy weather.

Lorn Strathclyde   **1 E 1**
Argyll. Lorn is the romantically beautiful hinterland of Oban, between the Firth of Lorn on the western seaboard and Inveraray on Loch Fyne, a parallel arm of the sea. From Oban the winding west coast road follows a succession of sandy bays south between rocky headlands to Lochgilphead. Loch Fyne's coast road, A83, north to Inveraray, runs through forests yet gives grand views across the water. The north westerly return route, back to Oban, runs by the tree-clad shores of Loch Awe, an inland freshwater loch 30 miles long, with the gaunt ruins of Kilchurn Castle at its head. After following the Oban railway through the Pass of Brander, it runs by Loch Etive and the Falls of Lora, where the seawater falls eastward or westward, according to the run of the tides.

The Lothians Lothian   **1 L 4**
The Lothians comprise the southern shores of the Firth of Forth, for 50 miles from Falkirk east to Dunbar. Throughout this good farming country, easily reached by boat before roads were built, great estates developed from the middle ages, and their pattern persists today. West Lothian, centred on the abbey and palace of Linlithgow, has become disfigured by industrial developments, including the red shale heaps which are relics of a defunct oil mining enterprise. Midlothian is nowadays largely hidden by the spread of Edinburgh. East Lothian, centred on Haddington, remains unspoilt, its sunny farms and hills a perpetual delight.

Mull of Galloway Dumf. & Gall.   **1 F 10**
Wigtown. Shaped like a hammerhead, the Mull's peninsula stands out west of the Galloway mainland, coming within 20 miles of Northern Ireland. The Mull itself is a headland of steep cliffs, topped by a lighthouse, and is the most southerly point of all Scotland. Around it sea currents flow ceaselessly—it is the spot 'where 7 tides meet'.

Rivers & lochs

River Clyde   **1 H 4**
The River Clyde, whose course has been the cradle of Scotland's industrial growth, starts as a moorland stream in the grassy Lowther Hills of northern Dumfriesshire, near the A74 Glasgow–Carlisle main road. One tributary runs from Queensberry Hill, 2,285 feet, within sight of the Solway Firth.

Flowing north past Lanark, and the industrial coalfield towns of Hamilton and Motherwell, the growing Clyde winds through the heart of the commercial and manufacturing capital of Glasgow. Here it becomes tidal and navigable, and wharves and shipyards line its banks towards Dumbarton. There it broadens out to become the Firth of Clyde, a broad arm of the sea running first west to Gourock, then south towards the open Atlantic.

Forth Road Bridge

River Forth   **1 J 3**
The great river rises very near Scotland's west coast, in Loch Chon, above Loch Ard. One tributary, the Dubh Water, starts on Ben Lomond, only 4 miles from the western sea. Falling quickly almost to sea level, the Forth wanders east, over a flat peaty wilderness called Flanders Moss, to Stirling. East of Stirling the River Forth broadens out into its long tidal estuary, the Firth of Forth, which carries cargo ships to Grangemouth on the south side, and naval shipping to Rosyth on the north shore. At the Queensferry Narrows, named after a historic ferryboat crossing, it is spanned by 2 bridges, each over a mile long.

Loch Lomond

Loch Lomond Central Strathclyde   **1 G 3**
Stirling & Dunbarton. The largest freshwater lake in Britain. At its southern end, near Dumbarton, the loch is like an inland sea, bordered by level fields and studded by tree-clad islands. In the north its narrow upper reaches are shut in between the 3,000-foot-high peaks of Ben Lomond and Ben Vorlich. Here is a true Highland glen, with torrents, crags and pinewoods. The best beaches are around Rowardennan, and holiday centres are at Balloch, Balmaha, Luss and Tarbet. At its broadest point 5 miles wide and 22 miles long, Loch Lomond is tapped as a water supply. What's left flows down the short River Leven to the Clyde at Dumbarton.

River Tweed   **1 L 6**
Springing from Tweed's Well on Hart Fell, near the Devil's Beef Tub Pass in the heart of the southern uplands, this fine unspoilt river runs north towards Peebles, then east through a steep valley that carries 15 miles of thriving pine, larch, and spruce forests. Near Galashiels the dale of the Tweed

widens; the river flows on past Abbotsford, home of Sir Walter Scott, and Melrose with its romantic ruined abbey. Crossed by bridges at Kelso and Coldstream, where it becomes the English border, the Tweed next glides through a rich agricultural landscape, with tall broadleaved trees, to Berwick-upon-Tweed. Flowing below the high railway viaduct and the old stone arch bridge, it gains the North Sea over a sandy bar at the mouth of Berwick Harbour.

Canals

The Crinan Canal   **1** D 2
Strathclyde
Argyll. This is a short canal, only 8½ miles long, which was constructed to cut off the long journey round the peninsula of the Mull of Kintyre. It passes through a very beautiful landscape of wooded mountains. Things to see: the terminal basins at Ardrishaig and Crinan, and the locks halfway between them.

The Crinan Canal

The Forth and Clyde Canal   **1** J 3
This waterway cuts across the Lowlands of Scotland, from Bowling Basin on the north bank of the Clyde through Glasgow, Kirkintolloch, Kilsyth, Bonnybridge and Falkirk to Grangemouth Docks on the Forth. It is sad and neglected, and some sections have been filled in so through navigation can never be restored. But the canal is excellent for walking along, and it sports one or two elegant and very substantial aqueducts. The waterway is easily accessible by road—and a passenger railway is never far away. The best lengths to explore are the basin at Bowling, the attractive wooded section around Kilsyth, a short tunnel near Bonnybridge and the remains of a flight of locks on the outskirts of Falkirk.

Archaeological sites

Antonine Wall Lothian   **1** K 3
Old Kilpatrick, Dunbarton, to Bridgeness, West Lothian. Shortly after the completion of Hadrian's Wall a change of policy under the Emperor Antoninus Pius led to the reconquest of the Lowlands, and in AD142–43 a new frontier work was constructed between the Clyde and Forth. By about AD180 it was abandoned in favour of Hadrian's Wall.
The Ditch. This ran in front of the Wall, separated from it by a berm 20 feet wide, and measured 40 feet wide and 12 feet deep. Well-preserved sections can be seen at Callendar Park, Watling Lodge, Seabegs Wood, Rough Castle, Croy Hill and Westerwood.
The Wall. Built of turf layers, the Wall probably stood some 9 feet high, with a wooden parapet above. The turf was laid on a stone foundation some 14 feet wide, and this can be seen in New Kilpatrick Cemetery and Roman Park, Bearsden. The Wall itself has not survived well, but a good section is visible at Rough Castle.

Forts. 19 forts and signalling stations are known along the Wall, usually attached to its back, at roughly 2-mile intervals. Three fortlets have been found. Only 1 fort survives well, at Rough Castle; 1 acre in size, it includes a headquarters building, officers' quarters, and has an annexe with a bath-house. The outlines of other forts can be traced at Castlecary, Westerwood, and Bar Hill.
Military Way. A service road running behind the Wall; the Way passed through the Wall forts. The forces building the Wall erected sculptured slabs recording their work, and most of these, with altars, tombstones, and models of the Wall, can be seen in the University of Glasgow Hunterian Museum; a smaller group of finds is housed in the National Museum of Antiquities, Edinburgh.

Ballochroy Strathclyde   **1** D 5
Mull of Kintyre, Argyll. The group of antiquities at Ballochroy probably dates from the Bronze Age, and includes 3 standing stones and a stone burial cist.

Burnswark Dumfries & Galloway   **1** L 8
Birrenswark, Dumfries. The Iron Age hill fort at Burnswark was one of the centres of the Selgovae, and, like the famous site at Masada in Israel, stormed by the Romans from a series of siege camps placed halfway up the hill.
The siege camps are distinguished by the round artillery emplacements on the side facing the fort. The interior of the fort has produced quantities of lead bolts, from when the defences were destroyed and the tumble spread down the hill. Probably the site of the battle of Brunanburgh in AD937.
The nearby fort at Birrens, Blatobulgium, was built as an advance post for Hadrian's Wall, and continued in use as part of the Lowland garrison while the Antonine Wall was occupied.

Cairn Holy Dumfries & Galloway   **1** H 9
Kirkcudbright. A group of Neolithic chambered cairns, with horn-like projections at the ends, which are peculiar to Scotland.

Cairnpapple Lothian   **1** K 8
Bathgate, West Lothian. On Cairnpapple Hill 1,000 feet above the Lowland Plain is a complex of henge, cairns and burials of the Bronze and Iron Ages. Upright stones mark a cairn with a 100-foot diameter.

Dun Mor Vaul Strathclyde   **1** A 7
Isle of Tiree, Argyll. The Iron Age broch is built on the edge of the seashore, and its recent excavation has provided much information about the inhabitants of these defensive towers. It was apparently used only in times of danger, when the local inhabitants sheltered there.
Towards the end of the 2ndC it became the home of the chief local family.

Edin's Hall Broch Borders   **1** O 4
Edin's Hall, Berwick. The defensive towers of Iron Age Scotland are rare in the Lowlands where, as in England, the usual defensive structure was a hill fort. The broch at Edin's Hall was short-lived, and belongs to the period after the first Roman withdrawal from Scotland at the end of the 1stC.

Eildon Hill Borders   **1** N 6
Eildon Hill North, Roxburgh. The large Iron Age hill fort was one of the centres of the Selgovae, an Iron Age tribe of Scotland, and was destroyed by the Romans in AD79. A signal-station was placed on the hill, in connection with the nearby fort of Trimontium (Newstead).

Ruthwell Cross Dumf. & Gall.   **1** L 9
Ruthwell Church, Ruthwell, Dumfries. 9 miles SE of Dumfries. The 18-foot-high runic cross at Ruthwell is one of the finest examples of Anglo-Saxon sculpture, and a major European dark age monument. It was carved towards the end of the 7thC and its good state of preservation suggests that it stood inside a church.

Traprain Law Lothian   1 N   3
Dunpender, East Lothian. The large Iron Age
hill fort at Traprain Law was a major tribal
centre (oppidum) for the Votadini, who
occupied the eastern Lowlands. Excavations
have produced numerous huts, and evidence
for a settled population throughout the
Roman period, suggesting that the Votadini
enjoyed friendly relations with the Romans.
The fort continued in use during the dark
ages, and a fine treasure of silver vessels was
buried here during the early 5thC, probably
raided from Britain or Gaul; it is now in the
National Museum of Antiquities, Edinburgh.

Wemyss Fife   1 M   2
Fife. In addition to carving free-standing
stones, the dark age Picts cut their symbols
and animal representations on the walls of
caves, as here at Wemyss.

Woden Law Hill Fort Borders   1 O   7
Woden Law, Roxburgh. A large Iron Age hill
fort with multiple bank and ditch defences.
Woden Law was a centre for the Selgovae,
and was abandoned after the Roman
conquest. The line of Roman siegeworks on
the hill probably represents training
manoeuvres, as the hill fort was unoccupied
when they were built.

Footpaths & ancient ways

Antonine Wall   1 K   3
Built 20 years after Hadrian's Wall, this
earth wall stretched for 37 miles between the
Firth of Forth and the Firth of Clyde.
(*See also* **Archaeological sites.**)

Dere Street   1 N   6
This great Roman military road was driven
through the Cheviot massif towards a
crossing near the Tweed near Melrose, and
thence through Lauderdale to Inveresk, near
Edinburgh on the Firth of Forth.
The line of this Roman road remains well
defined in certain sections. The Roxburgh
District Council have signposted the section
from the former county boundary to
Bonjedward, and have plans to do more.

Regional sport

Curling   1 L   4
There are rinks at Kelso, Edinburgh
(Haymarket), Falkirk, Glasgow, Kirkcaldy,
Lockerbie, and Stranraer

Fishing   1 K 9
At Glencaple on the River Nith in
Dumfriesshire traditional fishing methods
still live on: local fishermen operate their
stake nets for flounders, and even more of a
Solway speciality, catch salmon by use of a
'haaf' net. The haaf netters stand in a line
chest deep in water, facing the
current, holding a 14-foot spar to which is
attached a net. The bottom of the net is held
up so that it forms a series of open pockets.
When a salmon snags the net the fisherman
throws net and fish over the spar, stuns it
with a mell and deposits it in his creel. A
most profitable sport, but licences are hard
to come by.
Apart from the esoteric this area offers
superb sport. In the rivers Dee and Tweed
and their tributaries on the east coast is
excellent sea fishing, and the largest fresh
water lake in Britain, Loch Lomond, offers
varied sport.

Football   1 H   4
Football in Scotland means Celtic and
Rangers. The teams have dominated Scottish
football for years and are fierce rivals. This
rivalry finds its counterpart in the equally
fierce partisanship of their supporters. Celtic
was formed by Irish Catholics living in the
east end of Glasgow, and religious
differences being what they are, the other

big team in Glasgow, the Rangers, attracted
a large Protestant following.
The result is that when the two teams play
tickets are like gold dust. Celtic play at
Parkhead, and Rangers at Ibrox Park.

Golf   1 M   1
St Andrews, Fife, is famous the world over
as the home of the Royal and Ancient Golf
Club, the ruling body of world golf. The
game and its development is uniquely Scots.
Fife probably has more golf courses per head
of population than any other part of the
world.

Royal and Ancient Golf Club, St Andrews

Golf in Scotland is also cheap. There are
four courses in St Andrews: Old, New, Eden
and Jubilee. Other seaside Fife courses are
Crail, Elie and Earlsferry, Scotscraig at
Tayport, Leven, Kinghorn and Aberdour.
Inland there are excellent courses at
Canmore, Glenrothes, Ladybank, Pitreavie,
and Kirkcaldy and the testing hill courses
like St Michael's and Cupar. There are
hundreds of other first class courses, mainly
south of the Highlands. The Scottish Tourist
Board publishes a brochure detailing over
300 golf courses which welcome visitors (23
Ravelston Terrace, Edinburgh).

Sailing   1 F   5
The Clyde is the Scottish answer to the
Solent. Clyde Week has an international
reputation, and deservedly. If the rather
dodgy Scots west coast weather is taken into
account, this is probably one of the finest
places in the world to sail. Large areas of
semi-sheltered waters, exceptional scenery,
and the close proximity of other oustanding
sailing areas make this the *sans pareil* of
sailing.

Sub aqua   1 O   4
Berwick. Reliable, above average visibility
has made the coast between St Abb's and
Eyemouth in Berwickshire a popular area for
skindivers, and diving clubs. The clear
waters enable wrecks and the Cathedral Rock
to be seen to advantage. At the Scoutscroft
Diving Centre, Coldingham, air is readily
available at 3,500 psi.

Festivals, events & customs

There are a number of local festivals and
events—contact the local Information Centre
for details

'Braw Lads Gathering' Borders   1 M   5
Galashiels, Selkirk. A mounted procession
through the town which takes place every
year. *Jun.*

Common Ridings of the Border country
These annual ceremonies are reminders of
the turbulent past on the Borders and take
place in several towns. At Hawick 'Common
Ridings' have been held for centuries to
commemorate a victory over the English at
nearby Hornsole. At Selkirk 250–300
horsemen take part in a ride which recalls
gallantry at Flodden Field. The riders carry
symbols of the independence of the border
towns.

Edinburgh Festival, 'Beating the Retreat'

Edinburgh Festival Lothian 1 L 4
Edinburgh, Midlothian. Started in 1947, it's a grand festival of film, opera, music, drama, art and military pageant. 'Beating the Retreat' on Castle esplanade, *Wed and Sat evenings. Mid Aug-Sep.*

Handball Game Borders 1 N 6
Jedburgh, Roxburgh. On Shrove Tuesday a handball game is played through the town, a custom dating from the 16thC.

Royal Highland Show Lothian 1 L 3
Ingliston, Midlothian. 1½ *miles S of Kirkliston.* Scotland's national agricultural show with all the popular trappings. *Mid Jun.*

Stirling Festival Central 1 J 3
Stirling. Begun in 1959; Albert Hall is the centre of activity for this festival of concerts and recitals. The concert of popular Scottish music is a main attraction. *Mid May.*

Special attractions

Auchindrain Strathclyde 1 F 2
Argyll. Magnificent open-air museum set up by the Scottish Country Life Museum Trust in 1963, when they restored a deserted 18th and 19thC village. Of particular interest are the longhouses complete with byre, period furnishings and domestic utensils. There is an interpretative centre where various craft skills, including weaving, are demonstrated.

Camera Obscura Lothian 1 L 4
Outlook Tower, Castle Hill, Edinburgh, Midlothian. A Victorian toy for projecting onto a screen in a darkened room a panorama of the countryside surrounding the building in which it is housed.
This fine specimen has been operating since 1892 and is described in a 15-minute tour by a guide. Also houses an exhibition on the old town of Edinburgh. *Closed winter.*

Cruachan Power Station Strathclyde 1 F 1
Nr the Pass of Brander, Argyll. 7 *miles W of Dalmally.* An underground power station which takes water from a reservoir high up the side of Ben Cruachan and turns it into electricity at peak periods, and when the grid is lightly loaded takes water from Loch Awe and returns it to the reservoir.
During the summer the Scottish Hydro Electric Board run a minibus service down to the underground galleries from the car park.

Grants Distillery

Grants Distillery Strathclyde 1 F 7
Girvan, Ayr. This is a far cry from the whitewashed black-roofed little distilleries of the Highlands. Automated and among the most modern distilleries in Europe producing both grain and Lowland malt whisky.

Lochty Private Railway Fife 1 M 3
Fife. 6 miles NW of Anstruther on B940

Cupar—Crail road. On Sundays in summer a steam train with an observation car and a restored LNER streamlined pacific (similar to Mallard which holds the world's speed record for a steam engine) puffs up and down the line between Lochty and Knightsward.

Myreton Motor Museum Lothian 1 M 3
Castle Park, Dunbar, East Lothian. The largest motor museum in Scotland with a constantly changing exhibition including motor cars from 1896, motor cycles and bicycles from 1863, commercial vehicles and a collection of military vehicles.

Prestongrange Mining Museum Lothian 1 M 3
East Lothian. 2½ *miles E of Musselburgh between A1 and A198.* One of the few remaining working Cornish beam engines. This specimen was built in 1874 and ceased pumping in 1955. Collection of other old mining items and a colliery railway.

Preston Mill Lothian 1 N 3
East Linton, E Lothian, 5 miles W of Dunbar off A1. A rather rough building with great charm. This is the only working water mill left on the River Tyne and is the oldest working grain mill in Scotland. Dates from the 18thC.

Scottish Railway Preservation Society Central 1 K 3
Wallace St, Falkirk, Stirling. A collection of locomotives, coaches and waggons dating from 1875 to 1953; other items of railway history. Locomotives are occasionally steamed.

Regional food & drink

Black bun
This Edinburgh bun is a loaf-shaped rich fruit cake encased in pastry.

Butterscotch
A delicious concoction of butter, brown sugar, lemon juice and ground ginger.

Haggis
This traditional Scottish dish arrives at the table to the skirl of bagpipes. Made of sheep's stomach stuffed with oatmeal, suet, liver, hearts, onion and spices. It is served on Burns' Night and sometimes Hogmanay.

Jethart snails
A hard toffee that is a local delicacy in the Jedburgh area.

Kippers
Very fine kippers come from Scotland's east coast, Eyemouth being one of the centres.

Mussel brose
This is traditionally made from mussels which originate from Musselburgh where there is a famous mussel bed at the mouth of the River Esk.

Salmon
This universally favourite fish is at its best in Scotland. The River Tay and the River Tweed are the best known salmon rivers.

Scottish dunlop
This cheese is very similar to cheddar in flavour, but it is moister and eaten whilst young.

Selkirk bannock
This is a yeasted loaf shaped in a round. Very popular in the Lowlands, with local bakeries having their own recipes.

Whisky
There are two distinct types—malt which is made by the traditional pot still method and grain whisky which is made in the coffee still patented in 1831.
Most whisky is a blend of both types and any well known brand will be made up of between 15 and 40 different whiskies.
Malts are classified in four groups: Highland, Lowland, Islay and Campbeltown, all of which are to be found in this region.

Scottish Highlands and Islands

Tayside is a land of famous battles and heroic deeds, where battlemented strongholds stand guard on precipitous cliff-top perches or glare fiercely across a mediaeval nest of pantiled roofs. It is a majestic land washed by the Firth of Tay in the south, and sealed in the north and east by a wall of mountains. It is a region criss-crossed by rivers and streams, and great lochs submerged by scarred and crumpled hills. It has a brave stormy history, the people and the land untamed until long after Culloden. The wooded glens, escape routes of whisky smugglers and honourable heroes alike, rush in twisted torrents of green—from the soaring Grampians in the north to the lush undulating farmland of the Vale of Strathmore in the south. Quiet villages and towns with tiny winding streets make intricate patterns in an expanse of pasture land.

The glens and lochs in the counties of Perth and Kinross in the west are surrounded by a tide of greenery, while Glenshee to the north west is shrouded in misty hills rising steeply to the glacier-seared mountains. Perth was Scotland's capital until the 15thC and in neighbouring Scone, Scottish kings and queens were crowned for over 400 years. This is the land that was fought over by the Picts, as well as being the home of the legendary king, Macbeth. There are beautiful towns like Montrose with its broad main street and Flemish style houses, handsome Kirriemuir the home of the playwright Sir James Barrie, or Brechin, a mediaeval maze of streets stretched taut over a steep hill.

To the north east is Grampian, now an oil rich region, naturally embellished by mountains, green valleys, rivers and streams stocked with trout and salmon. It is bordered by the pastoral landscape of the River Dee in the south, to the east and north by scimitar-shaped bays, steep cliffs and sea, and to the west by a desert of moorland and mountains clawing skyward. The industrial centre is Aberdeen, the 'Granite City' and booming oil capital, situated at the mouth of the Dee. This was the land ruled over by the dreaded Comyns, the Norman earls of Buchan in the 13thC. And it was here that Robert the Bruce struggled to wrest Scotland from the English. There are snug harbours, like Peterhead, hiding behind the breakwaters; Stonehaven, a picturesque town by the mouth of a green valley; Braemar, a Deeside village and home of the Royal Highland Games, dominated by the massive wall of Cairn Toul. To the north west is fertile farmland bordered by a torn and jagged coastline. It is a wild land with Glen Coe, scene of the bloody 1692 massacre, sealed in the mountains, and Loch Linnhe ruled by towering Ben Nevis. This was where the Christian missionaries from Ireland first set foot in the 6thC. It was also the land burnt and pillaged by Viking raiders, warred over by battling clans and finally, the stage for bitter fighting during the Civil War. To the north is the gable end of the Grampians and rugged upland pastures flooded with sheep. But once this was a land populated by small crofting communities.

For centuries up to Culloden, the crofters had been at the beck and call of their clan chiefs at times of bloody struggle. The destruction of the clan system in the years following Culloden created a rift between the laird and the common islesman. Settled within metropolitan life, the lairds, in need of money, began to speculate. They discovered that the hardy sheep of the border country could be kept out all year on the northern hills and because demand for wool was so great and the profits so fat, the lairds began to introduce sheep to the central Highlands and western mainlands. A few of the crofters found employment on the new sheep farms, but the others, whole communities in some instances, were cleared off the land between 1820 and 1840. Many emigrated, but many chose to eke out a living on the wastelands along the coast, their fiery spirit and hardiness ennobling the giant emptiness. Here you will discover daunting scenery, the early morning mists shredded on razor-edged rocks and sharp hills.

To the west into the fury of the sea are some countless islands, rocks, reefs and jagged inlets. Some, like Lismore, are flat and bare like half-submerged barges. But Skye is the most beautiful of them all, a lush land filled with pointed mountains, its coastline painted by silvery sands. There is a feeling here of being on the edge of the world, but it was here that Christian Scotland first began, on pious Iona, a naked windswept island where St Columba landed in AD563 to establish a monastery that was to become the cradle of Christianity in Scotland.

oast

Aberdeen

Aberdeen Grampian   2 0 4

Aberdeen. Pop 200,000. EC Wed. MD Fri.
A slab of granite buildings elbowing each
other in a maze of rib-tight streets spread
round the busy harbour. Known as the
'Granite City', it is a place of many parts: an
oil boom town, the third largest fishing port
in Britain, a major holiday resort with 13
miles of sands and a handsome university
city. Entwined along the banks of the
snaking River Dee as it wriggles its way into
Aberdeen Bay, the city was once 2 separate
burghs, Old Aberdeen (2 miles north of the
city centre), a cathedral and university town
encircled by the River Don—and New
Aberdeen, an equally old fishing settlement
built on a creek of the Dee. Finally, to the
north west is the post-war city—now the
commercial and industrial centre of north
east Scotland and oil capital of the North
Sea. This is a booming, sky-reaching place
that has a gutsy, invigorating feel—an
indestructibility like a rubber ball, not a
beefy heartlessness.
Aberdeen has a history as old as the hills,
often turbulent, and never dull. Cobwebbed
legends, dug out for historians and children
alike, abound here. A township of the
Romans, it was already a thriving fishing
port at the time of the marauding Vikings. It
suffered its share of the agonising religious
and civil strife of Scotland's Middle
Ages,playing host to both heroic and tragic
figures. It was burned by Edward III in
1337, but a newer, more spacious city arose
from the ashes. In the 17thC it was occupied
3 times by Montrose and in 1651 the
Commonwealth military occupation began.
Religious, scholastic and commercial centre,
it was granted its first charter by William the
Lion in 1179 and another by Robert the
Bruce in 1319.

Districts
Old Aberdeen is today's university 'village',
but in the 12thC it was a separate burgh
which grew up around the ancient cathedral
and university. In the High Street is King's
College. Founded in 1494 and named in
honour of King James IV, the complex was
begun in 1500 and enriched and extended
until the 19thC. Of particular interest: the
chapel, with large traceried windows and
fine canopied stalls; Cromwell Tower built
1658 as a student hostel; the Library, a
magnificent Victorian shed with a froth of
fan vaulting built 1870–85. Dominating the
High Street is Old Aberdeen Town House
1788, a dignified Georgian building,
academic and correct, with crowning cupola.
To the north, standing reverently on a high
grassy bastion overlooking Seaton Park, is St
Machar's Cathedral, founded 1136 but
dating mostly from the 14thC. A twin-spired
sandstone fortress, inside it has a beautifully
painted 16thC heraldic
wooden ceiling
patterned with coats of
arms. Opposite, on the
other side of Seaton
Park, is the Brig o'
Balgownie built 1329 to
cross the River Don.
The College Bounds, at
the south end of the
High Street, are some
attractive 18thC
pantiled town houses.
Also of interest are the

Mercat Cross, Aberdeen

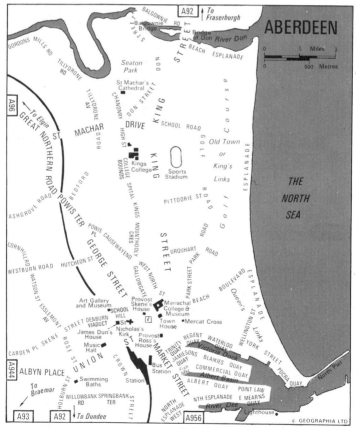

single-storey houses built in 1737 in Grant's Place and the grander 18th and 19thC houses in The Chanonry.

For 600 years the centre of Aberdeen was New Aberdeen, built round the junction of Union Street, King Street, George Street and Market Street. At the head of Union Street is the Town House, an extravagant amalgam of Scottish Baronial and Flemish Gothic styles, built in 1871. The Old Tolbooth, Castlegate, was built in the 17thC with a magnificent lead spire. Nearby is the Mercat Cross a circular arcade crowned by a columned pedestal, built 1686. Marischal College, built in Broad Street in 1593 was King's College's Protestant competitor. The Flemish Gothic frontage was added in 1905. The religious centre here is St Nicholas's Church, a majestic burgh church, founded in the 13thC, split in two at the Reformation and rebuilt as West Church in the 18thC and East Church in the 19thC. The latter contains an interesting 14thC crypt. The old transepts, which divide the two and which contain the largest number of carillon bells of any church, 48 to be exact, belong to neither East nor West Church but to the city. You can also visit some fine domestic buildings such as Provost Ross's House, built 1593 and the second oldest building in the city, and the 16thC Provost Skene's House with a fine painted ceiling of the 17thC. In Union Street, there are some splendid 19thC Regency houses. At the east end of Union Street is the boldly porticoed Music Hall of 1820.

Galleries & museums
The major museum is Aberdeen Art Gallery and adjoining museums, Schoolhill. A 19thC Neo-Classical building, it has a good collection of Old Masters, Impressionists and sculptures, as well as works of the Glasgow School of the 1880s. Nearby is 18thC James Dunn's House which has been carefully and thoughtfully restored as a children's museum. Early manuscripts, seals and charters are on exhibition at the Town House, King's College Library and St Machar's Cathedral. The Gordon Highlanders' Museum has colours, banners, uniforms and weapons of the famous regiment raised in 1794 by the Duke of Gordon. The University of Aberdeen Anthropological Museum has a fine collection, accumulated since the 1830s, of Egyptian antiquities, Roman glassware, Asiatic relics, boomerangs and blow-pipes, and shrunken heads of the Jivaro Indians, amongst other rare items.

Festivals
The International Festival of Youth Orchestras and Performing Arts, a fortnight of music and song, takes place in *Aug.* Highland games, Highland and country dancing, and pipe music are featured in the Aberdeen Festival, spread over 9 days every *Jun.*

Arbroath Tayside   2 N 8
Angus. Pop 22,600. EC Wed. Gaily coloured fishing boats crowd the harbour, landing the haddock which is turned into the local delicacy, Arbroath Smokies. Inland is a bustling pleasant work-a-day town with some fine old buildings. On the north side of the town is the restored and enlarged Hospitalfield and, more historically significant, the remains of Arbroath Abbey. The Declaration of Arbroath was signed in 1320 in the abbey and was Scotland's formal statement of independence after Robert the

Arbroath Abbey

Bruce's victory at Bannockburn. The large circular window in the abbey's south transept used to be illuminated as a guide to ships at sea. There are sandy beaches to the east and west of the harbour with good bathing.

Arisaig Highland   2 C 5
Inverness. Pop 700. On the road to the Isles where it first meets the open sea, this village provides exceptional views of the Inner Hebrides. When the weather is right the islands of Rhum and Eigg seem to float on the seas like gigantic prehistoric monsters. Sandy beach.

Auchmithie village

Auchmithie Tayside   2 N 8
Angus. Sharp line of gabled cottages with the village street seemingly plunging into the bottomless sea. Squatting on a 150-foot-high cliff top, with a steep track galloping down to the harbour. Boats can be hired here to visit the many caves in the neighbourhood connected with 18thC smugglers. Rock and shingle beach.

Balmedie Grampian   2 O 4
Aberdeen. A lane from dune-backed sandy beaches leads to a rambling hamlet hidden amongst trees.

Banff Grampian   2 N 1
Banff. Pop 3,700. EC Wed. An ancient Royal burgh and port standing on the mouth of the River Deveron, and linked to the town of Macduff on the opposite bank by a handsome 7-arched bridge designed by Smeaton. Banff still retains some attractive 17th and 18thC burghers' houses around High Shore; the old cemetery is reputed to be the resting place of some 40,000 old Banffers.

Banff

One famous old Banffer who does not lie there is James Macpherson who, on route to the gallows in 1701, now marked by the Biggar Fountain in Low Street, insisted on playing defiant music all the way on his fiddle. Of interest: Mercat Cross and the Town House with its 17thC steeple; Duff House, a fine 18thC mansion designed by William Adam. Beach—sand and shingle.

Broughty Ferry Tayside   2 M 8
Angus. Pop 12,500. EC Wed. Dundee's seaside, and once a ferry terminal for the Tay road ferries which were replaced by the new Tay Bridge in 1966. The whaling museum, in the old Broughty Castle, is well worth a visit. A fine sandy beach. Bathing is safe close inshore, but avoid the mouth of Dighty Water.

Buckie Grampian   2 M 1
Banff. Pop 7,900. EC Wed. The largest town in Banffshire and the busiest fishing port on the Moray Firth. Buckie, through no fault of its own, has developed into a long straggling town, as Buckpool, Gordonsburgh, Ianstown, Portessie and Strathlene spread into each other.

This Tayside town on the cliffs above the port is dominated by the twin spires of St Peter's Roman Catholic Church (1857). Almost a cathedral, it is a reminder that Banffshire remained a stronghold of popery despite John Knox and the Reformation. Rock, shingle and sandy beach.

Burghead Grampian   2 K 1
Moray. Pop 1,300. Bustling 19thC harbour port embracing a finger of land at the tip of the Moray Firth. Of interest are remains of Pictish fort and the annual Burning of the Clavie, *each Jan evening of the 11th.*

Carnoustie Tayside   2 M 8
Angus. Pop 7,400. EC Tue. Two golf courses, the Championship, considered to be one of the best in the world, and the Burnside. Lovely golden sands which at low tide contain gorgeous warm pools and a children's playground near the beach.

Catterline Grampian   2 O 6
Kincardine. The scenery here is as taut as a bow string, a delicate balance straight out of some fine painting—naked sea, curved bay, great wall of cliff and perched on top, a stern faced fishing village jammed firmly in place by a great expanse of sky.

Collieston Grampian   2 P 3
Aberdeen. Pop 100. Grey stone harbour village, with a swashbuckling air, that hogs the grassy slopes above a sandy cove.

Cove Bay Grampian   2 O 5
Kincardine. Pop 800. Rambling nest of buildings wrapped round a harbour in the sharp shadows of a cliff.

Cruden Bay Grampian   2 P 3
Aberdeen. Pop 2,000. EC Thur. Good swimming, good golf, and the dramatic ruins of Slains Castle make this a satisfying all round place. A couple of miles to the north is Bullers of Buchan, a spectacular amphitheatre 200 feet deep and 50 feet across, into which the sea flows through a natural arch. Doctor Johnson and Boswell nervously walked round this cauldron by a path which can still be used today. Several miles of sand and dunes.

Cullen Grampian   2 M 1
Banff. Pop 1,500. Classical vignettes ennoble this cliff-top Regency resort built between 1820-30 to replace an old fishing town. Seatown, Cullen's old fishing harbour is painted with gabled cottages squeezed colourfully together. Nearly 2 miles of good, sandy beach.

Downies Grampian   2 O 5
Kincardine. Homespun hamlet glued to the top of a crescent of cliffs on the edge of Cammachmore Bay. Pencil line of shingle and small fishing boats add to the character of the place.

Dundee Tayside   2 M 8
Angus. Pop 196,400. EC Wed. MD Tue. Bustling industrial city and commercial port, now bursting at the seams with the oil boom, but not yet buried in an avalanche of modernity. Although much of the historic centre has gone, there are still corners of intrigue to transport you back to more blood-chilling times—as in 1547 when English forces plundered and burned the town, or when William Wallace, the first to take up the gauntlet against the English in the 13thC, was outlawed for avenging an insult with his dagger. This is a city that has been fought over for centuries, first by the Romans who built camps in the vicinity, later by the Picts and then by the first King of the Scots, Kenneth MacAlpine, who set out to conquer the Picts from here in the 9thC. The busy sea port of today with its oil tankers and great cargo ships grew from a quiet sheltered bay along the spacious waters of the Firth of Tay. In 1190 William the Lion granted Dundee a Royal charter and the town began to expand. But in 1296 Edward I sacked the town. In 1385 it was once more pillaged by the English. Yet after each bout of destruction the city fathers began to re-build again. The city was torn apart yet again during the English Civil War and occupied by the Jacobites during the months prior to Culloden. Little wonder that the only remnant of the great 15thC town church, let alone anything else, is the Old Steeple. The only surviving town gate is 16thC Wishart Arch. William Adam's Town House of 1734 was shamefully demolished in 1931 and the rash of plaques does little to compensate. But this is a living town, not a historical museum. In the 17thC Dundee was a flourishing woollen centre and by the late 18thC it was the centre of the linen industry in Scotland. Already a prosperous

Mains Castle, Dundee

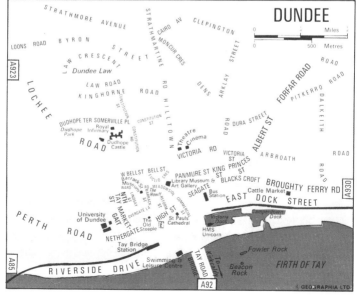

whaling port, it was providence that sent jute from India in 1822 and coupled with the oil from whaling, Dundee rapidly expanded as the world centre for the spinning and weaving of flax. The population exploded fourfold, with new factories and crowded tenements rammed tightly together around a rambling nest of streets and lanes scrambling outwards from the Tay. Today the city, which was known for 'jute, jam and journalists', also produces whisky, carpets, ships, and the traditional Dundee cakes.

Buildings of interest include: many fine Victorian churches such as All Saints, 1865-70, by George Frederick Bodley, a pupil of Sir George Gilbert Scott; and St Paul's Episcopal Cathedral 1853, by Sir Gilbert Scott himself.

With a flourishing university founded in 1881, Dundee today is Scotland's fourth largest city. Its industrial core is relieved by 4 golf courses and 28 public parks which tear great green inlets out of the city fabric. In the centre of the city is The Howff, a piece of land given to Mary Queen of Scots, now used as a cemetery, but for long the meeting place of the trade guilds. From the south, the city is served by 2 long bridges. The railway bridge replaces one that was blown down by a gale whilst a train was crossing it in 1879. The road bridge, opened in 1966, is over 1½ miles long, and Britain's longest road bridge over a river. Dundee Law (571 feet), which is the city's highest point, is the remains of a volcanic plug. From the top is a splendid vista of the city and the coast from Buddon Ness right up to the Firth of Tay.

Worth a visit: the fascinating Golf Museum at Camperdown House; the Barrack Street Shipping and Industrial Museum; Unicorn, a floating museum, housed in an early 19thC frigate.

Findhorn Grampian   2 K 1
Moray. Pop 700. Fishing village welded at the pinched gateway to Findhorn Bay. The third village to be built here—the first having been buried in an avalanche of sand in the 17thC, the second drowned by a great flood in 1701. Magnificent sandy beaches and good sailing.

Findochty Grampian   2 M 1
Banff. Pop 1,200. Gabled stone cottages, all spick-and-span, step down a steep slope to an attractive harbour. This fishing village, built on a saddle of land between 2 headlands, was founded in 1716 by the owners of 16thC Findochty Castle—a leering ruin west of the village.

Findon Grampian   2 O 5
Kincardine. Tiny hamlet piled high on a precipitous cliff top. Famous for the Finnan haddock, the name it gave to the curing of haddock over a peat fire.

Fraserburgh Grampian   2 P 1
Aberdeen. Pop 10,600. EC Wed. MD Wed.
A holiday and fishing town with an attractive and busy harbour founded in 1546 by Sir Alexander Fraser. The northernmost part of the town is on Kinnaird's Head which is surmounted by a lighthouse. Near it is the Wine Tower, the origin and use of which is unknown. The only entrance is on an upper storey. Sandy beach.

Gardenstown Grampian   2 O 1
Banff. Pop 900. Windswept fishing village on a sandstone hill above the glistening waters of Gamrie Bay. The picturesque harbour is screened by a huge leg of rock.

Gourdon Grampian   2 O 6
Kincardine. Pop 700. Fishing village exuding weather-beaten good health on the sunlit slopes above a rocky harbour. Prosperous port which grew in leaps and bounds in the 19thC.

Hopeman Grampian   2 L 1
Moray. Pop 1,200. 19thC harbour village dressed in a neat Sunday-best of golden stone. Fingers of sandy beach flank the

harbour, whilst a rich carpet of agricultural land washes the rear of the village. Of interest is Duffus Castle, 2 miles SE, a grimly magnificent 14thC keep, standing on the site of one of the finest motte-and-bailey strongholds of Norman Scotland.

Inverbervie Grampian   2 O 6
Kincardine. Pop 900. Strikingly situated on the south bank of the Bervie Gorge where the river forces its way to the sea. Hercules Linton, the designer of the famous tea clipper 'Cutty Sark' and an Inverbervie man, is honoured by a memorial here. The nearby town of Gourdon is worth seeing to watch the women baiting the hand fishing lines for their fishermen husbands—up to 1,200 hooks per line. Beyond the river mouth is a shingle bar of brilliantly hued pebbles. The beach is also shingle.

Inverness

Inverness Highland   2 H 2
Inverness. Pop 36,600. EC Wed. MD Tue.
Sandwiched between the Moray Firth and Loch Ness, the town is drawn in a sweeping arc across a winding fork of the River Ness. This so-called capital of the Highlands is a high Victorian town of sombre, spikey Gothic architecture, with lush gardens and leafy streets laid out in spacious meandering lines along the plank flat plain.

A strategic site since Pictish times with numerous remains of hill forts, burial cairns and carved stones, by the 12thC it was a thriving merchant city with its own Royal castle. The turreted redstone 19thC castle, built in a comically pompous, fairy tale Gothic style, was the site of the legendary Macbeth's stronghold. It was here that Mary Queen of Scots stayed and later it was occupied by Bonnie Prince Charlie, who subsequently blew it up. Inverness was of such strategic importance that Cromwell built a fortress here in 1652-57, but this too has disappeared, dismantled following the Restoration to appease nationalist clans.

At the centre of the city is the Gothic Revival Town House (1880), where Prime Minister Lloyd George held a British Cabinet meeting in 1921. Other buildings of interest include Abertaff House (1592), with turreted staircase-tower; Dunbar's Hospital, built 1688 as an almshouse for the poor; the clock-tower, the only remnant of Cromwell's star-shaped fort; the High Church, built 1770 onto a 14thC tower.

Inverness is still a port of medium importance and possesses its own fishing fleet which regularly passes through the Caledonian Canal to fish off the west coast. Historic Culloden Moor lies 5 miles SE of the city. A cairn marks the site of the Highlanders' last stand in 1746. Although Inverness is a popular holiday centre, fast currents make it dangerous for bathing. Muddy sand. *See town map page 64.*

Johnshaven Grampian   2 O 6
Kincardine. Pop 500. Cheery fishing village wedged neatly like a ruled line on a platform of land between the main road and rocky beach.

Kingston Grampian   2 L 1
Moray. Pop 200. Once a busy 18thC and 19thC shipbuilding village, now hugging the mouth of the River Spey in stony silence. Garmouth, 1 mile away, was also a busy timber port until forced to close by the ever-changing river channel. It was there that

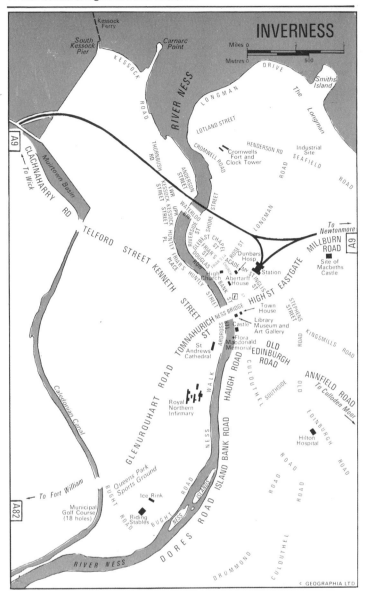

Charles II landed in June 1650, and where he signed under duress the two covenants in support of Presbyterianism.

Kinlochmoidart Highland   **2 D** 6
Inverness. A small crofting hamlet at the head of Loch Moidart, famous for its visit by Bonnie Prince Charlie on his way to raise the standard at Glenfinnan. The support of Moidart is commemorated by 7 beech trees planted in a meadow nearby, and called the Seven Men of Moidart. The 7 men are also remembered in a Highland reel of the same name. See Castle Tioram set on an island further down the loch.

Lossiemouth Grampian   **2 L** 1
Moray. Pop 5,700. EC Thur. A prosperous fishing port where initiative and enterprise have paid off. The administrative side of money-making is handled in the twin town of Branderburgh perched on the cliffs above the port. A holiday resort with good beaches and swimming, but avoid bathing near the mouth of the River Lossie.

Macduff Grampian   **2 N** 1
Banff. Pop 3,800. Bustling harbour town crowned by an early 19thC church, that stands on the crest of a wave of green hills. Steep streets plunge down to the waterfront like a big dipper at the fairground.

Mallaig Highland   **2 C** 5
Inverness. Pop 900. EC Wed. A full stop in all senses. It is the end of the road and the railway to the Isles. To the west, Skye is served by a ferry service to Armadale, and to the north and east is the roadless emptiness of Knoydart.
Apart from the ferry Mallaig supports itself from herring fishing, a kipper factory, and lobster tanks. The village is quite overpowered by the grandeur of the surrounding country. Rock and shingle beach.

Monifieth Tayside   **2 M** 8
Angus. Pop 6,400. Cheerful Charlie of a town. Lies at the centre of a 5-mile crescent of sand swept by the Firth of Tay, between

Carnoustie and Broughty Ferry. Interesting Iron Age settlement nearby. Good golf course and caravan sites.

Montrose Tayside   2 N   7
Angus. Pop 10,000. EC Wed. MD Wed, Fri.
The combination of recently-injected prosperity from nearby North Sea oil and its long-standing popularity as a holiday resort has surprisingly not spoilt Montrose's charm and peaceful tradition. The broad High Street, with Flemish-style houses, is almost pure 18thC from the tall steeple by the Town House at one end to the busy port at the other. When Glasgow was no more than a village, Montrose was already a flourishing port, a position it held well into the 18thC with its lucrative tobacco trade with Virginia and the New World. For centuries the rich merchants also prospered from trade with the Low Countries. And so, naturally, did the town, whose spatial sensibilities are clearly Dutch inspired.
Tucked away on either side of the High Street are numerous closes sandwiched between Baltic Street and Western Road.

montrose

Parallel with the High Street and running north from behind the nest of streets around the harbour is a belt of trees, lawns and bowling greens called the Mid Links. Lining it, almost like a wall, are some fine houses of warm rose-coloured stone, many with courtyards and high garden walls, built for the gentlemen farmers and prosperous merchants.
Everything is very urban in scale, with pedimented porticos and bold cornices, whilst the north end of the Mid Links narrows slightly before bursting out into a great estuary of green around the golf course. Montrose is a magnificent holiday resort with 4 miles of sandy beaches and good sailing in Montrose Basin. But the place still shuts down fairly early it seems, like a light switch, for at 22.00 each night 'Big Peter' the curfew bell cast in Rotterdam in 1676 is still rung from the 220-foot-high steeple in the High Street.

Morar, Inverness

Morar Highland   2 C   5
Inverness. EC Thur. The village sits on a narrow neck of land between the deepest lake in Britain, Loch Morar (1,080 feet deep), and the Atlantic. The road and railway compete for space to cross the gorge containing the falls of the River Morar. The blinding white singing sands of Morar set off the superlative landscape of this area.

Muchalls Grampian   2 O   5
Kincardine. Pop 400. 19thC village of bleached white houses tied firmly down on a cliff top. Waves, like giant ice-cream scoops, have carved huge 80-foot-high holes in the cliff wall. The 17thC castle, an L-plan tower house wrapped in a curtain wall, has fine plasterwork in the Great Hall. *Open summer Sun and Tue afternoons.*

Nairn Highland   2 J   2
Nairn. Pop 5,900. EC Wed. A popular and still developing holiday centre. Like all good resorts it claims to have a monopoly of fine weather, though to be fair all the Moray coast is noted for its warm and dry summer climate. Facilities include a heated indoor sea-water swimming pool, children's paddling pool and playground, and in fact all the trappings of a well equipped resort. Five miles to the south-west lies Cawdor Castle, a name well known to those who know their Macbeth. In the High Street see the old cross, the post office and Town House of 1818. There are excellent sandy beaches, and a picturesque river mouth harbour much used by pleasure craft and some fishing boats.

Newburgh Grampian   2 O   3
Aberdeen. Pop 500. Little seaport village sealed behind the dunes on the southern bank of the swollen basin of the River Ythan. Dune swept beach with fast current. Excellent fishing ground—sea trout, brown trout and salmon.

Pennan Grampian   2 N   1
Aberdeen. Hardy hamlet of stone cottages tucked up against a great red sandstone wall of cliffs. Its harbour gingerly points a finger out into the cold waters of Pennan Bay.

Peterhead Grampian   2 P   2
Aberdeen. Pop 14,200. EC Wed. A busy seaport and boat-building town as well as one of the major service ports for the North Sea oilfields. The harbour shelters behind two breakwaters built with the help of convict labour. The stark and dangerous way of life of the fisherfolk is echoed in the spare and economic buildings of the town, relieved only by the warmth of red granite. The Town House by John Baxter at the end of Broad Street is worth a visit. There is a bathing beach in the southern half of the bay.

Portknockie Grampian   2 M   1
Banff. Pop 1,200. Once a flourishing herring port built round a natural harbour, it is now a quiet village sitting on a rocky headland and staring out to sea in contemplation, like a retired sea-captain.

Portlethen Grampian   2 O   5
Kincardine. Pop 100. Picturesque fishing village clinging tenaciously to a cliff-walled cove that shelters a natural harbour.

Portsoy Grampian   2 M   2
Banff. Pop 1,700. Sharp and earnest with hints of the former greatness of bygone times. The village is battened down tight round an old harbour on the edge of a rocky bay. It was a busy fishing and commercial port in the 18thC. Local serpentine rock, known as Portsoy 'marble', was exported to France and even used at Versailles on 2 of the palace's chimneys.

St Vigeans Tayside   2 N   8
Angus. A lost world almost devoured by Arbroath. The hamlet is a mediaeval nest, piously peaceful, but dominated by a pompous church beaming proudly from a rocky hillside pedestal. Of particular interest is the cottage museum containing early Christian and mediaeval relics.

Stonehaven Grampian   2 O   5
Kincardine. Pop 4,800. EC Wed. A cheerful town nestling at the mouth of a sheltered valley formed by 2 rivers. It still has its fishing fleet, but Stonehaven today is better

stonehaven

Dunnottar Castle, Kincardine

known as a sailing centre. The harbour is attractive with an interesting 17thC Tolbooth used now as a museum on the quay. You shouldn't miss Dunnottar Castle. Bathing is off a shingle beach, or in comfort from the town's open air heated pool.

Islands

Canna Highland   2 A 4
Inverness. Lush green island called the 'Garden of the Hebrides'. At the east end is a sheltered harbour. In the north is Compass Hill, so named because the cliffs' rich iron deposits are supposed to have a magnetic effect on ships' compasses.

Coll Strathclyde   2 A 6
Argyll. Pop 200. Once part of the Lordship of the Isles, like Tiree, it also has many remains of brochs. The island is a shallow, rolling blanket of heather-carpeted peat hills, relieved by night-black lochs. The only village is Arinagour, a skimpy handful of houses where there is also a hotel. Most of the islanders survive by crofting. Breacacha Castle, now carefully restored, is a fine 14thC fortress. Miles of beach and shell sand dunes on the western side.

Eigg Highland   2 B 5
Inverness. Dramatic and mysterious, 6 miles long and dominated by a dark brooding basaltic peak, the Sgurr of Eigg, 1,289 feet high. The pressure of the molten lava has squeezed out a writhing mass of twisted columns, like great blobs of toothpaste, that decorate the rock like iced piping on a birthday cake. A cave in the south east of the island was the setting for a clan feud in the 16thC when the MacLeods of Skye are reputed to have murdered 200 men of the clan MacDonald. The famous 'singing sands' lie to the north of Eigg. The island contains remnants of old hazel scrub and is rich in many species of sea birds and mosses.

Eigg and Rhum, Inverness

Iona Strathclyde   2 A 8
Argyll. Christianity was first introduced to Scotland on a considerable scale during the late 5thC. It spread first through Strathclyde and the Forth valley from Whithorn and Carlisle. Reinforcement came in the 6th and 7thC from Irish missionaries, who set up a whole series of monastic foundations. Their first was that at Iona, established in AD563 by St Columba, who landed on the island with 12 followers. A man not only of great piety, but evidently also of great energy, Columba and his followers managed to start a movement which brought Christianity ultimately to all Scotland. St Oran's Chapel, built 1080, is the oldest surviving building and has a cemetry which is the burial place of 50 Scottish Kings; the ornately carved

16-foot-high St Martin's cross is 10thC; St Mary's Abbey, where St Columba is buried, dates from the 13thC. Also of interest are the numerous carved Celtic crosses.
The island itself is bare and windswept. Pillaged by the Vikings continually from the 9th to 10thC, it has a raw, knotted landscape swept by roaring winds, that accentuate the piety and peace of the monastic ruins.

Lismore Strathclyde   2 D 8
Argyll. Blocking the mouth of Loch Linnhe like a half-submerged barge, it is a flat, fertile green but treeless island. The former seat of the Argyll diocese, it has a tiny cathedral, now the parish church. Spectacular sea and land scenery.

Muck Highland   2 B 6
Inverness. Only 2 miles long this low island is very attractive, with some sandy beaches. The cliffs are full of sea birds of all varieties. No ferry service.

Mull Strathclyde   1 C 8
Argyll. Pop 1,600. Over 30 miles in length with mountains in the southern and eastern parts of the island—some peaks are over 3,000 feet high. This is the third largest of the Hebridean islands. Sea lochs and creeks erode the west and south coast in great Baroque swirls, whilst in the north, Mull is bracken green with woods flooding the sheltered valleys. The main town is Tobermory, a polychrome wall of early 19thC houses jammed tight in a curve round the harbour. In 1588 the 'Duque di Florencia', a remnant of the Spanish Armada, sank in Tobermory Bay with an alleged 3 million gold doubloons on board. Only a few trinkets from this legendary treasure trove have been found.

Mull Little Theatre

The attractive little village of Dervaig lies 8 miles NW of Tobermory. Consisting of 26 semi-detached houses built in 1799, the village hugs the crumpled end of a long, narrow sea loch. A popular attraction is the Mull Little Theatre which has regular performances throughout the summer and is Scotland's smallest professional theatre. The theatre is in a converted barn near the church.
Craignure, on the east coast fronting Loch Linnhe, is the main port of Mull. Salen, a small village sheltering in a wooded site, stands on the narrow neck of land between north and south Mull. Also of interest: 19thC Torosay Castle, near Craignure, a Scottish Baronial fairy-tale castle by David Bryce; Duart Castle, an aggressive 13th–17thC monolith raised on a great bastion of rock on the east point of Duart Bay.
A pleasant holiday island with plenty of hotel accommodation and amenities for sea angling, golf, walking, fishing, swimming and pony-trekking. There is also a 15,000-acre deer forest.

Raasay Highland   2 C 3
Inverness. A rocky, hilly and very pleasant island which has decreased in population from 600 to 200 over the last 100 years. This was helped by the disastrous potato famine in the last century but the main cause was the infamous 'Clearances'.

Rhum Highland   2 B 5
Inverness. Largest island in the 'Small Isles' group of the Inner Hebrides. Rhum had over 400 people in the late 18thC but the Highland Clearances of the early 19thC forced the islanders to emigrate to America.

Lying south of Skye, it is a mountainous island erupting into 3 peaks over 2,500 feet high. Since 1957 the island has been owned by the Nature Conservancy Council who use it as a huge open-air laboratory for Scotland's environmental and ecological problems. Animal life includes a herd of 1,500 red deer. Day visitors are welcome but camping is by special permission only.

Skye Highland   2 B 3
Inverness. Pop 7,400. The most beautiful of all the Scottish isles, seen best in the early morning—when a veil of mist is shredded by the scarred and crumpled mountains, when the sun rise sends sharp pencil lines of shadow to accentuate the rolling blanket of land. It is 50 miles long and 25 miles wide, with a sharp bright light and bracing air that makes you feel you are standing on the roof of the world. In the centre of Skye are the Cuillin Hills that tumble down to scimitar-shaped bays and the mirror-still waters of narrow sea lochs. Over 3,000 feet high they challenge the most experienced of rock climbers. The coastline is jagged and torn by hundreds of sea lochs and sweeping bays. In plan it looks like the silhouetted shadow of a giant bird of prey, its talons ready to claw.

Dunvegan Castle, Skye

The main occupations are a combination of crofting and fishing, with tourism providing a large slice of the island's income. The principal township and port is Portree, a polychrome wall of curving terraces with gabled dormers and an undulating skyline that seems to hug the boat-filled bay. Of particular interest: historic Kingsburgh House where Bonnie Prince Charlie sought refuge and where Flora Macdonald, who took the Prince to the outer isles disguised as her serving woman, later entertained Boswell and Dr Johnson; Dunvegan Castle, home of the chiefs of Clan MacLeod for several centuries, is a multi-facetted cliff wall of crenellated parapets and corbelled angle turrets on a sharp escarpment on the edge of Dunvegan Bay. Equally interesting are the pinnacles and 'Tables' of the Quiraing in the north of Skye. Also fascinating is the gigantic 150-foot-high pillar known as 'The Old Man' at the foot of the high plateau Storr.
The people are hospitable, dignified, respect the Sabbath, and mostly speak Gaelic.

Kyleakin (Skye)   2 D 3
EC Wed. One of the two modern gateways to Skye. Here the visitor will first see the island's characteristic whitewashed stone terraced cottages. Overlooking the town and the modern invaders are the remains of the 14thC Castle Maol, a small but important

Kyleakin, Skye

Highland strongpoint used to control the strait between Skye and the mainland. The '-akin' part of Kyleakin is said to come from the 13thC King Hakon of Norway who sailed by on his unsuccessful way to invade Scotland.

Portree, Skye

Portree (Skye)   2 B 2
Pop 2,000. EC Wed. Portree, or in English 'King's Haven' is the capital of Skye. A pleasing little place with a harbour delineated by whitewashed stone terraced houses. The town rises to the north and culminates in an attractive main square. An excellent touring centre for Skye and there are steamer trips from here to nearby Raasay Island.

Uig (Skye)   2 B 1
Pop 2,000. Like so many Highland villages Uig refuses to be pinned down by the cartographer's dots on a map, and is a picturesque conglomeration of crofts and cottages scattered over a hillside to the north of a harbour. From here car ferries leave for the Outer Hebrides.

Staffa

Staffa Strathclyde   2 A 8
Argyll. North of Iona, it is an uninhabited island famous for its remarkable basaltic caves, which writhe and froth at the edges in geometric convulsions worthy of the best kinetic art. Of particular interest is Fingal's Cave, the inspiration for Mendelssohn's 'Hebrides' overture. The cathedral-like cave is 227 feet long and 66 feet high above the mean tide water level.

Tiree Strathclyde   2 A 7
Argyll. Pop 1,000. For many just a name on a shipping forecast before Sunday lunch, rather like the mythical Desert Island of radio. In reality, this is a long, pancake flat island, 12 miles by 3 miles and, at most, no more than 25 feet above sea level. Edged by silvery crescents of sand, it has lush arable land with meadows bright with buttercups.

The inhabitants are engaged mostly in a combination of fishing and crofting. Many of the dwellings are traditional black houses with 6-foot-thick walls, narrow windows and thatched roofs. The chief centre is Scaranish, a scattered hamlet with the aura of a frontier town. Interesting remains of the earliest islanders' defences include duns and brochs, the most spectacular of which is Dun Mor Vaul, a round stone tower 35 foot in diameter and with 13-foot-thick walls. Christianity came to Tiree in the 6thC, and later it became part of the Lordship of the Isles. In the Atlantic 10 miles SW of the island is a magnificent piece of Victorian daring, the Skerryvore Lighthouse, built 1843 by Robert Louis Stevenson's uncle.

Treshnish Isles Strathclyde   2 A 8
Argyll. Curious shaped isles adrift west of Mull. One has a tall peak and wide brim and is nicknamed the 'Dutchman's Cap'.

Inland towns & villages

general watts bridge, Aberfeldy.

Aberfeldy Tayside   2 J 7
Perth. Pop 1,600. EC Wed. A peaceful
market town set in delightful countryside.
The Wade Bridge over the Tay is a little
masterpiece, showing very obviously the
assistance of William Adam in the design.

Aberfoyle Central   2 H 10
Perth. Pop 800. EC Wed. Romantic village
rolled up in a ragged carpet of tree-clad hills.
The area was the setting for two of Sir
Walter Scott's novels, 'Rob Roy' and the
'Lady of the Lake'. Of interest are the cast-
iron mort safes, once used to foil body-
snatchers, and now kept in the ruined
church. Nearby Inchmahome Priory,
standing on an island in the Lake of
Menteith, was the childhood home of Mary
Queen of Scots. The town is a good place
from which to explore the Trossachs.

Aberlemno Tayside   2 M 7
Angus. Crisp, ordered village, small scale and
friendly. Of particular interest are some
memorable examples of Pictish sculptured
stones, found in the churchyard and nearby
Flemington Farm. Ruined Melgund Castle
was the home of Cardinal Beaton.

Abernethy Tayside   2 L 9
Perth. Once a town, now a village, it has a
circular refuge tower for the preservation of
the local clergy, 1 of only 2 in Scotland. The
tower is 74 feet high with an entrance door 6
feet from the ground, and is built of hewn
square stones.

Aboyne Grampian   2 M 5
Aberdeen. Pop 2,300. EC Thur. MD Mon. A
neat and, for Scotland, unusually geometric
town arranged around a large flat green
surrounded by distant hills. It has its
moment of glory every September with the
very popular Highland Gathering held on
the green.

Alford Grampian   2 M 4
Aberdeen. Pop 1,800. EC Wed. MD Tue. A
pleasant little market town on the south
bank of the River Don in the centre of the
Howe of Alford. Alford came briefly to the
notice of history when the Royalist Marquis
of Montrose engulfed the Covenanting army
of General Baillie in 1645.

Four miles to the
south is Craigievar
Castle, an
extravaganza of
turrets, gables and
conical roofs built in
1626. Inside is a
superb Renaissance
ceiling.

Craigievar Castle

Amulree Tayside   2 K 8
Perth. Stern faced hamlet squeezed into a
roller coaster of green hills. Once an
important stopover on the drovers' road
south.

Ardgour Highland   2 E 6
Argyll. The large white lighthouse guards the
entrance to the narrows at the foot of Loch
Linnhe. From Ardgour is a ferry service to
the main Fort William road, and the frenzy
of the main road underlines the tranquillity
of this little village. The church was built to
a design produced by Telford for the
government's Highland church building
programme in the 1820s and '30s.

Archiestown Grampian   2 L 2
Moray. Pop 200. Model village, neat and
ship-shape as if on parade, with a central
square walled with houses. Begun 1761 by
Sir Archibald Grant.

Aviemore Highland   2 K 4
Inverness. Pop 700. EC Wed. Until the mid
1960s Aviemore was a pleasant sleepy little
village which had grown up round a railway
station. With the advent of commercially
organised skiing, change came with a
vengeance.
The Aviemore Centre, a complex of hotels
and indoor and outdoor sporting facilities,
restaurants, theatre and concert hall, was
designed to combat the Scottish weather's
assaults on the skiing season. Now the centre
offers all the year round holidays. An
environmental triumph.

Ballater

Ballater Grampian   2 L 5
Aberdeen. Pop 1,000. EC Thur. Attractive
town, crisp as an icicle amid forest-drenched
mountain scenery, with the River Dee
winding its broad, boulder-strewn way past.
Good golf course with spectacular views of a
wave of mountains from the Grampians in
the east to the Cairngorms in the west. The
town has done well out of its
neighbours—HM the Queen at Balmoral and
HM the Queen Mother at Birkhall.

Balquhidder Central   2 H 9
Perth. Pronounced 'Balwhidder'. The final
resting place of Rob Roy (died 1734), his
wife, and two of his five sons is near the
remains of the old chapel. The village is set
in a glen called the Braes of Balquhidder
which opens out on to Loch Voil. This
beautiful spot is perhaps too popular for its
own good.

Banchory Grampian   2 N 5
Aberdeen. Pop 2,400. EC Thur. Another
attractive and expanding Deeside holiday
village in a sylvan setting. Nearby the River
Feugh joins the Dee. The Brig of Feugh ½
mile upstream has an observation platform to
watch the salmon leaping the rapids.

Blair Castle, Perthshire

Blair Atholl Tayside   2 J 6
Perth. Pop 1,400. EC Wed. A dignified
village dominated by the fantasy Blair Castle,
seat of the Duke of Atholl, and swamped by
a main road.

Blairgowrie Tayside   2 L 7
Perth. Pop 5,600. EC Thur. A small town set
in a sea of raspberry farms which produce
half the total crop of Scotland. The road to
Perth passes a magnificent beech hedge
planted in 1746 in the grounds of Meikleour
House. Over 85 feet high, it borders the road
for 580 yards. The 19thC Brig O'Blair over
the swift running River Ericht links
Blairgowrie to Rattray. About 2 miles north
the river runs through a gorge with 200-foot-
high cliffs.

Boat of Garten Highland   2 K 4
Inverness. Pop 400. Little grey Speyside
village anchored amongst incomparable
scenery of forested hills rising to sharp
craggy peaks. The Strathspey Railway

Association runs a limited service to Aviemore using rolling stock from the Old Highland Railway.

Braemar Grampian   2 L 5
Aberdeen. Pop 1,000. EC Thur. Dominated by the massive Cairn Toul (4,241 feet) this Deeside village is world famous for its Royal Highland Gathering, held in September and normally attended by the Queen and Royal Family. Braemar Castle is worth a visit; still surviving are inscriptions made by the bored 18thC soldiery. Balmoral Castle, the Royal residence, is 6 miles east.

Brechin Tayside   2 N 7
Angus. Pop 6,600. EC Wed. An ancient historical town with precipitous streets. The cathedral is mainly 13thC but suffered from a disasterous early 19thC restoration.

Brechin Cathedral, Angus

Fortunately much has been put right and the choir is a pleasing and delicate example of lancet work. Next to the cathedral is an 11thC watchtower used as a refuge for the clergy and church treasures.

Callander Central   2 H 9
Perth. Pop 1,800. EC Wed. This natural gateway to the Highlands is entombed in a wall of mountains and heather-covered hills. Established in the late 18thC, it is a busy, bow-windowed Regency town, spaced airily around a broad main street and square. The River Teith meanders into the town from a foreground of lush green meadows, where it joins the River Leny.

Camserney Tayside   2 J 7
Perth. Lovely unspoilt village. Of particular interest are its thatched cottages and numerous examples of cruck-framed housing. One has a preserved hanging hood over the fireplace.

Carrbridge Highland   2 K 4
Inverness. Pop 400. A favourite skiing resort that straddles the main road north of Aviemore. Hearty back-slapping village ringing with winter laughter—the Cairngorms swamping the horizon to the south east. Of interest is the Landmark Centre with its illustrated history of the Highlands.

Comrie Tayside   2 J 9
Perth. Pop 1,800. EC Wed. A quiet holiday resort on the River Earn popular with walkers. A particularly good walk is up Glen Lednock to the Devil's Cauldron where the River Lednock rushes down a narrow channel and through a hole in the rock.

Coylumbridge Highland   2 K 4
Inverness. On the approaches to Cairngorm ski slopes and a good base for hill walkers with routes to Lairig Ghru and Braeriach.

Craigellachie Grampian   2 L 2
Banff. Pop 400. Terraced stone village, at the junction of the Fiddich and Spey, staring absent mindedly out across meadowland. The River Spey is crossed in a grand span of traceried iron work by the Craigellachie Bridge, designed by Thomas Telford in 1815.

Crianlarich Central   2 G 9
Perth. Railway village, at the junction of the Oban and Fort William tracks, framed in a dramatic landscape of breathtaking bleakness.

Crieff Tayside   2 J 9
Perth. Pop 5,600. EC Wed. MD Tue. Despite almost total annihilation in the two Jacobite rebellions, this attractive country town seems to have won back against history and to be at peace with itself. Look at Crieff Cross, a 10thC carved slab not to be confused with the market cross in front of the 17thC Tolbooth. Drummond Castle 2 miles south is worth a visit.

Deskford Grampian   2 M 1
Banff. Once the heart of an 18thC flax-spinning industry, it is now a quiet village. Of interest: a ruined church with a typical early 16thC sacrament house.

Dinnet Grampian   2 M 5
Aberdeen. Resilient little village embraced by hills in a basin of the River Dee. Of interest nearby: Crannog Island, Bronze Age earthworks in Loch Kinord; also the site of the Battle of Culbean 1335, turning point in the second War of Independence when the Scots destroyed the English forces that had previously been besieging Kildrummy Castle.

Drumlithie Grampian   2 O 6
Kincardine. Pop 200. Just north of Arbuthnott, it is a rambling nest of irregularities pinioned by a tall bell tower. A handloom village until put out of business by the development of the power looms in the late 19thC. The bell tower built 1777 was tolled to regulate the weavers' meal times.

Drumnadrochit Highland   2 H 3
Inverness. Pop 400. Hearty village draped casually on a podium of land, wedged between the west bank of Loch Ness and a wooded glen. Of interest: Urquhart Castle, battered 15thC giant lying harmless now on a huge pedestal of land above the loch; the Corrimony chambered cairn of the megalithic period. A popular place with tourists—good for walking, fishing, pony-trekking.

Dufftown Grampian   2 L 3
Banff. Pop 1,500. EC Wed. Planned by the 4th Earl of Fife in 1817 in the form of a cross pin-wheeling round a central square, this is the heart of malt whisky country. The town and surrounding district has numerous distilleries, many with visitor centres. Of interest nearby: Glenfiddich distillery; Balvenie Castle, moated ruins of the 13thC stronghold of the Comyns. South of the town is the 12thC church of Mortlach which has 2 ancient memorial stones within its precincts.

Dunkeld Tayside   2 K 8
Perth. Pop 1,100. EC Thur. A large but delightful village with the 600-year-old remains of a once great cathedral. The National Trust for Scotland has been very active restoring the little 18thC houses to the south of the main street. Pause to admire Telford's fine bridge over the River Tay.

Copper pot stills, Craigellachie Distillery

Dunning Tayside 2 K 9
Perth. Pop 600. Spirited vignette of houses
lying at the foot of the Ochils in a
delightfully brazen way. The parish church,
rebuilt in the early 19thC, has a magnificent
late 12thC square west tower of 3 stages. At
the top, there are crowstepped gables and
round arched windows, springing from a
central column.

Edzell Tayside 2 N 6
Angus. Pop 700. At the base of an idyllic
valley—Glen Esk—the village dates back to
the 16thC but was largely replanned in 1839.
Edzell Castle, with the wall of Grampians
behind, is a 16thC tower house to which a
mansion and lovely walled Renaissance
garden were later added. The garden wall is
decorated with superb heraldic and literary
symbols.

Elgin

Elgin Grampian 2 L 1
Moray. Pop 16,400. EC Wed. MD Fri. A
compact busy little shopping town built to a
cruciform plan. Approaching the town across
the Laich of Moray, the western towers of
the ruined cathedral are seen reaching up to
the sky.
The cathedral was first mentioned in 1190,
and what remains gives a sketchy portrait of
what was once one of the finest churches in
Scotland. Notice the old arcaded houses in
the High Street, and the fine early 19thC
church of St Giles designed by Archibald
Simpson. See also Thunderton House and
the mediaeval church of the Greyfriars
Monastery in Abbey Street.

Ellon Grampian 2 O 3
Aberdeen. Pop 2,300. Today a commuter
town for oil-boom Aberdeen, but known as
the ancient capital of Buchan. Its old granite
buildings are still glued tightly together
along the banks of the River Ythan.

Fettercairn Grampian 2 N 6
Kincardine. Pop 300. 18thC village on the
edge of the fertile Howe of the Mearns. A
Rhenish-Gothic triumphal arch of 1864
commemorates an incognito visit of Queen
Victoria and Prince Albert a few years
previously. Fettercairn House is an
interesting Restoration building, 1660.

Fettercairn, Kincardine

Fetteresso Grampian 2 O 5
Kincardine. Picturesque village crouched like
a rugby scrum around the skeleton of a
13thC church.

Fochabers Grampian 2 L 2
Moray. Pop 1,200. Abutting a forest on the
east bank of the River Spey, it is a Georgian
village of whitewashed houses around a large
market square. It was built in 1776 by
John Baxter, William Adam's mason, for the
4th Duke of Gordon who had the original
village cleared from its site close to Gordon
Castle to make way for a large extension to
the castle. The parish church built to one
side of the market square is a spirited
building with bold portico and spire.

Fordyce Grampian 2 M 2
Banff. Pop 200. Tiny village crammed
protectively round a 16thC tower house.

Forfar Tayside 2 M 7
Angus. Pop 10,500. EC Thur. MD Mon, Fri.
The county town of Angus keeps itself busy
milling jute. There seems to be some doubt
about the town's antecedents, as Cromwell's
merry men burnt the town records in 1651,
and the town was not re-incorporated until
1665.
The town hall was designed by William
Playfair (1789-1857) and houses some
portraits by Romney, Raeburn and
Thorwaldsen. It also houses the 'Forfar
Bridle'—a collar with a prong used in
mediaeval days to gag those about to be
executed. About 2 miles to the north east are
the remains of Restennet Priory, mainly
12thC with a 15thC spire.

Forres Grampian 2 K 2
Moray. Pop 5,600. EC Wed. King Duncan,
killed by Macbeth, held court in Forres.
Today an obelisk to a Crimean war hero
marks the spot where the Royal castle stood
at the west end of the High Street.
There is little pretension in this neat little
burgh, except perhaps for the market cross
(1844) modelled on the Scott memorial at
Edinburgh. The town museum has a famous
collection of local fossils, and at the eastern
end of the town, a few hundred yards along
the Kinloss road, is the Sueno Stone, a thin
shaft of sandstone 23 feet high, carved with
figures of warriors, animals and knots, and is
thought to commemorate the final defeat of
the Danes in 1014.

Fort Augustus Highland 2 G 4
Inverness. Pop 900. EC Wed. This village is
situated on the land separating Loch Oich
and Loch Ness, and originally grew up
round a fort built by General Wade in 1730.
The fort has now gone and in its place is a
Benedictine abbey and school.
The school and tower were designed by the
inventor of the hansom cab, Joseph Hansom.
The cloisters and other parts were designed
by Peter Pugin. On the south side of the
school runs Wade's Road over the
Corrieyairack Pass which was used by
Bonnie Prince Charlie's army on its march
to Edinburgh.

Fortingall village

Fortingall Tayside 2 J 7
Perth. Unusual for Scotland, a village of
thatched cottages. It has an ancient yew tree
in the churchyard which is thought to be
over 2,000 years old. At the west end of the
village is Glenlyon House, formerly the
home of Captain Robert Campbell who led
the Glencoe massacre.

Fort William Highland 2 F 6
Inverness. Pop 4,200. EC Wed. Originally an
important outpost guarding the southern end
of the strategically important Great Glen.

Fort William, Inverness

Named after William III who ordered the building and garrisoning of a stone fort in 1690. Now an important tourist centre. The old town consists of a high street of typical West Highland buildings nestling at the foot of Ben Nevis, and straggles out to absorb nearby villages on the banks of Loch Linnhe towards Oban. See the West Highland Museum with important relics of the Jacobite rebellions of 1715 and 1745.

Fowlis Easter Tayside   2 L   8
Angus. A village noted for its splendid restored 15thC church of St Marnock. See the preserved screen door, 4 fine pre-Reformation paintings, sculptured font, and most unusual for Scotland, a tabernacle with an annunciation. Note the iron collars or jougs beside the south west door for wrong-doers.

Glamis Castle, Angus

Glamis Tayside   2 M   7
Angus. Pop 1,000. A picturesque village given a bogus connection with Macbeth by Shakespeare. The castle, which was almost completely rebuilt in the 17thC, has a fine collection of armour, furnishings and paintings. In contrast, the Angus Folk Museum focuses on the life of the peasantry. The village jougs are near the churchyard gates.

Glamis Village

Glenfinnan Highland   2 E   6
Inverness. A clachan—the local name for a small Highland village—at the head of Loch Shiel. There is a tower surmounted by a statue of a kilted Highlander marking the spot where Bonnie Prince Charlie raised his father's standard on the 19th August 1745. The little Roman Catholic chapel has an intriguing bell mounted outside in a frame on the ground.

Grantown-on-Spey Highland   2 K   3
Moray. Pop 1,700. EC Thur. From Georgian times a holiday town with a pleasant spacious atmosphere. In the winter 'après ski' life is well catered for, and in the summer there is fishing and golf. The parish church contains a fine black oak pulpit and some old panelling.

Huntly Grampian   2 M   3
Aberdeen. Pop 4,100. EC Thur. MD Wed. Cupped in the Strathbogie hills at the junction of the River Deveron and its tributary the Bogie, Huntly is an oasis of classic, gridded order. The town was planned in the 18thC around two tight straight streets and a central square. Of particular interest is Huntly Castle which evokes the whole history of Scottish castle development from Norman times to the 17thC. All that now remains of the French château-style Renaissance palace, 1597–1602, is a roofless ruin, with lovely oriel windows. For centuries, Huntly Castle was the home of the mighty Gordon family who were responsible for building most of the town.

Inchture Tayside   2 L   8
Perth. Pop 100. Hamlet of red sandstone cottages cradled in a green valley between the estuary of the River Tay and the foot of the Sidlaw Hills. The ruins of Moncur Castle are to the east of the village.

Inver Tayside   2 K   8
Perth. Picturesque village, lyrical in intensity, dancing along the banks of the River Tay. Of interest is the cottage where the famous Scots composer, Neil Gow, lived until his death in 1807.

Inverurie Grampian   2 N   3
Aberdeen. Pop 5,400. EC Wed. MD Fri. An innocuous little town on the banks of the River Don, characterised by wide open streets bordered by granite houses. Until recently the home of a minor railway works. In the churchyard of the ruined Kinkell Church 2 miles south is the inscribed Pictish 'Brandsbutt Stone'. The church itself contains a fine sacrament house. See also The Bass, a 50-foot-high mound which was probably an important motte-and-bailey stronghold.

Keith Grampian   2 M   2
Banff. Pop 4,200. EC Wed. MD Tue. A neat country town still benefiting from its planned re-building at the hands of the Earl of Findlater in 1750. Keith's oldest building is the Milton Tower (1480); its ruins stand near the Milton Distillery, founded in 1785, and one of Scotland's oldest working malt whisky distilleries.
The Roman Catholic church of SS Peter and Paul has its pediment embellished by two enormous figures of its patron saints; look at the altarpiece presented by Charles X of France.
If you're morbidly inclined, cross the Auld Brig O'Keith (1609) to Fife Keith. Near the churchyard there is the Gaun Pot or pool in which witches were drowned.

Kenmore Tayside   2 J   7
Perth. Pop 700. EC Thur. A pretty little model village at the eastern end of Loch Tay. The church (1760) is by William Baker. Don't miss the village inn where Burns wrote lines about his pleasure in the view from the bridge. They are kept over the fireplace in the inn parlour.

Killiecrankie Tayside   2 K   7
Perth. EC Thur. A hamlet best known for being the site of a furious, bloody battle in 1689—at the head of the Pass of Killiecrankie 1 mile north. The Jacobite Highlanders' army under Viscount Dundee—the 'Bonnie Dundee' of Scott's ballad—routed William III's army under General Mackay. Sadly Dundee was killed at the moment of victory. A steep footpath descends to the narrow opening of the gorge known as 'Soldier's Leap', after the formidable jump across the River Garry by a fleeing trooper. Much of the area is owned by the National Trust for Scotland.

Killin, Perth

Killin Central   2 H   8
Perth. Pop 600. EC Wed. Attractive stone built village wedged in along the banks of the River Dochart at the western edge of Loch Tay. Houses nestle under an umbrella

of trees, but the major spectacle, from kitchen window or road, is the towering 4,000-foot mass of Ben Lawers. In summer its slopes are a garden of rare Alpine plants. Skiers congregate there during winter. In the grounds of nearby Kinnell House is a prehistoric circle of standing stones. See also St Fillan's 8 healing stones at the tweed mill near the Bridge of Dochart.

Kincardine Grampian   2 N   6
Kincardine. Once a straggling village which took its name from mighty Kincardine Castle and gave it to a county. The castle and village, with the exception of the disused kirkyard of the vanished St Catherine's Chapel, have all disappeared.

Kingussie Highland   2 J   5
Inverness. Pop 1,100. EC Wed. Replanned in the late 18thC as a woollen centre, it is a handsome town ducking for cover along the banks of the River Spey. Crowning a grassy table of land across the river are stark ruins of Ruthven Barracks built in 1718 for the Redcoats. It was here that 1,500 clansmen

Ruthven Barracks

rallied after their defeat at Culloden only to be dispersed by Prince Charles Edward Stuart. Of particular interest is the Highland Folk Museum with a magnificent exhibition of Highland life over the last 2 centuries, including Highland dress, tartans and a furnished black house. The town is also both a winter and summer holiday resort with good outdoor sporting facilities.

Kirkmichael Tayside   2 K   7
Perth. Handful of houses thrown in delightful abandon on rising ground along the banks of the River Ardle. One of the former drovers' roads from the north east of Scotland ran through nearby Glen Fernalt.

Kirriemuir Tayside   2 M   7
Angus. Pop 4,100. EC Thur. A bijou town of red houses with narrow streets. J. M. Barrie was born at No 9 Brechin Road. In a pavilion behind the cemetery (in which Barrie is buried) is a camera obscura. Visit the gardens of Logie House about 1 mile south.

Northmuir, Kirriemuir

Knockando Grampian   2 L   3
Moray. Quiet village tucked up in a wooded valley of the River Spey, with Ben Rinnes glaring hungrily down at it across the river. Interesting parish church with galleried interior. Also worth seeing: the Tamdhu distillery, complete with visitor centre, but *closed in winter.*

Laurencekirk Grampian   2 N   6
Kircardine. Pop 1,400. EC Wed. MD Mon, alt

Sat. In the rich heartlands of the Howe of Mearns it is hard to imagine how this burgh with its 1¼ miles of main street was planned. The town owes its inspiration and original economy to Lord Gardenstone who encouraged hand-loom weaving and the making of snuff boxes.

Letham Tayside   2 M   7
Angus. Pop 800. Model village founded in 1788 by George Dempster of Dunnichen as a linen-weaving centre.

Lochearnhead Central   2 H   8
Perth. EC Wed. 19thC village of solid substance on a raft of land in rugged Highland hills. Standing at the western bank of Loch Earn it is a good centre for sailing and water skiing. Of interest nearby is a romantic castellated mansion, Edinample Castle, built 1630 and mirrored, like a Hollywood epic, in the Loch.

Logierait Tayside   2 K   7
Perth. Once the site of a former Royal court, it is a quiet contemplative village at the junction of the rivers Tay and Tummel. Logierait Hotel yard has a few foundation stones of the gaol where Rob Roy was once imprisoned. In the churchyard are iron mort safes used to prevent body-snatching.

Longforgan Tayside   2 L   8
Perth. Pop 500. Characteristic lowland village, unpretentious and hospitable, gathered at the foot of Huntly Castle—a giant of a tower built in the 15thC on a rocky plinth.

Milton of Clova Tayside   2 L   6
Angus. A lonely hamlet overlooked by the very attenuated ruins of Clova Castle. Glen Clova is one of the loveliest of Angus glens and the road which finishes at Clova follows the course of the River South Esk. On the banks of the South Esk grow many rare plants and ferns.

Monymusk Grampian   2 N   4
Aberdeen. Pop 200. Small village draped on a green hill above the River Don. Of particular interest is the parish church (1140), with magnificent Norman entrance portal and chancel arch. There is also a 16thC tower house along the river bank. Much of the village was rebuilt by Sir Archibald Grant, an agricultural reformer, in the 18thC.

Muthill Tayside   2 K   7
Perth. Pop 700. Nestling in a wooded site, the village was burned by fleeing Highlanders after the Battle of Sheriffmuir in 1715. It was rebuilt in the late 18thC with monolithic houses of thick stone walls and deep-set windows as if to repel a thousand armies—let alone a Highland storm. nearby is Drummond Castle with its magnificent gardens and museum.

New Deer Grampian   2 O   2
Aberdeen. Pop 600. Model village, exuding straightforward dignity, built by James Ferguson in 1802. It has a tree-lined street dominated by the bell tower of St John's Episcopal Church.

New Pitsligo Grampian   2 O   2
Aberdeen. Pop 1,100. The peat moss wilderness of the Buchan plain was transformed in the late 18thC by the draught-board straight streets of this large village, pinned to the eastern slope of a hill. It was financed by Sir William Forbes, the banker. There is a magnificent Victorian church by George Edmund Street, the Gothic Revival genius of 'High Victorian' England.

Newtonmore Highland   2 J   5
Inverness. EC Wed. This Speyside summer holiday resort doubles in the winter as a skiing centre. There is good fishing, golf and tennis. The tennis courts, with typical Scots economy, convert into curling rinks in the winter. Of interest is the Clan Macpherson Museum which includes the famous 'Black Chanter' and 'Green Banner' both used as lucky talismans by the Macphersons in war.

The Old Perth Bridge

water tower, Perth

Perth Tayside   2 K 9

Perth. Pop 43,000. EC Wed. MD Mon, Fri.
Inland port as well as market centre for the
rich agricultural hinterland, this was the
capital of Scotland before Edinburgh. It was
a busy maritime harbour as long ago as the
13thC. Nearby Scone Palace was both court
and Royal residence in feudal times, and
even further back in time, Agricola's army is
said to have established a camp here in the
1stC. The Royal burgh was established in
1210 and Perth was the centre of Scottish
government until 1452. From the 13thC the
city acted as host to the major religious
orders whose councils met here. During the
turbulent 14thC the city frequently changed
hands, first to the English, then to the Scots
and so on. It was here that James I was
assassinated in 1437, and it was here that
the fiery reformer John Knox first reaped
the rewards of his sermons—when the city's
famous monasteries were destroyed. Perth
fought and lost with the Royalist cause
against Cromwell and was also a Jacobite
stronghold in 1715 and 1745.
Described as the 'Fair City' and the real
'Gateway to the Highlands', Perth is built on
the banks of the River Tay, sandwiched to
the north and south by two lush green parks,
North Inch and South Inch. The main
historic site is St John's Kirk, a handsome
15thC town church with choir and transepts
built 1440-48, and tower in 1511.
The violence of the Reformation was
launched here from the pulpit by John
Knox, with a sermon on idolatry in 1559.
Pin-wheeling around the church and opening
out, north and south onto the spacious
Inchs, are fine crescents and terraces of a
quality to match those of Edinburgh's New
Town. To the north is Rose Terrace, a
handsome Georgian street designed by
Robert Reid in 1805. Barossa Place is a
ravishing street of Regency
villas, whilst to the
south, Marshall Place,
designed 1801 by
Robert Reid, is perfect
and discreet.
From tree-lined Tay
Street along the banks
of the river, there is a
good view north to
Queens Bridge, designed
1766-72 by Smeaton.
Charlotte Place, near
the bridge, is a
sinuously curved,
delicate piece of
townscape built 1830. Other buildings of
interest include: the Round House, a
Classical style rotunda built 1832 as the
Perth Waterworks and now housing the
Tourist Information Centre; the Art Gallery
and Museum, designed 1824 with miniature
domed Roman temple and bold Ionic portico
articulating the ends; Balhousie Castle, a
16thC tower house and used since 1962 as a
regimental museum for the Black Watch;
City Mills, an 18thC corn mill has been
converted into a modern hotel; King James
VI Hospital, built 1750. Scone Palace, a
19thC castellated mansion was the successor
to the former Renaissance palace and
mediaeval abbey. Inside there are good
collections of porcelain and furniture.
Famous people associated with Perth are:
Bonnie Prince Charlie who stayed at the
17thC Salutation Hotel, South Street, in
1745; novelist John Buchan, who later
became Lord Tweedsmuir, was born in the
city and lived in York Place; John Ruskin
had a residence in Rose Terrace; the
supposed house of the 'Fair Maid of Perth',
penned by Sir Walter Scott, stands in
Curfew Row.

Perth Art Gallery

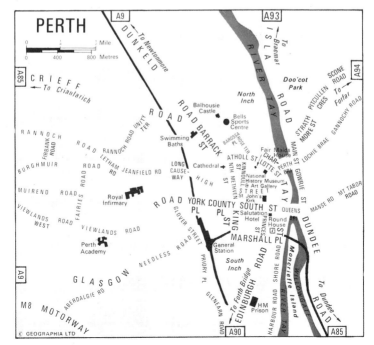

Pitlochry Tayside   **2 K 7**
Perth. Pop 2,600. EC Thur. Famous holiday resort, welcoming in the bracing mountain air, and superbly situated in a wooded saucer of land, surrounded by magnificent countryside. With a history going back to a Pictish fort some 2,000 years ago, it was through here that Robert the Bruce led the remnants of his army following his defeat at the Battle of Methven in 1306. But the town's prosperity really dates back to the rebellious days of the 17th and 18thC. When General Wade was sent to subjugate the Highland rebels in the early 18thC, he constructed a network of military roads to facilitate troop movements. These later became turnpike roads with tollhouses. Such a great improvement in communications brought new wealth to the town.
Additional good fortune occurred when Queen Victoria's personal physician described the mountain air here as the finest in Scotland, and on that basis the town was catapulted into being as a fashionable health resort of the late 19thC. It is also the home of the Pitlochry Festival Theatre, where a broad spectrum of plays are performed in the summer. Across the River Tummel at the entrance to the mausoleum of Dunfallandy House stands one of the finest examples of a Pictish sculpted stone in Scotland.
The town became a burgh in 1947 and possesses 2 distilleries and a tweed mill. Good fishing, sailing, walking, climbing and pony-trekking facilities. Pitlochry's link with extensive hydro-electric development has, fortunately, not spoilt its scenic appeal.

Port of Menteith Central   **2 H 10**
Perth. A quiet holiday resort on the north side of the Lake of Menteith. Boats may be hired here to visit the 13thC ruins of the priory on Inchmahome Island. Mary Queen of Scots stayed in the priory as a young girl.

Scone Tayside   **2 K 9**
Perth. Famous in Scottish history, Scone (pronounced 'scoon') was a seat of government in Pictish times and the coronation place of Scottish kings; the home of the Stone of Destiny until its removal by Edward I to Westminster Abbey in 1296.

Spean Bridge Highland   **2 F 6**
Inverness. Pop 200. EC Thur. The bridge itself is one of 1,200 that the great Scots engineer Thomas Telford built in his native country. The village church was built in 1812. Of interest nearby is Neptune's Staircase, a series of 8 locks carrying the Caledonian Canal 80 feet high. Also designed by Telford, it is at Banavie to the south west of the town.
Glen Spean, extending eastwards from Spean Bridge, gives access to Roy Bridge, and to the 'parallel roads' of Glen Roy: scars left from former shore-lines of Ice Age lakes, some 10,000 years ago.

Tarland Grampian   **2 M 5**
Aberdeen. Pop 500. EC Wed. Old world village floating in a lush green vale, washed by the river valleys of the Don and Dee. Houses are parcelled neatly round a spacious central square.

Tomintoul Grampian   **2 L 4**
Banff. Pop 300. Strong claimant for the status of being the highest village in the Highlands. This is a sharp, intense place (1,160 feet up) and consists of one main street, with a central grassed square stretched taut on a sandstone ridge. It was planned in 1779 by the Duke of Gordon and built by local masons with local stone. Nearby is the Glenlivet distillery, complete with visitor centre. Guided tours *Apr-Oct.*

Turriff Grampian   **2 N 2**
Aberdeen. Pop 3,000. EC Wed. A busy place spread flat on a fertile plateau at the centre of a prosperous agricultural district. The old church 12th-14thC, belonged originally to the Knights Templar, but only the choir and the double belfry remain. The area around is rich in castle architecture.

Craigston Castle, 4 miles NNE, built 1604-07, has a central tower with projecting wings, and an ornately sculptured balcony thrown across the upper part of the recess. *(Open by appointment only.)* Also of interest: Delgatie Castle, 2 miles W, 13thC stone keep extended in the 16thC; Tousie Barclay Castle, 3 miles S, built 1587 but drastically altered in the late 18thC.

Regional features

Many entries that could appear under this heading apply equally to other regions of Scotland, in particular the North. To avoid unnecessary repetition of information, it is suggested that you refer to the following entries listed under 'Regional features' in the **Northern Scotland** section, i.e. burghs, clans, crofters, hydro-electricity, peat, the Sabbath, etc.

Loch Ness Monster
The monster has been rearing his ugly head from as early as the 14thC and people have been claiming that there is something down there ever since. The loch itself is cold though it never freezes, and its surroundings are rather scarey. Photos purporting to depict the creature have been taken, so keep your eyes open.

Pearl hunting
The Lower Spey in summer is the centre of a pearl-fishing industry. Mussels from the river bed are scooped up and about 1 in 100 contains a pearl. Great quantities of these mussels are found in the river estuaries on both the east and west coast, and you might be lucky enough to find your own pearls.

Cross, Aberlemno   Cross, Kirkinner

Pictish crosses
Can be found in villages and churchyards across the Highlands. Several of these stones, which date from the 5thC, can be seen in the Meigle Museum in Perthshire. Another example, carved with animals and battle scenes, is in Aberlemno churchyard.

Round towers
The tall, round towers that you find at Abernethy, Perthshire, and at Brechin, Angus, are Irish in origin. Built of hewn stone, and generally with an entrance door high above the ground, they were virtually impregnable. Clergy used them as a place of refuge in times of danger. The Abernethy tower is 74-foot-high and was built in the 11thC. The Brechin tower, 10th-11thC, is 87-foot-high, and 15 foot in diameter at the base. It is attached to the church. Both structures narrow towards the top and are capped by a conical roof. Their principal purpose was to serve as bell towers.

Wildlife
The Highlands, because of their peace and isolation, have retained some very special wildlife. The golden eagle builds its eyries around 2,000 feet up in the lonely mountains. Ospreys, which live on fish, came back to rear their young at Loch Garten in 1958. Reindeer, which long ago roamed the Highlands, were brought back from Lapland in 1952. The pine marten and the wildcat, both native hunters of great speed and agility, still abound, protected in nature reserves. Less wild, but equally adapted to the cold are the long haired shaggy Highland cattle which are the hardiest breed in Britain.

The Scottish language

Throughout much of the Highlands, which are covered by this section, and Northern Scotland, the people's first language is Gaelic. It is a soft lilting tongue derived from old Irish, which fits well with the quiet friendly nature of the Highlanders. The Anglo-Saxon may well be confused by the way place names are pronounced as opposed to how they are spelt. 'Ch' for instance either sounds like someone gently clearing the back of his throat as in 'loch' or as the letter 'h' in 'Acharacle'. The letter 'B' is frequently sounded as a 'V' so that 'Beag' (meaning little) sounds like 'Veck'. Below are a few of the more common Gaelic root words found in place names:

aber	mouth or confluence of a river
ben, beann, beinn	mountain
caolas	a strait or firth
car	bend or winding
coire, corrie	hollow
dubh, dhu	black, dark
dun	hill fort
eilean	island
inch, innis	island
inver, inbhir	mouth of a river
mor, more	great, extensive
ross	peninsula, forest
ru, rhu, row, rudha	point
strath	broad valley
tobar	well
uamh	cave
uig	nook, sheltered bay

Famous people

J. M. Barrie (1860–1937) 2 M 7
9 Brechin Rd, Kirriemuir, Tayside. The birthplace of the creator of Peter Pan is now a Barrie Museum, and it was the inspiration of many of his other writings. In particular Kirriemuir was the model for his town of Thrums.

Bonnie Prince Charlie (1720–88) 2 E 6
Glenfinnan, Highland. Loch nan Uamh beside the Fort William-Mallaig road was where Bonnie Prince Charlie landed in 1745 in his attempt to win back the English throne. The cave where he spent his first night is clearly marked from the road down a small footpath where it is possible to follow Charles's first few days' journeyings. Follow the road back to Lochailort and turn right to Kinlochmoidart where there is a row of 6 (originally 7) beech trees called the Seven Men of Moidart, to commemorate the Prince's bonnie most faithful companions. On an island in Loch Moidart stand the remains of Castle Tioram (visible from the road) which was destroyed in the abortive rebellion of 1715, and was originally Clanranald's home. Charles then went on to Glenfinnan at the head of Loch Shiel where he set up his standard on the 19th August 1745. The place is marked by a tower surmounted by a statue of a kilted Highlander.

HM Queen Elizabeth II 2 L 5
Balmoral Castle, nr Ballater, Grampian. Whenever possible the Royal Family have always gone to Balmoral in the summer. This is not a state residence but belongs to the Queen personally, an inheritance of Queen Victoria's enthusiasm for all things Highland.
The house was designed by William Smith of Aberdeen with a great deal of consultation with Prince Albert, the Prince Consort. A magnificent Baronial mansion.

James Ramsay MacDonald 2 L 1
(1806–1937)
Lossiemouth, Highland. Ramsay Mac' was Britain's first Labour Prime Minister. He was born in a little backroom at No 1, Gregory Place, Lossiemouth in 1886. The

cottage was originally thatched, and is now marked by a stone plaque; his first school was a little Free Church General Assembly School which is still there.

St Columba (AD543–615) 2 A 8
Island of Iona, Mull. Iona was the home and headquarters of St Columba, who set out from here in AD563 to convert Scotland to Christianity. The island is more than a collection of old ruins, it's a living religious experience that one can share with countless thousands of others from times gone by.
St Columba's original mud and wattle chapel disappeared centuries ago, but the Norman cathedral remains a magnificent testament to faith, and its restoration by the Iona community a continuance of the same. Nearby is St Oran's Chapel, the oldest building on the island, said to occupy the site of St Columba's original chapel. The chapel cemetery is the oldest Christian burial place in Scotland and contains the graves of 50 kings. Among the monarchs buried at Iona is Macbeth who was preceded there by Duncan I, killed in 1040.

Robert William Thomson 2 O 5
(1822–1873)
Stonehaven, Grampian. A bronze plaque on the side of the house sited at the southern end of the Market Square is all that marks the site of the great engineer and inventor's birthplace. Robert Thomson best known for creating the first resilient tyres, both solid and pneumatic, when only aged 23, is less remembered for giving us the first fountain pen, rotary engine, the drydock, road steamers, sugar machinery and the donkey-engine type of travelling crane.

Cathedrals, abbeys & churches

Ardclach Church Highland 2 K 2
Nairn. 8 miles S of Nairn. The church, built in 1655, has a 2-storey belfry which stands apart from the church at the top of a hill.

Bellie Parish Kirk Grampian 2 L 2
Fochabers, Moray. John Baxter's splendid little classical church (1798) with pillared portico and spire mirrors the time's sophistication in thought and faith.

Birnie Kirk Grampian 2 L 2
Moray. Built on a site hallowed since early Celtic times, this is one of the few surviving Norman churches in Scotland still used for worship. Inside is the Ronnel Bell, said to have been made in Rome of silver and copper, but probably of Celtic origin. A gentle reminder of simplicity of faith and daily life.

Deer Abbey Grampian 2 P 2
Old Deer, Aberdeen. 10 miles W of Peterhead. Threadbare remains of a Cistercian monastery hidden in a wooded valley on the banks of the River Ugie. Founded in 1219 on the site of a Celtic monastery, where monks produced the famous 9thC 'Book of Deer', which is now in Cambridge University Library.

Dunblane Cathedral Central 2 J 2
Perth. A beautiful 13thC Gothic building with a Norman tower incorporated in the south wall of the nave. The west front is pure early English.

Elgin Cathedral Grampian 2 L 1
Moray. A product of the intense building activity of 13thC Scotland, it is a glorious cathedral that was rebuilt after a fire in 1270, with the addition of double aisles flanking each side of the nave—a rare feature in Britain. Burnt by the enraged Earl of Buchan following his excommunication in 1390, it deteriorated further after the Reformation. Now a gaunt but pious skeleton lurching across the landscape like a blinded camel.

Grandtully Church Tayside   2 K   7
Perth. Pronounced 'Grantly'. Outside a plain
little 16thC church, but inside the arched
ceiling is extravagantly ornamented with
painted wooden medallions depicting
subjects from the Bible.

Iona Abbey Strathclyde   2 A   8
Argyll. The great religious orders of the
Benedictines, Cistercians and Augustinians
were encouraged to settle in the 12thC and
they gradually replaced the earlier Celtic
monasteries. In conformity with the religious
orthodoxy of Western Europe, they adopted
a standard plan church with living quarters
grouped round a cloister. Iona Abbey, a
Benedictine foundation built from the
13thC to the early 16thC, is particularly
interesting as it is virtually complete, having
been recently restored.

Pluscarden Abbey Grampian   2 L   2
Moray. 7 miles SW of Elgin. This 13thC
Cistercian abbey is an intriguing cross
between the Romanesque and early English
styles. Used as a secular building for 400
years it was taken over in 1948 by the
Benedictine order at Prinknash Abbey in
Gloucestershire. A happy, hopeful rebirth
which sadly so many of Scotland's fine old
ecclesiastical buildings cannot share.

Pluscarden Abbey, Moray

Restenneth Priory Tayside   2 M   7
Restenneth, Angus. Cobwebbed ruin loaded
with reverence. Founded in 1153 by
Augustinians here through Jedburgh Abbey on the
site of an 8thC church, that had been built
by a Pictish king. There is a beautiful 13thC
chancel and an extraordinary tall, square
tower crowned by a 15thC spire. The
primitive lower part is pre-Norman.

St Machar's Cathedral Tayside   2 O   4
Aberdeen. As blunt and as uncompromising
as the religious beliefs of many of the
worshippers here through the centuries. The
only ancient granite cathedral in Britain, the
main body of the work was executed
1424-40, although earlier work was
incorporated.
The twin spires were added in 1552. The
west front contains an original 7-light
window and a round-arched doorway. The
nave has a good clerestory. See also the
charter room and the restored ceiling.

St Nicholas's Church Grampian   2 O   4
Aberdeen. The East and West Churches are
separate and divided by the arches of the
steeple and the walls of a 12th–13thC
transept. Part of this transept is called
Drum's Aisle which has fine mediaeval brass.
There is a portrait of the mathematician and
physician Duncan Liddel in his laboratory.
Daily during summer a 48-bell carillon is
rung.

St Serfs Tayside   2 K   9
Dunning, Perth. Dominated by its massive,
seemingly square and simple Norman tower,
which is in fact cunningly tapered. The light
from the small windows gives a subdued
effect to the nave, and one's gaze is drawn
into the chancel and beyond to the altar
glittering with candles.

Tullibardine Collegiate   2 K   9
Cathedral Tayside
Perth. A simple 15thC place of worship, and
one of the very few of its kind in Scotland
still unaltered. It has a remarkable open roof
and heraldic decorations. The gables have
typical Scots crow stepping.

Castles & ruins

Claypotts Castle Tayside   2 M   8
Near Broughty Ferry, Angus. Built like an old
armoured car, heavy and slow but all angular
and lethal, ready to kill. The best preserved
Z-plan tower house in Scotland, built
1569-88, it consists of a tall, central block
with two round corner towers on the
diagonal, with oversailing crowstepped
gabled upper storeys. There was a problem
combining domesticity with defence as can
be seen in the presence of a gun-loop in the
kitchen.

Craigievar Castle Grampian   2 M   4
Aberdeen. 4 miles S of Alford. Built 1626, it
epitomises the Indian summer of Scottish
Baronial style tower houses. Nostalgia for
yesteryear was very strong in such
buildings—as seen in the machicolated
parapets and the angle pepper-pot turrets,
originally a French feature and borrowed by
the mediaeval builders. This is a particularly
well-preserved example having been spared
later alterations. Cliff-like façades, 7 storeys
high, flower into a skyline of corbelled
turrets. Given to the National Trust for
Scotland in 1963.

Doune Castle Central   2 J 10
Perth. Brute of a castle, but timid also—a
product of that transitional phase when the
belligerent nature of castle architecture was
gradually giving way to domestic
considerations. Built in 1419–24 and
particularly well-preserved, it was originally
intended to be a more palatial residence.
What was built, consisting of Great Hall and
kitchen, with the lord's hall above the
gateway, is still spectacular.

Drum Castle Grampian   2 O   5
Aberdeen. A thick walled, 70-foot-high 13thC
tower house full of slit-eyed fierceness.
Becalmed by the decorum of the 17thC
crowstepped gabled mansion linked to it.
Closed winter.

Duart Castle Strathclyde   2 D   8
Duart Point, Isle of Mull, Argyll. A dark
brooding, sinister building on a rocky
eminence, or a fairy tale castle of
enchantment, it all depends on the weather.
Duart was commenced about 1250, extended
in 1633, ruined in 1691 and restored in
1911. The Tobermory Galleon prisoners
were held in the dungeon. *Closed winter.*

Duart Castle

Dunnottar Castle Grampian   2 O 5
Stonehaven, Kincardine. A breathtaking island stronghold with a savage history matched by the wild beauty of its position. The important parts of the remains are a 14thC tower and chapel and 16thC gateway. At one stage the Crown Jewels of Scotland were kept here but they were smuggled out before the castle fell to Cromwell.
Of interest is the Convenanters' memorial which commemorates a Scottish version of the Black Hole of Calcutta when 122 men and 45 women were herded into one dungeon where many died.

Dunvegan Castle, Skye

Dunvegan Castle Highland   2 A 2
Dunvegan, Skye, Inverness. Probably the oldest continuously inhabited castle in Scotland. A massive, square, uncompromising building with very few exterior frills. Parts of the building are said to date back to the 9thC, but the main body of work was executed between the 15th and 19thC. The moat is now bridged.
The castle is the seat of Clan MacLeod and is full of many of the clan's historical relics such as the 'fairy flag' and the 12thC chief Rory More's two-handed sword and drinking horn. *Closed winter.*

Fraser Castle Grampian   2 N 4
Kemnay, Aberdeen. A swaggering product of castellated architecture, huffing and puffing with corbelled upper storeys, pepper-pot turrets and pedimented dormers. Begun in 1575, it has a fine Great Hall. *Closed winter.*

Fyvie Castle

Fyvie Castle Grampian   2 N 3
Fyvie, Aberdeen. The swan-song of Scottish Baronial architecture. A swashbuckling, dare devil building of the early 17thC, with a 150-foot walled front, corner towers, corbelled turrets, gables and a monumental central entrance gate. Hidden in a wooded vale of the River Ythan, this colossus leers at you through the leaves. *No admittance.*

Glenbuchat Castle Grampian   2 L 4
Aberdeen. Ruins of a fine Z-plan tower house, with gun-loops designed more for display than hostility. *Irregular opening.*

Huntly Castle Grampian   2 M 3
Huntly, Aberdeen. Sometimes called Strathbogie Castle, this ancient pile, once the home of the Gordon family, represents a veritable pot-pourri of different ideas and periods. The earliest part of the castle is the Norman motte or earthmound; there is a mediaeval keep with enormously thick walls,

but perhaps pride of place goes to the Renaissance works by the first Marquis of Huntly between 1597 and 1602. Notice the delicately angular first floor windows, the carvings round the entrance to the north east tower, and finally the richly featured fireplaces.

Inverlochy Castle Highland   2 F 6
Inverness. 2 miles NE of Fort William. The development of castle enclosures in 13thC Scotland was a West European influence. The defence of the curtain wall, by projecting towers, or reinforced by a plinth complete with archer slits and battlements, was imperative. Many were provided with a keep. Inverlochy Castle, with quadrangular courtyard and massive round angle towers is a classic example. The keep was made by enlarging the north west tower.

Kildrummy Castle Grampian   2 M 4
Nr Mossat, Aberdeen. This is the best example of a 13thC stone courtyard castle in Scotland, and still possesses a complete layout of domestic buildings. Powerful and massive it is hard to believe that it was captured by Edward I who cruelly put to death here Robert the Bruce's youngest brother.

Midmar Castle Grampian   2 N 4
Aberdeen. W of Echt. Muscle-bound product of the Scottish Baronial style, with tall crowstepped gabled central keep and flanking towers off the diagonal angles—one round, one square, with stair turrets on the inside angles. Begun in 1570. *No admittance.*

Rait Castle Highland   2 J 2
Nairn. 3½ miles S of Nairn. A remarkably complete 13thC castle, notable for its round tower and remains of Gothic traceried windows. The scene of a bloody massacre in 1424 when the Mackintoshes attacked the Comyns.

Slains Castle Grampian   2 P 3
Aberdeen. 1½ miles N of Collieston. Dramatic ruins of a 15thC keep marooned on a high rocky headland. Destroyed by James VI in 1594, after he discovered a plot by the owner to land Spanish troops along this section of the coast.

Unusual buildings

Baxter's Lower   2 M 8
Dens Jute Mills Tayside
Dundee, Angus. Designed by Peter Carmichael in 1866, these mills are an excellent example of the architect-engineer's work. The name architect-engineer was given to the pioneers in the field of structural engineering who created works of artistic merit. It was the functional aspect of these which has had such a profound appeal for the architects of the 20thC.

Bell Rock Lighthouse Tayside   2 N 8
Angus. The oldest sea-swept lighthouse in Britain, it is everyone's idea of where the lighthouse keeper stands his lonely vigil. Built 1807–11, the tower was made of interlocking granite blocks to the same design as Smeaton Tower on the Eddystone Rock.

Brechin Round Tower Tayside   2 N 7
Brechin, Angus. Built nearly 1,000 years ago, it is one of two remaining round towers in Scotland: 87 feet high, 15 feet in diameter at

Huntly Castle

Round Tower, Brechin

the base, 12¼ feet at the top, and surmounted by a 14thC conical roof. Some 6 feet from the ground is a narrow round-headed doorway through which frightened clerics used to squeeze themselves to safety in times of danger.

Spey Bridge Grampian   **2 L 2**
Craigellachie, Banff. Designed and built in 1815 by the engineer, Thomas Telford. The castellated pair of stone turrets guarding the bridge at both ends are an interesting concession to the taste of the time, though of greater significance is the use of prefabricated cast iron in its construction.

Houses & gardens

Balmoral Castle Grampian   **2 L 5**
Nr Ballater, Aberdeen. A well-forested park on the River Dee which complements the Baronial style of this famous Royal summer residence bought and restored by Prince Albert in 1852.

Balmoral Castle

Blair Castle Tayside   **2 J 6**
Blair Atholl, Perth. A large whitewashed mansion of various dates in the Scots' Disneyland/Baronial style is the home of the Atholl family. Situated in wooded grounds and approached through an avenue of lime trees. Originally built in 1269, this imposing structure was restored in 1869 by Robert Bryce. The castle has a lovely tapestry room, Jacobite relics and a fine collection of armour and musical instruments. *Closed winter.*

Blair Castle, Perth

Branklyn Gardens Tayside   **2 L 8**
Perth. 12 miles E of Perth. A 2-acre garden created by Mr and Mrs John Renton and bequeathed to the National Trust for Scotland, it has a particularly fine collection of alpines, clematis and roses and old fruit trees, beneath which can be found a wide selection of herbaceous plants such as bearded iris, lilies and the heavenly blue meconopsis. *Closed winter.*

Brodie Castle Grampian   **2 K 2**
Moray. 15thC tower house with 17thC addition. Good collection of Dutch, Flemish and English paintings. *Closed winter.*

Coxton Tower Grampian   **2 L 1**
Moray. 3 miles E of Elgin. High spirited odd

coxton Tower, moray

ball, like Don Quixote, dreamily searching for the heroics of yesteryear. Tall, stone gabled tower with corbelled turrets and machicolated parapets, built in 1644 but belonging more to the intrigue and style of the preceding century.

Craigievar Castle Grampian   **2 M 4**
Nr Lumphanan, Aberdeen. One of the finest tower houses in Scotland, completed in 1626 and has remained unaltered and continuously inhabited. The building with its turrets and high pitched roofs was built by William Forbes. The fine hall has a magnificent Renaissance ceiling with pendants and retains its screens and a huge fireplace. Over the fireplace is the family motto, 'Do not waken sleeping dogs'. *Closed winter.*

Crathes Castle Grampian   **2 N 5**
Nr Banchory, Kincardine. Crathes dates from the late 16thC and is one of the finest Jacobean castles in Scotland. It contains some remarkable paintings of the Muses, the Virtues, and the Nine Worthies, and an oak panelled ceiling unique in Scotland. The Green Lady's Room is said to be haunted. The lovely garden dates from 1702 when the east wing was added.

Cullen House Grampian   **2 M 1**
Cullen, Banff. The castellated house, home of the Earl of Seafield, contains portraits by George Jamesone and R. Waitt, old weapons and fine painted ceilings.
Of interest: the library and the Monks' Passage, an underground passage which runs to the parish church—a relic of the days when the oldest part of the house was a monastic school. *Closed winter.*

Delgatie Castle Grampian   **2 N 2**
Delgatie, Aberdeen. The seat of Clan Hay. Rebuilt by the Hays 1315-16 on earlier foundations. Painted and groined ceilings (1570). Mary Queen of Scots stayed here in 1562. There is an interesting museum on armour and weapons. *Limited opening summer.*

Doune Park Gardens Central   **2 J 10**
Perth. 12 miles W of Doune. Laid out in the 19thC, it is divided into distinct areas: the walled garden with herbaceous plants and roses, glens with azaleas, rhododendrons and shrubs, a pinetum and parkland with spring bulbs.

Drummond Castle Tayside   **2 J 9**
Perth. 3 miles S of Crieff. A magnificent garden in the form of St Andrew's Cross dominates the scene from the terrace. Note the interesting sundial dated 1630 at the centre of the cross. The castle was built in 1491 but was partly demolished in 1745. Only the square tower of the original building still stands and contains an interesting collection of armour. *Closed winter.*

Duff House, Banff

Duff House Grampian   **2 N 1**
Banff, Banff. Noble, powerfully passionate country mansion designed by William Adam in 1730. It stands on an arcaded ground storey, with curving steps flanking a pedimented centre, articulated by boldly drawn Corinthian pilasters. The square corner towers and attic storey, crowned by urns, bring what might have been a delicate pastoral symphony to a noisy crescendo worthy of Vanbrugh at his most Wagnerian. *Closed winter.*

Glamis Castle Tayside   2 M   7
Glamis, Angus. What a complicated
confection this place is, with its clusters of
turrets, bartizans, and extinguisher roofs.
The castle owes its pleasant aspect to the
remodelling by the 1st Earl of Strathmore,
1675–87, but portions of the high square
tower, 15 feet thick, are much older. The
drawing room has a fine cradle-vaulted
ceiling. *Closed winter.*

Haddo House

Haddo House Grampian   2 O   3
Nr Ellon, Aberdeen. Built in 1732 to the
design of William Adam and greatly altered
inside by the first Marquess of Aberdeen in
1880. It contains interesting paintings, a
private chapel by G. E. Street and a
magnificent drawing room. *Closed winter.*

Leith House Grampian   2 M   3
Nr Kennethmont, Aberdeen. Austere, but
dignified 17thC courtyard house with gabled
dormers and corbelled turreted towers.
Home of the Leith family since 1650, the
house has some fascinating family treasures
and Jacobite relics. Attractive grounds with a
fine rock garden. *Closed winter.*

Leith Hall, Aberdeenshire

Pitmedden Grampian   2 O   3
Nr Udny, Aberdeen. 14 miles N of Aberdeen.
A formal garden originally planned by
Alexander Seton in 1675, it was neglected
until reconstructed by the National Trust for
Scotland using surviving yews and Seton's
pavilions as a guide line. There are 4
parterre gardens edged with miles of box
hedging and planted with 30,000 annuals
grown in the glasshouses here.

Provost Ross's House Grampian   2 O   4
Shiprow, Aberdeen. Built in 1593, it takes its
name from Provost John Ross of Arnage who
owned it as a town house in the 17thC. As
an excellent example of early domestic town
architecture it was restored in 1954 by the
National Trust for Scotland. *Limited opening
times.*

Provost Skene's House Grampian   2 O   4
Guestrow, Aberdeen. The home of a 17thC
provost or mayor of Aberdeen has been
restored as a museum. The Duke of
Cumberland stayed there in 1746 before
marching to Culloden where he defeated
Prince Charles Stuart.

Scone Palace Tayside   2 K   8
Scone, Perth. The present castellated mansion
is the early 19thC successor to a Renaissance
house and a mediaeval abbey. The latter was
the home of the Stone of Destiny until 1296
when Edward I of England removed it to
Westminster Abbey. There is a fine
collection of French furniture, china, ivories
and 16thC needlework, including bed
hangings worked by Mary Queen of Scots.
Closed winter.

Traditional dwellings

Black Houses
The characteristic black house is found
primarily in the outer isles today. The black
houses of Skye have hip-ended roofs and
overhanging eaves of thatch. The older plans
included house and byre under one roof.
The fire was in an open hearth with a small
smoke vent above. Traditionally, the house
was always built on sloping ground with the

black house

chimney added later

byre at the lower end. When the byre was
finally built as a detached building, the plan
was re-arranged and fireplaces built into the
end walls. A distinctive feature is the way
the thatch is dressed and bound around the
protruding chimney. The walls were built of
undressed stone, with the corners rounded.
The thatch was usually roped to the roof
and weighted by stones tied just above the
eaves, or hanging down the face of the wall.
Floors were normally beaten earth, whilst
most rooms were open to the roof. Windows
were few and small, and on some houses a
porch was added.

Clay Houses
The stone used to build the traditional black
houses was not always readily available. In
17thC Aberdeenshire, now part of the
Grampian Region, mud walling was used not
only for building the humble cottages but
also for the building of manses, churches and
town houses. Clay was mixed with straw and
the walls built up like the cob cottages of
Devon. But at the vulnerable points, such as
the sides of doors and windows, and the
corners of houses, hewn stone was used
whenever possible. The walls were built in
varying depths on stone or cobble footings to
keep out the damp. In parts of Moray, Banff
and Buchan, clay was mixed with sand and
straw. During the late 19thC this mixture
was combined with large stones in the
construction of many houses built in Banff,
Aberdeen and Turriff.

Cruck Houses
The shape and form of most Highland
houses were conditioned primarily by the
fierce Atlantic winds and secondly, by the
availability of materials. For instance, in the
outer islands, such as Tiree where there were
no trees, wood for the roof timbers of houses
was taken from the numerous ships wrecked
along the cost.
Most houses were built of crucks, but unlike
those in the Lowlands which were single
pieces of curved timber, here in the
Highlands they were jointed at the level of
the wall, the lower blade scarfed and pegged
to the upper. There are many examples of
cruck-framed buildings surviving in the
central and western Highlands, as well as in
south west Scotland.

Dalriadic Houses
A characteristic primarily of the Lowlands,
but also found here. The stone walls are
usually about 2 feet or more in thickness, the
stones roughly dressed to provide square
corners, jambs and lintels. A typical feature
is the use of the backs of box beds to form a
partition between the lobby and kitchen.

Industrial Housing
The late 18thC saw the establishment of the
cotton industry in Perth and Kinross, with
an industrial village of 2-storeyed stone and
brick houses being built around the Stanley
Cotton Mills in 1785. Other village

model village, Robres

communities were found at Fochabers, in the District of Moray in Grampian, and industrial housing at Deanstone Park in Perthshire. A characteristic of both developments is that the houses were whitewashed.

Seaport Houses
Many of the houses of the east coast towns are characterised by roll-moulded surrounds, crowstepped gables and angle turrets typical of the 17thC. Walls were invariably built of granite, while roofs were usually of stone slate. Some mid 18thC houses were built of blocks of peat, stone and broom, and others had their street façades especially stuccoed or rubble harled.

Museums & galleries

Abbot's House Tayside   2 N 8
Arbroath, Angus. The remains of a 12thC monastery which is now a folk museum with Robert the Bruce associations.

Aberdeen Art Gallery   2 O 8
& Museums Grampian
Schoolhill, Aberdeen. Good collection of Scottish art; painting and sculpture, watercolours and prints. Marine exhibits.

Angus Folk Museum Tayside   2 M 7
Kirkwynd Cottages, Glamis, Angus. Housed in a row of restored cottages, this is a museum displaying 200 years of domestic and farm life in the area.

Broughty Castle   2 M 8
and Museum Tayside
Broughty Ferry, Angus.. Local history, including whaling and armoury. Also Scottish Tartan Society Information Centre.

Doune Park Gardens &   2 J 10
Motor Museum Central
Doune, Perth. A fine collection of historic cars including many sports models collected by Lord Doune. Also woodland gardens with rare conifers. *Closed winter*.

Dundee City Museum   2 M 8
and Art Gallery Tayside
Albert Square, Dundee, Angus. Local history and archaeology, well documented. Has the oldest known astrolabe (a navigational instrument) which dates back to 1555.

Glenfiddich   2 L 3
Distillery Grampian
Dufftown, Banff. A museum attached to a whisky distillery showing the history of 'Scotch'.

St Vigeans Museum Tayside   2 N 8
Nr Arbroath, Angus. A cottage museum with a fascinating assortment of early Christian and mediaeval sculptured stones.

Skye Cottage Museum Highland   2 A 1
Kilmuir, Isle of Skye. Highland crafts and furniture in a restored island house. Also history of the island's past. *Closed winter*.

Spalding Golf Museum Tayside   2 M 8
Camperdown House, Dundee, Angus. Devoted to that most Scottish of games, with exhibits dating back to 1680.

West Highland   2 F 6
Museum Highland
Fort William, Inverness. Smacks of the Jacobites and Bonnie Prince Charlie but also includes local history and geology.

Zoos & aviaries

Aberdeen Zoo Grampian   2 O 4
Hazlehead Park, Aberdeen. A modern zoo with an emphasis on educational studies and native Scottish animals. The Exhibition House is especially interesting.

Blair Drummond   2 J 10
Safari Park Central
Blair Drummond Castle, Perth. Lions, giraffes, elephants, zebras and eland roam free. Monkey jungle. Performing dolphins, sealions; boat service to Chimpanzee Island. Also cheetah reserve. *Closed winter*.

Camperdown   2 M 8
Wildlife Centre Tayside
Camperdown Park, Dundee, Angus. A 10-acre zoo with wallabies, monkeys, goats, rabbits and donkeys. Also waterfowl including flamingoes.

Nature trails & reserves

Achlean Nature Trail Highland   2 J 4
Achlean, Inverness. Rich variety of birds on lower Cairngorms slopes; heather moorland. Two miles long. Also red deer and observation tower. Guide and details from Achlean Croft at the end of the road down Cairngorms' side of Glen Feshie—enter the glen from B970 near Feshiebridge.

Ben Lawers Nature Trail Tayside   2 H 8
Perth. Start at car park, turning left 5 miles N of Killin on A827. Outstanding alpine flora, but also good for mountain birds including buzzard and raven. 1½–2 miles. Leaflet from National Trust for Scotland Centre at car park.

Cairngorms National Nature   2 K 4
Reserve Highland
Cairn Gorm, Inverness. Highest mountain massif in Britain with arctic/alpine plants and a fine variety of breeding birds. Easy access to high tops via Cairn Gorm chairlift above Glen More (Speyside), and other good areas are above Glen Feshie at Allt Ruaidh and Achlean (Carn Ban Mor). Details from Nature Conservancy Council, 12 Hope Terrace, Edinburgh.

Cairngorms in winter

Highland Wildlife Park Highland   2 J 5
Kincraig, Inverness. Wolves, bears, wild cats, sea-eagles, as well as herds of European bison and deer in 250 acres of Speyside scenery. There is a café, shop and picnic area. *Closed Nov–Feb*.

Landmark Highland   2 K 3
Carrbridge, Inverness. Off A9 at Carrbridge on Aviemore–Inverness road. A free nature trail with Speyside forest species forms part of this unique centre. Excellent exhibition on Highland history, wildlife, etc. Car park and restaurant. *Closed winter*.

Loch An Eilean Highland   2 K 4
Inverness. Left from B970 after leaving from Rothiemurchus. Picturesque Speyside loch with typical forest birds and historic castle—associated with Wolf of Badenoch, and by nesting ospreys in the 19thC. 2½ miles. Guide from information centre on north side of the car park. *Closed winter*.

Loch of the Lowes   2 K 8
Nature Reserve Tayside
Perth. Leave Dunkeld on A923, fork right after about 1½ miles onto minor road which runs S of the loch. Scottish Wildlife Trust reserve with breeding ospreys and waterfowl, great crested grebes and woodland birds. Observation post and visitor centre open to the public.

Queen Elizabeth Forest Park   2 H 10
Nature Trail Central
Perth. Off A821 2 miles S of Aberfoyle. Starts at Cobleland caravan site. Birds and plants of

plantation and natural woodland, 5 routes,
1½–8 miles. Guide from Forestry
Commission, 6 Queen's Gate, Aberdeen.

Queen's Forest   **2 K 4**
Nature Trail Highland
*Glenmore, Inverness. Start at campsite at Loch
Morlich.* Superb scenery and birds of
Speyside forest and lower Cairngorms slopes.
Guide is available from Camp Warden.

Birdwatching

Flanders Moss Central   **2 H 10**
Perth. S of Lake of Menteith. Good for black
and red grouse, for the grey geese and often
also for hen harriers. The disused railway
line from Buchlyvie provides excellent
viewing of part of this large area, and other
access points are via B835, Buchlyvie to
A81, and from B822 south of Thornhill.

Fowlsheugh Grampian   **2 O 6**
*Kincardine. Crawton S from Stonehaven on
A92; turn left after about 3½ miles.* An
important stretch of seabird cliffs, with
breeding fulmars, razorbills, guillemots and
kittiwakes. Excellent views can be had from
many points along the clifftop footpath north
from Crawton.

Lake of Menteith Central   **2 H 10**
Perth. Good for winter wildfowl, including
whooper swans and, in the evenings, roosting
pink-footed geese. It is overlooked by B8034
from Arnprior to Port of Menteith, but
access via the Big Wood (enter from the
minor road south of the lake) is better as it
brings a chance of black grouse, capercaillie
and woodcock, among many woodland
species.

Spey Bay Grampian   **2 L 1**
Moray. Where the Spey meets the sea there
is an excellent area for breeding common
and Arctic terns, winter wildfowl and waders
and a good selection of migrants in season.
There are good viewing points at Spey Bay
village on the eastern side, while to the west
the river can be reached from Garmouth and
Kingston (from B9015 from Mosstodloch,
west of Fochabers).

Speyside Highland   **2 K 4**
Inverness. The valley of the Spey, a huge
area lying between the Monadhliaths to the
west and the Grampians to the east, has long
been a Mecca for birdwatchers. There are
dozens of good spots, and virtually
everything may be found by exploring from
the roads and numerous footpaths. Good
general areas include Rothiemurchus and
Abernethy Forests, Loch Morlich and Glen
More, and Glen Feshie. Parts of the marshes
below Loch Insh can be seen from B970; the
RSPB have a new reserve here. Birds of the
rivers and lochs include goosander, osprey,
common sandpiper and dipper, while forest
specialities include capercaillie, crested tit
(virtually confined to Speyside as a British
bird), crossbill and siskin. Buzzards and
sparrowhawks are not uncommon, and both
golden eagle and peregrine may be seen
around the fringes of the mountain massifs.

Troup Head Grampian   **2 O 1**
Banff. 10 miles E of Banff. Walk north to
the large gully and via its left bank to the
cliffs: a large seabird colony with breeding
fulmars, kittiwakes, razorbills, guillemots and
puffins, and with cliff-nesting house martins.

Ythan Estuary Grampian   **2 P 3**
Aberdeen. 13 miles N of Aberdeen. A long,
rather narrow estuary, excellent for migrants
of all kinds, in autumn especially, and
famous for its eiders at all seasons. Waders
and duck are abundant in winter, sea duck
included, and both grey lag and pink-footed
geese occur in good numbers. The adjacent
sands of Forvie National Nature Reserve
have large breeding colonies of terns
(common, Arctic, Sandwich and little). Much
of the area can be covered from the A975
north from Newburgh.

Fossil hunting

Visit the local museum. Its fossil collection
usually states where individual fossils have
been found. When visiting quarries always
seek permission to enter if they look
privately owned or worked. Be careful of
falls of rock.
Mostly unfossiliferous rocks in this area, but
small outcrops of Jurassic beds occur in
Skye, at Broadfoot and Loch Staffin and on
the island of Raasay and locally in Mull, in
which are ammonites, belemnites, gastropods
and bivalves. Also on Mull is some
cretaceous chalk with fossil echinoids,
belemnites, sponges, bivalves and some
ammonites.

Forests

The ancient 'Wood of Caledon'
Only small portions of this magnificent old
forest are left—the largest is in the basin
between the Cairngorms and Aviemore and
consists of the Abernethy, Glen More and
Rothiemurchus forests (where the native
Scottish wild cats prowl at night). Mostly
pine with some oak and birch. Good
examples of this old forest in the Forest of
Mar in the valley of the Dee. Many forests
of old pines occur in the Inverness glens.
Areas also exist precariously at Crannock
Wood as it reaches the Moor of Rannoch in
Argyll.

Birch forests
Natural birch forests occur in many places
below 2,000 feet. Craigellachie in Moray has
one of the most mature and extensive.

Oak forests
The remnants of the ancient oak forests still
exist in Argyll and extend up the Great
Glen. Also in the Trossachs in the Tay
Valley and along the shores of Lochs Earn,
Rannoch and Tay. They are normally below
700 feet.

Mountains

Approximately three-quarters of this area is
mountains and is very wild and inaccessible.
The main mountain groups are the
Monadhliath Mountains, the Cairngorms
and the Grampians. Don't venture off the
beaten track alone; weather conditions can
change suddenly and be very severe; tell
someone where you are going and have some
knowledge at least of how to survive.

Ardgour Highland   **2 E 6**
Inverness and Argyll. Reached by car ferry
across the Corran Narrows south of Fort
William. This is the short-cut to
mountainous Ardgour, whose peaks,
particularly Sgurr na h'Eanchainne, 2,597
feet, afford superb scenery when viewed
from Ballachulish.

Atholl Tayside   **2 J 6**
Perth. The central Perthshire highlands,
form the ancient dukedom of Atholl, and
much land is still owned by the present
Duke of Atholl, who has his seat at Blair
Castle. It is a richly-wooded country. Great
forests of larch, spruce and pine, all skilfully
tended by foresters, clothe its hillsides
between the heather moors above and the
flat fertile fields of the low straths. From the
north the River Garry flows down over rocky
cascades through the narrow Pass of
Killiecrankie to join the Tummel.

Ben Lawers Tayside   **2 H 8**
Perth. Rising steeply above Loch Tay, and
the A827 road from Aberfeldy to Killin, Ben
Lawers comes just short of the 4,000-foot
level. Rare alpine plants, including saxifrages
and mountain rhododendrons, survive here,
and the upper slopes have been declared a
national nature reserve.

Bennachie Grampian   2 N 3
Aberdeen. 5 miles W of Inverurie, nr the A979.
Named from the Gaelic *beinn a' ciche*, or
peak of the pap, from its shapely silhouette,
this fine isolated summit is called in Scots
'The Mither Tap', for the same reason. It
rises to 1,733 feet. Last outpost of the
Grampians, it commands wide views over
the broad plain of Buchan towards the North
Sea.

Ben Nevis, Inverness

Ben Nevis Highland   2 F 6
Inverness. The highest mountain in Britain,
the 'mountain of snows' towers up
majestically within a mile of the west coast
town of Fort William. In shape it is half a
plum pudding with the steep face to the
north west. In summer it's a gruelling climb,
5 miles of pack-pony track. Winter climbing,
under snow and ice, and the crags of the
north face, test the hardiest mountaineers.
On the rare clear days the views from Ben
Nevis' 4,406-foot summit extend over all the
Highland peaks, and far out to sea over the
Hebrides.

Cairngorm Mountains

Cairngorm Mountains   2 K 4
Highland
Scotland's largest group of high mountains,
the granite Cairngorms stand as a 30-mile-
broad, 4,000-foot-high range between
Aviemore and Braemar. No roads cross
them, and a drive round involves 140 miles!
The northern group, including Ben Macdhui
(Britain's second highest mountain at 4,296
feet) and the Cairn Gorm are separate from
the southern group of Braeriach and Cairn
Toul by the deep defile of the Lairig Ghru,
or 'gloomy pass'. The Cairngorms give the
toughest walking in Britain as well as severe
mountaineering. Near Aviemore are
Scotland's finest skiing grounds.

Lochaber   2 F 6
The wild hill country around Fort William,
east of Loch Linnhe. Ascend the lower Nevis
Glen and a steep path climbs above
waterfalls to the seclusion of the upper glen,
hidden amid the peaks. Grim Loch Leven is
an arm of the sea trapped within the
mountains. Glen Roy is crofting country and
famous for its 'parallel roads', gravel beds
high on the hillside that mark the shores of
an Ice Age glacier-dammed lake.

Monadhliath Mountains   2 J 4
Inverness. The Gaelic name, 'the grey
mountains', aptly describes this huge, dull,
50-mile range between Loch Ness and

Speyside. Good deer stalking and salmon
fishing, but lacking any other attractions.

Sidlaw Hills Tayside   2 L 8
Angus. A stately range of basalt hills,
running up the eastern side of Perthshire
and Angus for 40 miles from Perth to
Montrose, the Sidlaws shield Dundee from
northern blasts. Rich arable farms are carried
surprisingly high up their flanks, then give
way to heather-clad moorlands. The highest
point is Auchterhouse Hill, 1,492 feet.

Strathspey Highland   2 K 4
Known also as Speyside and Badenoch, this
upland strath, here 800 feet above sea level,
has frosty, snowy winters, fine for skiing,
and dry, sunny summers. Birchwoods and
pine forests clothe the lower slopes up to
2,000 feet, and beyond the high Cairngorm
range soars steeply to over 4,000 feet,
rimmed with snowfields even in June. Top-
spots include the Aviemore Visitor Centre
and Glen More Forest Park.

The Trossachs Central   2 G 9
Perth. An attractive mountain group centred
on Loch Katrine (the setting for Scott's
'Lady of the Lake'). Ben Ledi (2,873 feet) is
the highest point. Classical Scottish scenery
of woods, rugged mountains and lakes.

Glens

Angus Glens   2 M 7
From the fertile plain of Strathmore several
long glens run north from old stone foot-hill
market towns, to the heart of the Grampian
mountain mass. North of Blairgowrie the
main Braemar road, A93, winds up Glen
Shee to its highest level at Cairnwell, 2,000
feet. These uplands are always deep in snow

Glen Isla, Angus

each winter, but snowploughs maintain a
clearway to the Glen Shee skiing slopes.
Glen Clova and Glen Doll, north of
Kirriemuir, end at a magnificent
amphitheatre of crags, below the slopes of
Dreish, 3,105 feet and Glas Maol, 3,504 feet.
North of Edzell, Glen Esk winds through
sheep pastures and pinewoods to remote
Loch Lee, hemmed in by the eagle-haunted
deer-stalking hills of Mount Keen, 3,077
feet, and Muckle Cairn 2,699 feet.

Buchan Grampian   2 P 2
Aberdeen. Though little visited, this 'cold
shoulder of Scotland' has a most attractive
countryside. Its undulating raised plain, well-
farmed for grain and fat cattle, is broken at
intervals by the deep glens of winding rivers
like the Deveron, lined with ash trees, oaks
and alders. Stray ranges of hills are topped
by pinewoods, and the rugged coast has
staggering sandstone cliffs.

Glen Affric Highland   2 F 4
Inverness. The exotic name of this long glen
is derived from Gaelic *Glean Affaraich*,
meaning the 'glen where the oats are grown'.
It runs inland from Beauly just west of
Inverness for nearly 40 miles. The road that
winds up Loch Benevian's north shore gives
wide views over natural woods of Scots pine
and birch, managed by the Forestry

Glen Affric, Inverness

Commission. The southern road from Cannich leads to the Guisachan pinewoods and the Plodda Falls, the northern one through sprucewoods to remote Loch Mullardoch, where anglers seek trout and deer-stalkers range the mountainsides.

GlenCoe

Glen Coe Highland   2 F 7
Argyll. 'Just the place for a massacre!'—has been the comment of more than one tourist descending the gloomy Pass of Glen Coe on a stormy day, for the towering hills shut in the high road from Tyndrum to Fort William where it drops from the Highland plateau towards Ballachulish and Loch Leven on the coast. Inevitably memories of that dread day, the 13th February 1692, linger here where 40 Macdonalds were slain because of the tardiness of their chief MacIan in declaring allegiance to King William III. But on a clear day the majesty of Glen Coe's steep peaks, now protected as a National Trust for Scotland property, impress every beholder. North of the road stands the 'notched ridge' of Aonach Eagach, which ends on the west in the shapely Pap of Glen Coe, 2,403 feet. The southern buttresses are called, in the Gaelic, the 'shepherds of Etive', after the great sea loch on their southern flanks. The eastern, lesser one, is Buchaille Etive Beag, 3,129 feet, and the western higher one is Buchaille Etive Mor, with a summit buttress called Stob Dearg, the 'red post', of 3,345 feet.

The Great Glen Highland   2 H 3
Inverness. Glen More, or the Great Glen, cuts straight as a knife through the central Highlands, from Fort William on the west coast for 60 miles north east to Inverness on the east coast. A string of lochs in deep narrow basins are set between steep-sided mountains that rise past forested foothills to high moors and remote rocky summits.

Strathmore Tayside   2 O 5
The 'great valley' runs for 50 miles north east of Perth towards Stonehaven. Sheltered by the Grampians on the north and the Sidlaws to the south, its warm rich red-brown sandstone soils yield heavy crops of grain, raspberries and nowadays flower bulbs, grown under the world's thriftiest farming conditions.

Rivers & lochs

Deeside and River Dee   2 O 4
Grampian
Aberdeen. Running inland from Aberdeen for 70 miles, the level strath over which the river wanders carries thriving crops and herds of sleek beef cattle. Foothills as far as the eye can see are clothed in woods of the native Caledonian pines, with the snow-tipped Grampian peaks in the distance.

Lochs Linnhe, Leven,   2 F 6
Eil and Lochy
Every visitor to Fort William is sure to pass along the shores of one or all of these lochs, narrow waters set deep amid high hill ranges. Loch Linnhe is a 30-mile-long tidal inlet of the sea. Near Corran the deep and dismal Loch Leven runs 14 miles east; Loch Eil, also salt water, extends 9 miles west from Fort William; Loch Lochy is a 10-mile-long freshwater loch, fringed with the Forestry Commission's thriving conifer forests.

Loch Ness

Loch Ness Highland   2 H 3
Inverness. Longest loch in Scotland, Loch Ness lies in a deep trench of the hills between Inverness and Fort Augustus, 24 miles long and 1 mile wide. Mystery surrounds the Loch Ness Monster, a legendary dinosaur-like beast said to show itself occasionally above the surface.

Spey Grampian   2 G 5
The great River Spey rises in the very heart of the Highlands, in remote hills above Loch Spey. A turbulent river, subject to sudden spates, it often floods its higher valley, called Upper Strathspey, around Kingussie and Aviemore. Below Grantown-on-Spey it cuts through a scenic, forested gorge, rushing steadily north east to gain entry to the North Sea at the sandy bar of Speymouth, near Fochabers.

Strath Earn Tayside   2 J 9
Perth. Loch Earn, the headwater of this lovely salmon river, extends from Lochearnhead to St Fillans. Below the loch, the Earn winds through a wooded glen past the charming towns of Comrie and Crieff. Then it leaves the hills for its broad fertile strath, below the breezy hills of Gleneagles and Auchterarder, to join the larger River Tay near Bridge of Earn township.

River Tay Tayside   2 H 8
Perth. Loch Tay, fed by the River Dochart from Crianlarich, is the starting point of this great Perthshire river. From Aberfeldy to Dunkeld the River Tay winds through steep wooded hills, then crosses fertile Strathmore to Perth, the ancient bridgehead, where it becomes navigable by coastal craft. Slowly its estuary broadens out towards the handsome, industrial city and port of Dundee.

Canals

The Caledonian Canal   2 F 5
This very fine waterway, designed by Thomas Telford, is rare in at least two respects. Firstly it was commissioned by the Government, mainly to afford to ships that would have sailed round Cape Wrath protection from both the weather and any potential aggressors: the French were on the warpath at the time. (The canal is still much used by coastal fishing vessels.) Secondly the

Caledonian Canal

Caledonian Canal is only a true canal for about a third of its 60-odd miles in length. The rest of the way the navigable channel follows the several deep lochs that stretch along the Great Glen: lochs Linnhe, Lochy, Oich, Ness and up to the Moray Firth. There are 29 locks on the canal itself, which climbs up from either end to a summit level at Laggan. The great cutting here is the main engineering feature of the canal. Many of the locks are in 'staircase' formation (the best places are at Muirtown, Banavie and Fort Augustus). Indeed one of the best things about this waterway from the tourist's point of view is that good roads follow the canal virtually from end to end.

The 'Scot II', which in winter functions as the canal's official icebreaker and tug, runs daily trips (except Sunday) along the canal every summer. The boat leaves the top of Muirtown Locks, passes through Dochgarroch Lock and then cruises down Loch Ness to Castle Urquhart and back.

Archaeological sites

An Sgurr Highland   2 B 5
Eigg, Inverness. The Iron Age fort at An Sgurr, with bank and ditch defences, occupies one of the most spectacular fort-sites in Scotland.

Ardoch Roman Fort Tayside   2 K 8
Ardoch, Perth. The defences of the Roman fort are among the most impressive of their kind in Britain. Originally a fort of over 5 acres with triple ditches, it was the largest camp in Britain and held 40,000 Roman soldiers. 2 more ditches were added on the north and east sides, making 5 in all; these would have held attackers within the range of missiles thrown from the fort.

Clava Cairns Highland   2 J 3
Clava, Culloden Moor, Inverness. The group of Neolithic cairns on Culloden Moor belongs to a type of monument confined to this area of north east Scotland. The burial cairns are roughly circular, with a passage for access to the central chamber, and are supported round the edge by a kerb of heavy slabs; around each cairn is a ring of free-standing upright stones. The associated ring cairns lack the passage, and now consist of an open ring with retaining kerb; they also have a surrounding place structure.

Dun Bhuirg and Dun Nan Caeard Strathclyde   2 A 8
Iona, Argyll. Dun Bhuirg and Dun Nan Ceard are Iron Age duns, small sub-circular forts with a thick surrounding wall of drystone masonry. The single entrance passages were apparently defended with timber bars set in sockets.

Dyce Sculptured Stones Grampian   2 O 4
Church of St Fergus, Dyce, Aberdeen. Two pagan Pictish symbol-stones are preserved in the old parish church.

Finavon Tayside   2 M 7
Nr Forfar, Angus. Finavon is a classic example of a 'vitrified' fort, a type of Iron Age hill fort apparently peculiar to Scotland.

These were originally defended with a stone wall about 20 feet thick, braced with timber beams, and timber buildings probably stood against the back of the wall.
In a subsequent fire, presumably during a siege, the buildings and bracing timbers caught fire; the stone was fused (vitrified) by the heat, and the complete length of wall collapsed.

Glenelg Brochs Highland   2 D 4
Glenelg, Inverness, 10 miles S of Kyle of Lochalsh. This well-preserved group of monuments illustrates 2 types of Iron Age defensive structures peculiar to Scotland. Dun Grugaig is a *dun*, a small fort, usually less than 60 feet across, which could be round, oval or D-shaped in plan. They had thick drystone walls, sometimes with an inner stair up to the parapet, and an entrance passage defended by timber barriers. Dun Telve, and Dun Troddan are *brochs*, defensive towers dating from the late Iron Age. The base is a massive masonry ring on which stands a hollow wall built of 2 concentric drystone shells; these are bonded at intervals by continuous rows of slabs, forming galleries inside the wall connected by winding stone stairways. The entrance passage was defended by guard cells and a wooden barrier.

Inchtuthil Tayside   2 K 8
Caputh, Perth. The Roman legionary fortress (Pinnata Castra) was built during the Scottish campaigns of around AD80, and guarded the main exit from the Highlands down the River Tay. The rampart and ditch of the rectangular fortress, and those of the nearby stores compound, can still be seen; excavation has shown that the fortress was never completed.
A short distance to the north is the contemporary Cleaven Dyke, a Roman boundary earthwork with a watch-tower.

Loanhead of Daviot Grampian   2 N 3
Daviot, Aberdeen. The Bronze Age site is of a type called a 'recumbent' stone circle and is peculiar to this part of Scotland. The irregular circle of uprights increases in height up to 2 large stones which flank a massive flat block. In the centre is a low ring cairn, a circle of stones with a kerb of upright slabs.

Maiden Stone Grampian   2 N 3
Nr Inverurie, Aberdeen. The Maiden Stone is a fine example of the symbol stones carved during the dark ages, and shows early Christian influence. One side has an elaborately carved Celtic cross, the other has symbols used by the native pagan Picts.

Pitcur Earth-house Tayside   2 L 8
Pitcur, Angus. The Iron Age 'earth-houses' of Scotland, of which Pitcur is a typical example, belong to the class of monuments known elsewhere as fogous or souterrains, and are usually attached to domestic or defensive settlements.
Most earth-houses are smaller than Pitcur which, at 190 feet long, is the largest known. They consist of a narrow underground gallery, curved in plan, entered by descending a flight of stairs and a narrow 'creep'. Others in the county are at Ardestie, Carlungie, and Tealing.

Raedykes Roman Camp Grampian   2 O 5
Raedykes, Kincardine. The Roman camp at Raedykes covers some 120 acres, and probably belongs to the campaign conducted in Scotland by the Emperor Septimus Severus during the early 3rdC. Such camps were essentially temporary, and accommodation would have been in leather tents.
Raedykes is unusual in its irregular outline, which follows the natural contours. It has a single bank and ditch defence, and probably had 6 entrances, of which 5 survive; there are simple breaks in the bank with a short bank placed in front to provide defensible cover.

Rubb'an Dunain Highland   2 B 4
Skye, Inverness. The Iron Age dun at Rubh'an Dunain is of the type known as 'galleried' from the method of building the defensive wall. The overall plan follows the sub-circular form of a standard dun, but the drystone wall is built in 2 concentric shells, with the hollow between spanned by horizontal slabs.
There is also a chambered Neolithic cairn on the site, built of drystone masonry.

Footpaths & ancient ways

Glenuig Path Highland   2 C 6
Inverness. The hamlet of Glenuig, situated on a tiny bay between Loch Moidart and Loch Ailort, has only recently been given a road. Until then everything came by sea, or via a 6-mile path to the nearest road at Kinlochmoidart. The coffins of the dead had to be carried out along this path and at the top of the pass between the 2 villages, where the corteges halted for a rest, cairns were erected. The old path, which has breathtaking views, can still be used. It also extends through Glenuig to Inverailort 7 miles to the north.

Regional sport

The entries under this heading in the following section—**Northern Scotland**—apply equally to this section.

Canoeing   2 C 6
This area offers unrivalled variety and opportunity. The fast flowing rivers such as the River Tay and River Spey are a test for the experts. The chain of fresh-water lochs linked by the Caledonian Canal between Fort William and Inverness offer great scope for canoe camping.
The west coast between Ardnamurchan and Mallaig offers a unique chance to view marine wildlife, and just north of here the canoe is the only real alternative to foot for exploring the remote area of Knoydart.

Climbing and hillwalking   2 F 6
The magnificent desolation of the Highlands provides exhilarating climbing and walking. Britain's highest mountain, Ben Nevis (4,406 feet), offers a challenge both to the hillwalker who toils up one of the several well known paths, and to the climber who insists on fighting his way up the precipitous north face.
The saw-toothed Cuillin Mountains on the Island of Skye are the steepest and rockiest in Britain and there are only a few summits which can be reached without rock climbing or at least a good deal of scrambling. The Cairngorm Mountains offer good climbing, with the added attraction of the recognised climbing bases of Aviemore and Kingussie. For the man on foot the western and central Highlands offer unparalleled freedom. Don't forget that in summer the weather is very unstable: in a matter of an hour brilliant sunshine can change to a thick wet driving Scottish mist.

Curling   2 H 2
Played all over Scotland for at least 350 years, and in essence rather like bowls on ice. The curling stones look like old fashioned earthenware bedwarmers and are made from polished granite with handles let into the top. The object of the game is to slide the curling stone down the ice so that it stops inside the tee; the team with the most stones at the centre of the tee is the winner. There are curling rinks at Aviemore, Aberdeen, Inverness and Dundee.

Highland Games   2 K 7
Every year some 35 Highland games or gatherings are held throughout Scotland,

Typical event at a Highland gathering

mainly in August and September. Their origin is obscure but they have a history going back to the 11thC. More than a Pictish athletics meeting, beside the traditional Highland sports there are bagpipe and dancing competitions. The nice thing about these events is that they are still run and entered in by the locals, although no one minds if the visitor wants to enter a competition. However, beware of offering to toss the caber. The largest of the cabers at the Braemar Gathering is over 19 feet long and weighs 120 lb. It is claimed that this has been tossed successfully less than 5 times. Other traditional sports are throwing the heavy hammer and putting the stone. You can see the games at Portree in Skye, Crieff, Glenfinnan, Pitlochry, Braemar and Aboyne.

Shinty   2 J 5
If skiing is the new sport of the Highlands, shinty is very much the traditional game; described as the fastest game played on foot in the world. Like the related game of hurley played in Ireland, it is graceful and thrilling, a species of hockey unshackled. There is no rule on how high the stick can be raised to strike the ball. The game is played all the way up the Great Glen, in Skye, along the course of the River Spey, and in other parts of the Highlands. Shinty is primarily a winter sport and skiing visitors can see the game played at Kingussie, near Aviemore, at the Dell Ground.

Skiing   2 K 4
It is only in recent years that the magnificent potential for skiing in Scotland has been discovered and exploited. There are now 3 very modern skiing centres, 2 in the Cairngorms at Aviemore and Glenshee, and the third in Glen Coe near Fort William. They all possess chair lifts, ski tows and schools and in fact everything one has come to expect from the long established Swiss resorts. Indeed Scots skiing, when conditions are right, is every bit as good as Switzerland. The only real drawback is the unpredictable weather. The official season is *Dec–May.*

Festivals

There are a number of local festivals and events—contact the local Information Centre for details.

Aberdeen Festival Grampian   2 O 4
Aberdeen. A 2-week festival during which the Highland Games take place. *Jun.*

Montrose Festival Tayside   2 N 7
Montrose, Angus. Concerts, art exhibitions and drama are presented at this festival, founded in 1963. A military pipe and drum band is usually on hand. *Sep.*

Pitlochry Festival Theatre   2 K 7
Tayside
Pitlochry, Perth. Started as a theatre festival under canvas. The spirit is still maintained, although there are many new additions. *Apr–Sep.*

Royal Highland Gathering   2 L 5
Grampian
Braemar, Aberdeen. A world-famous gathering of the Clans and a festival. *First Sat in Sep.*

Skye Provincial Gaelic Mod   2 B 3
Highland
Portree, Skye, Inverness. A festival of song is
held in *Jun.* Also at Portree the Skye
Highland Games are held on the third *Thur*
in *Aug,* and piping competitions at
Dunvegan Castle also during *Aug.*

Special attractions

Aberdeen Fish Auctions Grampian   2 O 4
Fish Market, Commercial Quay, Aberdeen. For
early risers only. At 7.30 in the morning this
lively market starts its fish auction which the
public can watch.

Flambeaux Procession Tayside   2 J 9
At Comrie in Perthshire one of the most
exciting Hogmanay or New Year's Eve
celebrations takes place. Townspeople in
fancy dress, led by pipers and torchbearers
march to the main square. There the
costumes are judged and prizes given.
Dancing, singing and general merry making
follow, and all revels come to an end when
the torches have burnt out.

Landmark Visitor Centre Highland 2 K 4
Inverness. S of Carrbridge. Described as
Europe's first visitor centre, Landmark
consists of a multi-screen theatre showing the
history of the Highlands, an exhibition of
man's survival in the Highlands from the Ice
Age to the 20thC, and a shop of Scottish
crafts. Nature trails run through its pine
woods. In the restaurant with bar, salmon
and venison are served as a speciality. The
terrace has a lovely view across the mirror
waters of a small loch.

Pitlochry Dam   2 K 7
and Power Station Tayside
The North of Scotland Hydro-Electric Board
has a display of their activities and provides
tours of the power station during daylight
hours. But perhaps more fascinating is the
large fish ladder which is fitted with an
observation chamber so that the passage of
some 5,000 salmon a year can be viewed.

Pitlochry hydro-electric scheme

Strathisla Distillery Grampian   2 M 2
Keith, Banff. Established in 1780, it is
another claimant for the status of being the
oldest working distillery in Scotland. Guided
tours in *Jun, Jul,* and *Aug.*

Whisky Distilleries
There are hundreds of whisky distilleries in
the Highlands. They can be recognised by
the pagoda-shaped tops of the kiln houses
where the barley is dried before malting. For
security reasons not all that many throw
their doors open to visitors. Among those
which you can visit, Glenfiddich Distillery
gives guided tours. There is also a bar and a
Scotch Whisky Museum.

Regional food & drink

For additional Scottish delicacies, refer to
some of the entries in the next section which
are also common to this area.

Aberdeen sausage
The home of the Aberdeen Angus—famous
for steaks—this granite city has also given us
Aberdeen sausage. A mixture of minced beef,
bacon, oatmeal and spices which have been
boiled in a greased cloth.

Arbroath smokies
These are smoked haddock which have been
salted before smoking in the 'Arbroath
Smoke Barrel'.

Caboc
A small soft cream cheese rolled in oatmeal.

Cloutie dumpling
Boiled in a cloth and similar to Christmas
pudding, this is eaten very often at
Hallowe'en.

Cock-a-leekie soup
This is a very rich clear soup, more akin to a
stew of chicken and leeks. Stewed prunes are
sometimes added.

Crowdie
This is an example of one of the many local
cream cheeses. The curd is mixed with
double cream and salt and served with
oatcakes and butter.

Cullen skink
This local soup is based on smoked haddock,
preferably from Findon, which is thickened
with mashed potato.

Dundee cake and marmalade
Keillers of Dundee first made orange
marmalade commercially in the late 18thC.
The cake is a rich fruit mixture, whose top
is decorated with almonds.

Finnon haddie
Findon is the home of this fine smoked
haddock. It is ideal poached and also in
kedgeree.

Forfar bridie
A tasty half-moon shaped pasty filled with
meat and onions. Local delicacy of the town
of Forfar.

Grouse
Shooting of grouse begins on the 'glorious
twelfth' of August and the birds will be on
the table of many restaurants that night. For
best results the bird should be 'hung' for
about a week.

Isy Tunkle's smokie pie
A fish pie made with Arbroath smokies and
served bubbling brown and hot.

Scottish flummery
For those who like a drop of the hard stuff
in their pud—a rich mixture of honey, cream
and whisky. A favourite of Flora MacDonald
who smuggled Bonnie Prince Charlie to Skye
and was said to have been arrested whilst
eating a bowl of it.

Whisky
There are many distilleries in the area
around the Dufftown, Craigellachie and
Rothes—that of the major Highland Malts,
the Glenlivets and Glenfiddich. Many of the
distilleries are open to visitors.

Northern Scotland

3

Northern Scotland begins with a jagged belt of mountain and moorland stretching from the North Sea in the east to the Atlantic in the west. This is the land of Wester Ross, East Ross and the Black Isle. Wester Ross, with its long, torn coastline strewn with narrow sea lochs and formidable cliffs, has a craggy wall of mountains, a myriad of steep sharp twisting glens, and giant waterfalls like those of Glomach plunging down 370 feet from scarred, brutish mountains. Its plants are exotic and sub-tropical, its beaches covered in golden sand, and the whole coast is bathed in the mild Gulf Stream climate. To the east is East Ross and the Black Isle, roped in by the Moray Firth and by a horizon ringed with mountain peaks. There are huge, fertile peninsulas and pine-clad hills rolling into the sunset; deep, shaded, wooded river valleys and a grey-green gouache of moorland skirting the mountains. Dominating it all, like a great thunder cloud highlighted by the sun, is Ben Wyvis, from the top of which seven counties, one ocean and a sea can be seen on a clear day. It is a land of broad river estuaries and vast salt marshes; hills like stranded whales are sprinkled with tiny hamlets, and the sheltered harbours like Fortrose or Cromarty are fronted by long sandy beaches and elegant promenades.

It was here that William the Lion built strong fortresses at Dingwall, Redcastle and Dunskaith to check the ever violent Norsemen of the Black Isle. It was also here that Robert the Bruce's queen was kidnapped from the sanctuary of the Church of St Duthus, Tain; and it was here that the clan battles were at their most bloody. In one incident the Mackenzies surprised a large force of Munros along a ridge of land. So great was the slaughter that the foot of the slope was piled high with severed heads which had rolled down. This was the land settled by the first Neolithic farmers over 5,000 years ago, and the land later to be ruled by Vikings.

To the north is Caithness and Sutherland, a giant loch-filled country bordered on three sides by moorland, high cliffs and wild seas, while the fourth side, in the south, is walled in by mountains. The land is rich in ancient rock formations and raked by glacial scars. To the north east lie the larger towns like Thurso and Wick; Scrabster is the ferry port for the Orkneys, Faroes, Iceland and Scandinavia. Fishing harbours are glued to headlands and sweeping bays are edged in golden crescents of sand. Caithness, a triangular tract of land long ruled by the Vikings, is also rich in chambered Bronze Age cairns and Iron Age brochs. There are high cliffs sculpted by the furies of the Pentland Firth into architectural wonders like the Stacks of Dunscansby, the soaring five rock pillars which resemble the remains of a giant mythical temple. Although John O'Groats is popularly known as land's end, Dunnet Head is in fact the most northerly point of Britain's mainland. At Dounreay stands Britain's first atomic fast-breeder reactor. Along the mountainous north coast, guillemot and razorbill can be seen, and puffin frequent the area near neighbouring Sutherland.

Orkney and Shetland are the Viking Isles, a mosaic of some 170 islands, of which only one third are inhabited. They became part of Scotland 500 years ago. It was on these islands that Stone Age man settled and built the village of Skara Brae, and the inspiring chambered tomb of Maes Howe, possibly the finest remains in Western Europe. Over in Shetland, Mousa Broch is one of the best preserved prehistoric towers in existence. The Orkneys are edged by silver beaches and surrounded by seas filled with skate, halibut and shark, whilst inland the numerous lochs are filled with trout. Kirkwall is the Orkney capital, a handsome stone-floored city of narrow streets carved from a cliff of buildings. This was the Viking stronghold, dominated by their monumental Romanesque cathedral. Shetland was colonised by the Vikings in the 8thC and they did not relinquish their control until the mid 15thC. But the Viking presence still prevails in numerous place names as well as much of the dialect. Towns like Lerwick and Scalloway are picturesque nests of tight-fitting buildings. Inland, Aith and Voe are scattered crofting communities, hugging the bare coast at the edge of uninhabited moorland. The cliffs and headlands are alive with puffins, guillemots and kittiwakes. In the moorland you can find Arctic skuas and red-throated divers, while colonies of gannets nest at Noss and Herma Ness.

Lerwick

Forty miles north west of Scotland are the Western Isles which comprise the Outer Hebrides. A long sweeping chain of islands from Barra Head in the south to the Butt of Lewis in the north. Here you will find the last stronghold of Gaelic. The islands to the south are predominantly Catholic, but in the Protestant northern islands, the Sabbath is strictly observed. Lewis

cliffs, Hermaness

is the largest and most northerly; a broad sweep of lush, green hills and moorland running down to the rugged mountains of Harris in the south. After the Clearances and the introduction of sheep to the fertile pastures inland, the evicted crofters eeked out a desperate living along the rocky east coast, or amongst the foot hills of the west where they were forced to move. You can still see their black houses or remains of their shielings, the small stone huts erected in the summer pastures of the uplands. The capital of Lewis is colourful Stornoway, seaport, market and manufacturing town, and now the home of Harris Tweed. But it was not always so, for it was Harris, in the south, where the tweed was first made and where weavers still practise the old craft of hand-weaving.

North Uist is a rich meadowland lined with long, sandy beaches and dotted with chambered cairns and prehistoric forts. Mute swans thrive here and winter brings great gangs of geese. Further south is flat Benbecula with its moorland, machair and many lochs. At Milton, on South Uist, a monument marks the birthplace of Flora MacDonald, who helped Bonnie Prince Charlie to escape to France. But possibly the most idyllic of all the islands is tiny Barra. Converted to Christianity in the 6thC, it is a rolling blanket of meadowland punctuated by ragged peaks and endowed with a carpet of 1,000 different wild flowers. This is the 'Garden of the Hebrides' where the only runway is a sandy strip of beach washed daily by the sea.

The coast

Applecross Highland   3 D 8
Ross & Cromarty. Pop 600. On a good day it is an exhilarating experience to follow the hairpin bends of the 'Pass of the Cattle'—the steepest road in Britain—which leads to the remote hamlet of Applecross. The views from the top of the pass (2,054 feet above sea level) are magnificent. Previously, the only other way to reach Applecross was by ferry from the Kyle of Lochalsh. But since 1976, the new road to Cuanig has improved accessibility. Red sand bay, with cliffs

The Road to Applecross

Armadale Bay Highland   3 K 2
Sutherland. West of Strathy, it is a handful of farm cottages, low dunes and sandy bay. On a wet day, there is an air of grey doom like the end of the world, but when the sun is out the change is electric—a sharp Mediterranean light streams out and makes you want to pack up and live here for ever in the cathedral quietness.

Avoch Highland   3 J 7
Ross & Cromarty. Pop 800. Thriving fishing village of whitewashed cottages clambering round the edge of a sheltered bay overlooking Moray Firth. An interesting feature is the way the houses are turned with their gable ends facing the furies of the winter seas like a shield. Boats could be drawn up between the houses for shelter. It is said that the villagers, who have a particularly distinctive appearance and dialect, are descendents of the survivors of a wreck of the Spanish Armada. The beach is sandy with a shingle backing. Strong currents make bathing unsafe.

Badbea Highland   3 L 7
Caithness. Ruins of a 19thC crofting hamlet overhanging the cliff edge. It was here that the crofters sought to start a new life after being cleared from the lush pastures inland. A 22-foot-high, 10-foot-square slab stands reverently in memory of the families who lived a bleak existence here a 100 years ago.

Balblair Highland   3 K 7
Ross & Cromarty. Handful of cottages with almost as many churches scattered on the southern bank of the mouth of Cromarty Firth, and connected by ferry to Invergordon on the northern bank. The parish itself has 7 churches, 4 of which are ruined. The Church of St Martin, now a rubble ruin, was built in the 13thC. Also of interest: the church of Cullicudden 1609; and the 18thC parish church with a porch at either end. Inside are pews allocated to various farms and estates, while the Laird's pews are reached through a separate entrance.

Balintore Highland   3 K 6
Ross & Cromarty. Pop 400. Straggling fishing village and harbour dug in round a gentle sandy bay.

Berriedale Highland   3 L 7
Caithness. A handful of houses clinging to the wooded slopes by the junction of 2 rivers and a small harbour. Rising steeply behind are 2 narrow green valleys. The tiny beach is reached by a suspension bridge sealed in a wall of perpendicular cliffs. To the NW is a monument to King George V's youngest son, who was killed here in an air crash during the Second World War.

Berriedale

The Black Isle Highland   **3** J   7
Ross & Cromarty. The Black Isle is
mysteriously named as it is not an island but
a green fertile peninsula with a ridge of
forested land crowning the patchwork of
undulating fields: in the summer roses bloom
in profusion. Tradition maintains that it
owes this name to its mild climate—which
never allows the landscape to become white
with settled snow.
Though some resorts have sandy shingle-
backed beaches, and between Rosemarkie
and Cromarty there are steep cliffs and rocky
bays, the coastline is mainly fringed with
muddy saltings—the haunt of wading birds.
Ornithologists will find this a particularly
rewarding area.

Bonar Bridge Highland   **3** J   6
Sutherland. Pop 500. Sprinkling of houses
guarding the narrow inlet between the Kyle
of Sutherland and the long, curving sea
waters of the Dornoch Firth. The fishing
hamlet was named after the bridge built by
Telford in 1811- 12 to cross the narrows.
This was rebuilt following a flood in 1892
and finally replaced by a steel bow-string
bridge in 1973.

Brora Highland   **3** K   5
Sutherland. Pop 1,000. EC Wed. With its
beach, golf course and excellent fishing river
Brora is a predictably popular resort. Rather
more unexpected is the fact that it also has a
coal mine (which has been worked since the
16thC) and owes its development as much to
industry as to tourism. There is a tweed
mill, a distillery and a brickmaking plant. Of
interest—the tiny, decayed harbour and the
Victoria Jubilee drinking fountain. Long
sandy beach.

Castletown Highland   **3** L   5
Caithness. Pop 900. A 19thC village built by
James Traill of Castlehill, one of Scotland's
enlightened agricultural improvers, to house
the workers of the flagstone quarry, which
he established in 1824. The small harbour,
from where the flagstone was shipped all
over the world, stands on the western side of
Dunnet Bay. This neat village is entered
under an umbrella of trees planted by Mr
Traill. It is an oasis of wooded greenery in a
windswept bare land.

Cromarty Highland   **3** K   7
Ross & Cromarty. Pop 500. EC Wed. A
labyrinth of winding narrow streets and rose-
covered, brightly painted houses nestle on a
lip of land curling out into the mouth of
Cromarty Bay. A once prosperous 16th and
17thC port and Royal burgh that slid into
rapid decline—to be rescued momentarily in
the late 18thC by the entrepreneur George
Ross, who built the harbour and established
a healthy portfolio of industry including a
brewery and cloth factory. The eventual
eclipse of the harbour and subsequent
crumbling decay of the town has been
daringly rescued in recent years in a
commando style raid of conservationists. The
National Trust for Scotland in collaboration
with the local development council have
sensitively restored many 18thC cottages and
consequently much of the fishing village
aura of some 2 centuries ago. But the talk
now is more of pottery and knitwear than
bow-sprits and sail cloth.
Of interest is the restored courthouse, 1782;
14thC cross; Gaelic Chapel, built by George
Ross in the late 18thC for the Highlanders
working in his cloth mills; Hugh Miller's
cottage, an early 18thC thatched cottage
where the stonemason, turned famous
geologist, was born in 1802. Muddy shingle-
scattered sandy beaches. Bathing safe except
when heavy rain produces strong currents.

Dingwall Highland   **3** J   7
Ross & Cromarty. Pop 4,200. EC Thur.
County town built of sunset pink stone in a
meandering hideout at the head of the
Cromarty Firth. Former mediaeval
stronghold of the earls of Ross, it was made
a Royal burgh in 1226. Fine 18thC

Tolbooth. There is a tall stone tower, built
in the 19thC to the memory of 'Fighting
Mac', the able general Sir Hector Macdonald
who rose from the ranks.
The mudflats and saltings of the Conon
Estuary make it unsuitable for bathing.

Dornie Highland   **3** E   9
Ross & Cromarty. Pop 100. Highland
landscape of mountain, loch and sea entombs
a handful of cottages lining the narrow,
rocky mouth of Loch Long where it joins
the broad waters of Loch Duich. Nearby is
Eilean Donan Castle, a formidable 13thC
fortress rebuilt in 1932.

Dornoch Highland   **3** K   6
Sutherland. Pop 800. EC Thur. Dornoch with
its mellow sandstone buildings set round the
cathedral, which dominates the land for
miles around, is the nicest town in northern
Scotland. It has three other claims to fame:
the best sunshine record in northern
Scotland, the third oldest golf course in the
world, and it burnt the last witch in
Scotland. Make time to take the gentle walk
up Ben Struie: the view is excellent.
Miles of safe sandy beaches curve away from
either side of the town.

Dunbeath Highland   **3** L   7
Caithness. Pop 200. Fragmented collection of
houses and tiny harbour scattered like seeds
along the mouth of a river. To the south, on
a precipitous pedestal of cliff, stands the
brooding menace of a 15thC keep, much
enlarged in the 19thC. Of interest in the
village is the Laidhay Croft Museum, a
restored croft with period furniture, which
evokes the hardy life in a homestead of a
century ago.

Dunnet Highland   **3** L   5
Caithness. Pop 100. Smattering of houses
under shelter of convenient cover in a corner
of Dunnet Bay, which has bulldozed its way
inland with an epic sweep of sandy beach.
The cabbage-white church has a 14thC
tower. North to Dunnet Head, in a heather
wilderness of peat bogs and pools, stands a
lighthouse crowning the 300-foot-high cliffs
above the rollers of the frothing seas of the
Pentland Firth. Dunnet Head itself is the
most northerly point of mainland Scotland.

Cliff, Dunnet Head

Durness Highland   **3** H   2
Sutherland. Pop 100. Crofting village
dispersed in irregular clusters of cottages,
that hug a loch-filled limestone headland.
There is a ruined church, built 1619. To the
east of Durness is Smoo Cave, consisting of
three chambers. The first is as cavernous as
a cathedral, the other two, one having a
magnificent 80-foot waterfall, are for pot
holers only.

Embo Highland   **3** K   5
Sutherland. Pop 300. Weather-beaten fishing
village hidden behind a wall of gables, like
the shields of an embattled highland clan,
facing the onslaught of the North Sea.
Sandy, dune-backed beach to the north.

Fortrose Highland   **3** K   7
Ross & Cromarty. Pop 1,100. Most of the
buildings of this demurely attractive village
are perched decorously on the plateau above
Chanonry Point, encircling the ruins of
Fortrose Cathedral. Near the harbour some
of this discipline is lost and the houses spill
colourfully down the grassy slopes towards
the golf course and the fine sand and shingle
beach.

Gairloch Highland   3 E 6
Ross & Cromarty. Pop 1,800. EC Wed. A
village built round a small harbour, with
magnificent views to the south of Ben
Alligan (3,232 feet) and Baeishven (2,869
feet) and across to the Outer Hebrides. The
large fleet of trawlers have to wait their turn
in the loch outside the little harbour before
unloading their catch at the quay. An
immense 8-mile sweep of white sand
stretches westwards from the village.

Golspie Highland   3 K 5
Sutherland. Pop 1,400. Huddled nest of
houses and harbour punctuate a sweeping
crescent of sand and rock. A thriving fishing
port in the 19thC, its harbour is now a
bright tangle of pleasure craft. Golspie is the
shopping centre for the inland farms and
crofts. Of interest is 18thC St Andrew's
Church; a giant statue of the 1st Duke of
Sutherland crowns a 1,300-foot peak to the
south west; Dunrobin Castle, 1 mile north of
the town, consists of a huge square turreted
13thC keep with 18thC additions. The castle
underwent drastic remodelling in the 19thC
by Sir Charles Barry, who transformed it
into a Scottish Baronial style extravaganza.
Dunrobin is still the seat of the dukes and
earls of Sutherland.

Helmsdale Highland   3 L 8
Sutherland. EC Wed. A small fishing port at
the mouth of the lovely Strath of
Kildonan, famous for its lobsters, which are
flown to France from Wick. Visitors are
welcome at the lobster sheds.
To the north the bay is wild and rocky, but
a stretch of shingle leads to a sandy beach on
the south side.

Hilton of Cadboll Highland   3 K 8
Ross & Cromarty. Pop 200. Polychrome wall
of cottages lying like a giant entablature on
the edge of a shingle beach.

Inver Highland   3 K 8
Ross & Cromarty. A hamlet of bone-white
cottages entrenched at the mouth of a
narrow inlet. Panoramic views across the
water to a perspective of flat wilderness,
terminated by the swollen foothills and
mountain peaks of Sutherland on the
horizon.

Invergordon Highland   3 J 7
Ross & Cromarty. Pop 2,200. EC Wed. The
gleaming towers and orange roofs of this
outpost of industry look splendid when
viewed from the northern shores of the Black
Isle. The natural harbour is one of the
deepest and most sheltered of the British
Isles; it was used as a seaplane and naval
base during both world wars, and in more
recent years has attracted the development of
a whisky distillery and aluminium smelter.
There are beaches of silty, pebbled sand.

John O'Groats Highland   3 M 8
Caithness. The tourists's goal: the north
eastern tip of the county, with enjoyable
views over the tide race of the Pentland
Firth towards the Orkneys. Steeped in the
legend of the Dutchman John de Groot, a
local ferryman who gave his name to the
place. The beach has rocks, shingle and
white sand, where small shells known as
'groatie buckies' are found. Safe bathing
close inshore on an incoming tide.

John o' Groats

Keiss Highland   3 M 5
Caithness. Pop 300. A cluster of houses
grouped around a colourful line of lobster
pots and a pin-cushion of masts in the tiny
harbour. The village is built on the northern
end of a long, gently curving beach of sand
in Sinclair's Bay. Of interest is the village
church, built by Sir William Sinclair in
1750—it was the first Baptist church built in

Scotland; remains of 2 brochs; Ackergill
Tower, a 15thC tower house standing on a
rocky plinth on the southern end of Sinclair
Bay.

Kilmuir Highland   3 J 8
Ross & Cromarty. Tiny cottage hamlet
hidden by a camouflage of roses.
Shipwrecked north of North Kessock, it is
beached in a forgotten countryside dressed in
rich greenery.

Kinlochbervie Highland   3 G 3
Sutherland. Pop 100. Thriving fishing village
on a platform of land sticking out from the
mouth of Loch Inchard.

Kyle of Lochalsh Highland   3 E 9
Ross & Cromarty. Water-flanked mountains
glower down from all sides on this small
town, whose facilities include a large and
famous hotel, a terminal railway station
complete with steam-powered crane, and a
ferry service to Mallaig, Skye (just across the
water), and the Applecross Peninsula. The
rocky headlands and strong tidal races are
not suitable for swimming.

Latheronwheel Highland   3 L 7
Caithness. Two villages in one. The first half
consists of a fishing village cascading gently
down the side of a hill to a sheltered
harbour. To the north, 1 mile inland, is the
second half—Latheron—a tiny hamlet blessed
with 3 churches. Of interest is the whale
bone arch built in 1869 from the skeleton of
a stranded whale; the former parish church
has been converted into Clan Gunn
Museum.

Lochcarron Highland   3 F 8
Ross & Cromarty. Pop 1,100. Fishing village
of grey stone cottages hugging the banks of a
mile-long, sea loch that is walled in by steep
wooded rock. At the mouth of the loch,
where the rock wall narrows before opening
out to sea, stand the gaunt ruins of Strome
Castle.

Lochinver Highland   3 F 4
Sutherland. Pop 300. Self-effacing fishing
village, knitted in a huddled stonework
pattern round a small harbour on the north
east banks of a sea loch. All around is a
thrilling, tortured landscape of twisted rocks
and jagged peaks squeezed skywards. A
magnificent haunt for geologists. Nearby is
the Inverpolly Nature Reserve.

Lybster Highland   3 M 7
Caithness. Pop 600. Large 19thC fishing
village along the east coast with a bustling
harbour, a sanctuary from the snarling grey
cliffs. Sturdy houses of quiet dignity,
classically spacious streets. Of interest nearby
are the Cairns of Camster, Bronze Age burial
chambers; the Hill o'Many Stones; the
Achananich standing stones.

plockton

Plockton Highland   3 E 8
Ross & Cromarty. Pop 300. 18thC village
consisting of a winding line of stone built
cottages and palm trees clinging to the
crumpled rocks and shingle beach of a
natural harbour at the mouth of Loch
Carron. All around great, jagged mountains
shoot skyward in dark shadows out of the
glass-still waters. Good sailing and fishing.

Portmahomack Highland   3 K 8
Ross & Cromarty. Pop 200. Quiet fishing
and holiday village brushed in briskly along
the eastern banks of a sheltered sandy bay.
Long vistas across the dark waters of the
Dornoch Firth to the shaded cardboard cut-
out of the blue hills and mountains beyond.
To the north, pinned indestructibly to a flat

nose of land poking out to sea, is the Tarbat Ness lighthouse, a 180-foot-high tower.

Portskerra Highland   **3 K** 2
Sutherland. Pop 200. A handful of houses, enclosed like a curtain wall to fight off the hostile furies of the sea, stands on a grassy cliff.

Reay Highland   **3 L** 5
Sutherland. Pop 300. 19thC picture postcard village standing a little aloof from its pint-sized harbour and idyllic sandy beach, which is backed by a rolling wave of dunes and crossed by tiny winding streams. Fine 18thC church with loft and external tower stair. The hills behind are a habitat for the golden eagle.

Rosemarkie Highland   **3 K** 7
Ross & Cromarty. EC Thur. Chanonry Point, a grassy promontory which has been made into an excellent golf course separates this village from Fortrose. Rosemarkie is a quiet continuation of its twin. The A832 climbs steeply out of the village offering a superb view across the voraciously swirling currents of the Moray Firth to the 18thC Fort George. Its fine sandy beach gives way to rocky bays backed by cliffs to the north.

Sandwood Bay Highland   **3 G** 2
Kinlochbervie, Sutherland. Flat golden sands, immense and beautiful, are the rewards for a 4-mile walk from where the road at Kinlochbervie ends. Strong tides; unsafe for bathing.

Scarfskerry Highland   **3 M** 5
Caithness. Crofting village of greystone cottages crouching round a natural harbour in a sheltered opening of this rocky coast.

Scourie Highland   **3 G** 3
Sutherland. Crofting village and tiny harbour sealed amongst scar-faced hills.

Scrabster Highland   **3 L** 5
Caithness. Pop 300. Stacked in workmanlike manner on the high grassy cliffs above the fishing harbour, from where the car ferries operate to the Orkneys and Shetlands. The setting is on the north west bank of Thurso Bay. Here the sturdy stone built houses are tucked snugly away from the furies of Pentland Firth. It was also from here that Lord Kitchener sailed in 1916 aboard the ill-fated cruiser sunk by a mine. Conger eels are a frequent sight in the harbour.

Shiel Bridge Highland   **3 F** 9
Ross and Cromarty. Trapped by a wall of mountains one side and the long, ice-cold waters of Loch Duich on the other, it is a small village of stone cottages encircling the bridge over the River Shiel.

Skerray Highland   **3 J** 2
Sutherland. North east of Tongue it is a straggling crofting village that climbs a hill overlooking Torrisdale Bay. In the sheltered bay at the foot of the hills is a tiny harbour.

Spinningdale Highland   **3 J** 6
Sutherland. A heroic failure standing on the north bank of Dornoch Firth between Bonar Bridge and Clashmore. It consists of 20 houses and the shell of a cotton mill. Inspired by Arkwright it was built by a 'do-gooder' from Skibo in 1790. The mill was burnt in 1880 and because of the escalating costs of transportation in such a remote area, it was left a skeleton, a gaunt memorial to misguided philanthropy.

Stoer Highland   **3 F** 4
Sutherland. Remote crofting village wedged in at the beginning of a rocky peninsular with just a finger of land out to sea. Many trout-filled lochs and numerous sandy beaches. Also of interest: 2 cairns and a broch at nearby Clachtoll.

Strathy Highland   **3 K** 2
Sutherland. A scattered hamlet hugging the ground as if trench warfare had just broken out. It is connected by a winding lane to a spacious beach. On Strathy Point is a bone-white lighthouse, built in 1958.

Sutherland's North Coast   **3 H** 2
The main road A836/A838 that strikes west from Thurso in Caithness to follow Sutherland's north coast towards Cape Wrath runs through a countryside of dramatic beauty. Usually it traverses bare unfenced moorland a mile or so inland from the sea, and the few small crofting villages scattered along the coast are only distantly seen amid their green fields. Occasionally, as at Melvich and Durness, it touches on lonely beaches of white sand where you can swim in the clear caressing waters of the warm Gulf Stream. Elsewhere it winds around two deep cliff-bound inlets of the Atlantic, called the Kyle of Tongue and Loch Eriboll. To the south three grey-brown bold mountains soar to the clouds, namely Ben Loyal, 2,304 feet, Ben Hope, 3,040 feet and Ben Spionnaidh, 2,837 feet. For 80 miles there is no town, but wayside hotels provide refreshment for deer stalkers, birdwatchers, salmon fishers, and those who come simply to watch the waves pound on the craggy shores. People sometimes wonder how this far northern county came to be called 'Sutherland'. The Vikings came from the north, and settled first in the Orkneys and Caithness; then they moved south into this, to them, the 'southern land'.

Tain Highland   **3 K** 6
Ross & Cromarty. Pop 2,000. The market centre in a sea of rich farmland. It sits politely and quietly in a gentle amphitheatre of land overlooking a spacious sandy beach. Turreted 17thC Tolbooth and handsome collegiate church built in 1371.

Thurso, Caithness

Thurso Highland   **3 L** 5
Caithness. Pop 9,100. EC Thur. MD Tue. Originally the Viking gateway to and from the mainland, Thurso spreads out along the edge of an almost boundless bay. It is the most northerly town in Britain. There are still strong undertones of its origin as a Viking settlement; the town's name, which is derived from the Norse 'Thor's-a', literally means river of the god Thor. Viking power was at its height in the 11thC and lives on in the names of many streets such as Olaf and Haakon.
Since the opening of the nuclear power station at Dounreay to the west nearly 30 years ago, the town has expanded in leaps and bounds but its essential appearance, that of a handsome market town, has hardly changed. As long ago as the 14thC, it was a major centre for the grain trade with Scandinavia and by the 17th and 18thC was a busy exporter to the Low Countries. By the early 19thC the flagstone industry had been established and for the next 100 years Thurso prospered on the shipment of flagstone from the surrounding quarries to the towns and cities of the Continent.
The town straddles the meandering banks of the River Thurso, which is rich in both salmon and trout. There is a long, narrow, bustling fishing harbour spied on by the ruins of 17thC Thurso Castle. This is the ancestral home of the earls of Sinclair and it stands matriarchally on the east bank of the river. Behind the harbour is a cobwebbed maze of 17th and 18thC fishermen's cottages. The broad streets and noble Neo-Classical houses of 19thC Thurso were planned by Sir John Sinclair who, during the

Thurso, Caithness

worst excesses of the Highland clearances, campaigned for a whole series of improvements in the living standards of crofters and farm workers alike. St Peter's Church, dating back to the 13thC, is Thurso's oldest building. Although partially rebuilt in the 17thC when a new nave and transepts were added, the work was abandoned in the early 19thC. A new church was built in 1833. The Town Hall square was the centre of mediaeval Thurso. Still the market square, it was here that the new Town Hall was built in 1872. In the old town, beside the church, is the Old Turnpike. Montrose once stayed here on his return from Orkney. Its name comes from the circular stair-turret corbelled out over the pavement. There is another similar example in the High Street. Also of interest is the Folk Museum, opened in the Town Hall building in 1969, which illustrates the history of Thurso and Caithness with a collection of photographs, antiques and ephemera; the Library, where the collection of Robert Dick, a local baker turned leading botanist and geologist of his day, is on view. Sandy beach backed with pebbles. Safe bathing away from the river.

Tongue Highland **3** J **2**
Sutherland. Pop 100. Undulating line of houses that lies a stone's throw from the east bank of a narrow inlet, the Kyle of Tongue. The horizon to the south is edged by a fretwork silhouette of jagged mountain peaks.

ullapool

Ullapool Highland **3** G **5**
Ross & Cromarty. Pop 1,500. EC Tue. Unlike most of the villages created by the British Fisheries Society in the late 18th and early 19thC, Ullapool continues to draw its income from its fisheries. The excellence of the catch has also provided the basis of much of the tourist industry. For years men have loaded their wives, nets and rods into the car and headed for this village. Most sea-fishing widows enjoy their bereavement— what better solace than the magnificent scenery of this corner of Wester Ross. Passengers for the first steamer of the day to Stornoway (Isle of Lewis) will find their early rise well rewarded if they drive into the town from the north. This route leads through the Inverpolly Nature Reserve. Worth making time for: a boat trip from the harbour to see the birds of the Summer Isles.

Whaligoe Highland **3** M **6**
Caithness. Tiny 19thC harbour south of Ulbster, at the foot of a sky-reaching wall of cliffs as sheer as the façades of 5th Avenue in New York.

Wick Highland **3** M **6**
Caithness. Pop 7,600. EC Wed. MD Thur. Sturdy, grey nest of stone buildings and narrow streets built in a fortified huddle as protection against the furies of the North Sea. Created a Royal burgh by James VI in 1589, it is the county town of Caithness.

Wick, Caithness

Straddling a broad loop in the winding river, Wick is really two towns in one. The original town was built on the inside of the loop to the north. On the outside of the loop, to the south, the British Fishery Society planned a fishing village and harbour in 1808 under the direction of Thomas Telford. It was called Pultneytown, named after Sir William Pultney, Chairman of the Fishery Commission. This was Britain's major herring port during the heyday of Scotland's fishing industry. In 1902 Wick and Pultney became one, combined under the name of the older settlement, Wick. There are 3 harbours, inner and outer harbours and a river harbour, broad quays, with a hill of streets behind. But as the herring shoals moved mysteriously away from the eastern coastal waters of Scotland, so did much of the hustle and bustle of Wick. A major blow, but Wick survived, quieter but possibly more idyllic. Described by Robert Louis Stevenson as 'the bleakest of God's towns on the baldest of God's bays'. It's certainly austere, but handsomely so. Today it is the market centre of the rich farmland of the region and tucked down a side street you will discover the delightfully old-fashioned auction rooms.

Wick.

Of interest: the Caithness Glass Factory; the parish church, built 1830 and said to have the widest unsupported roof span of its time in Scotland; the Andrew Carnegie Library and Museum; Nors Head Lighthouse, with views to the Orkneys and Pentland Skerries on a clear day; the ruins of the castles of Sinclair and Girnigoe which lie together 3 miles north east of the town; the ruins of the 14thC castle of Old Wick, known to seamen as the 'Old Man of Wick', situated some 1½ miles south east. The remains are a skeleton of a 4-storey keep, perched on a rocky ridge flanked by 2 gullies.

Islands

The Outer Hebrides Western Isles
The name is taken from the Norse *haf bred eyr*—'islands on the edge of the ocean'. The climate reflects this, being moderated by the Gulf Stream but lashed with Atlantic gales that batter the western shoreline. The winter nights are long and the living is hard for the majority of the people who are crofters. There are very few trees and pasture is limited, though seaweed is harvested for its alginates. They are a friendly, courteous and intelligent people and look 'foreign'. In fact they still speak a soft Scots Gaelic. Their economy is based on small farms, fishing, home weaving and tourism, and the impression given is that of a peasant community.

croft, hebrides

Power comes from peat (cut on the islands), coal and hydro-electricity. Roads are sufficient, but narrow and winding.
A visit here will stir your soul, and remind you of some of the basic values missing from town life.
There are many safe, sandy beaches, but enquire locally before swimming.

Barra Western Isles   **3 A 9**
The central island of the remotest group of the Outer Hebrides: the steamer from Oban takes a day to reach the harbour at Castlebay. Here Castle Kisimul, started in 1030, is the seat of the Macneil of Barra, and can be visited by taking a boat from the post office. The island is attractive, but barren. It is known as 'the Garden of the Hebrides' because there are more than 1,000 wild flowers that can be found here. Superb beaches with miles of empty sand.

Barra

Harris Western Isles   **3 C 4**
The southern part of the 'Long Isle,' where grey gneiss creates a 'moonscape' of bare rocks and craters filled with peaty water, softened only by large water lilies growing in profusion in the pools. Here we find Clisham, at 2,622 feet, the highest mountain in the Outer Hebrides. Crofting villages shelter behind rugged headlands and in tiny bays the fishing, particularly for lobsters, remains profitable.
Harris tweed is dyed and handwoven here in the cottages to the traditional colours and patterns, and exported throughout the world. There are several long, sandy beaches.

Leverburgh (Harris)   **3 B 5**
Pop 200. EC Thur. Tiny fishing village transformed in shape and name by the generosity of Lord Leverhulme into a small port in the early 20thC. It was conceived not so much as a commercial venture, but one of improvement in the manner of the 19thC humanitarian, Sir John Sinclair. But Lord Leverhulme died before the work was completed. The village was originally called Obe. Still to be seen are the wooden 'Swedish' style houses. The only good feature of the harbour that remains is its view across the Sound of Harris.

Rodel (Harris)   **3 B 5**
Glued to the southern tip of Harris at the foot of Roneval—a high hill squat as a duck—Rodel nestles around its sheltered

St Clement's, Rodel

harbour. It is famed for the 16thC church of St Clement's. Built as a chapel and MacLeod burial place, it crowns a small hill sealed in larger hills beside the bay and has some fine stone carving, particularly MacLeod's Tomb.

Tarbert (Harris)   **3 C 4**
Pop 500. EC Thur. Tarbert is strategically placed on the isthmus connecting the peninsula of South Harris with the rest of the Long Island; cars and coaches automatically pass through the town while car ferries regularly make the 2-hour trip to Skye. The seething activity of the place is heightened because it is the centre of Harris's tweed industry. Viewed from the south west the village is striking, with lines of houses radiating along the banks of its twin lochs.
There are some excellent beaches to the south west: take the A859 out of Tarbert—you will have to drive for about 10 miles, but the wide choice of sandy bays will be ample reward.

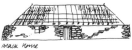

black house

Lewis Western Isles   **3 D 2**
The northern part of the 'Long Island.' An exciting landscape of peaty-moorlands with menacing outcrops of grey rock and sheer cliffs forming sandy bays and numerous lochs.
Over the years the crofters have improved the pastures, now rich with wild flowers, and have cultivated oats and potatoes. The traditional 'black houses' of stone and thatch are being replaced with modern buildings, standing open to the winds. There are few trees.

Loch Erisort, Lewis

Arnol (Lewis)   **3 D 1**
Pop 100. Picturesque village hugging a shallow basin of land, called 'Little Holland' because of the many stone dykes. Of interest is the Black House Museum. To the south west is the crofting village of Bragar with its giant whalebone arch.

Balallan (Lewis)   **3 C 3**
Pop 300. Long straggling line of stone cottages near a narrow sea loch. The longest village in Lewis, it is engulfed in a patchwork of ragged lochs, moors and saw-toothed mountain peaks.

Carloway (Lewis)   **3 C 2**
Pop 200. Hamlet hugging a narrow inlet on the north west coast of Lewis. Of particular interest is the Iron Age Dun Broch, standing in an impregnable position on a high hill. Circular tower with cavity walls of drystone. The outer wall is canted inwards.

Maivaig (Lewis)   **3 B 2**
Typical crofting village of scattered cottages pinned down on convenient terraces of land, sloping down to the sea loch beyond.

Stornoway (Lewis)   **3 D 2**
Pop 5,200. EC Wed. The largest town in the Hebrides and the unofficial capital. It is more bright and breezy than beautiful, but always surprising. A community of Pakistani shopkeepers speak Gaelic. Turreted Lewis Castle overlooks the town. The Harris tweed industry is centred here. The town has 2

Stornoway harbour

harbours, sheltered and accessible in all tides and weathers. Of interest are the Nicholson Institute and St Peter's Church. Excellent sandy beaches, with safe bathing.

Tolstachaolais (Lewis) 3 C 2
Colourful village of stone cottages dancing along a lush, green, roller coaster of land. A little to the south is the stone circle at Callanish; a megalithic Stone Age temple some 3,000 years old.

Tolsta, Lewis

Uig Bay (Lewis) 3 B 2
Tucked away on the south west of Lewis lie Uig Sands—a vast expanse of white velvet bordered by sweet smelling clover meadows. A haven in the strangely menacing 'lunar' landscape of this corner of the island. Beware of the area of quicksands at the western edge.

Valtos (Lewis) 3 C 2
The scattered houses of this tiny crofting village conform to the usual rather dismal architectural standard of the Long Island, but the beach is superb. Heaped high with orange and brown limpets, razor shells, tiny pink delicacies and sea-worn stones of an agreeably portable size, it's a beachcomber's paradise. Those with an insatiable lust for shells should also visit Reef, the next bay along.

St Kilda Western Isles 3 A 4
This group of tiny rocky islands, the westernmost of all Britain, lies 110 miles west of the northern Scottish mainland. These were inhabited until 1930, when the last group of Gaelic-speaking crofters was evacuated. Now belonging to the National Trust for Scotland, St Kilda has only temporary visitors today, usually naturalists on study tours run by the Nature Conservancy Council. Its cliffs, up to 1,396 feet high, are the tallest in Britain, the wildest, and most dangerous. The goat-like Soay sheep, the only truly wild sheep in Britain, survive and maintain their numbers, and thousands of sea birds nest.

St Kilda

North and South Uist and Benbecula Western Isles 3 A 6
These southern Hebridean islands form a long, broken chain, running for 35 miles south of Lewis and Harris. They average 8 miles wide, but their coasts are deeply indented everywhere by sea lochs. Inland lie wastes of rock and peat, broken by a maze of

countless freshwater lochs, with rocky peaks springing steeply from the wilderness. Down the west coast, however there is fertile land of the *machair* (see **Regional features**) beside the long sandy beach washed by the fierce Atlantic waves. Here stands a string of crofting villages along the single main road, A865. The 3 main islands of North Uist, Benbecula and South Uist are now linked by causeways. A ferry from Uig in Skye carries cars to Lochmaddy in North Uist, and other ferries link Lochboisdale in South Uist with Oban and Mallaig on the mainland. Most visitors come to fish, watch birds, or get-away-from-it-all, for the islands have no attractions save their wild scenery and clear air. There are miles of safe, sandy beaches, but beware of the tidal currents that flow swiftly through the channels between the islands.

The Orkneys 3 M 3
Many of the islands of Orkney cluster around the 'Mainland' (the largest island—Orcadians refer to the Scottish Mainland as 'The Sooth'). They are low lying, with a few gentle hills. The exception is Hoy—mountainous with grandiose coastal scenery including the 'Old man of Hoy', a tempting vertical carrot to intrepid mountaineers.

Old Man of Hoy, Orkney

Surprisingly, Orkney is not a fishing community: beef cattle and hens are the mainstays of the economy, both heavily mechanised. The Orkneys and the Shetlands were donated by the King of Norway and Denmark in 1468 as part of the dowry of Princess Margaret on her marriage to James III of Scotland. The Norse flavour is still very evident. Communications with the Scottish mainland are good, and there is a well-run internal air system. There are many stretches of sandy beach where bathing is safe close inshore.

Kirkwall (Orkneys) 3 N 3
Pop 4,600. For centuries the capital of Orkney, it was also the principal Viking stronghold for 6 centuries up until the 15thC. The town is dominated by the Cathedral of St Magnus 12thC, an impressive, weatherbeaten, cruciform church built in a monumentally fierce Romanesque style, with a yellow and red patchwork of sandstone. A mediaeval maze of streets wind tightly around the cathedral. Kirkwall has really 2 distinct parts. The earliest area, rebuilt during the last 2 centuries, was around Shore Street. Here you will find crooked streets of crowstepped gabled houses enriched by bright colours and a wall-to-wall carpeting of stone as in the shopping centres

Earl's Palace, Kirkwall

at Albert Street and Broad Street. The cathedral stands on the edge of this earlier settlement. The next phase of development was The Laverock, a district galloping outwards from Victoria Street. Adjacent to the cathedral is the Bishop's Palace, a 12thC building largely reconstructed in the mid 16thC. The Earl's Palace, 500 yards away, is a handsome Renaissance building erected at the turn of the 17thC by local slave labour. Also of interest is Tankerness House Museum, a 16thC building where the history of Orkney is depicted.

Scapaflow (Orkneys)　　　　3 N　3
Was the scene of intense activity in both world wars, but now only thistles invade this submarine base.

Stromness

Stromness (Orkneys)　　　　3 M　3
Pop 1,600. EC Thur. Magnificent harbour town scrambling around the foot of a beautiful backdrop of steep green hills. The main street is a narrow canyon winding through a cliff of buildings, begun in the 17thC when the town became a major port in Scotland's Baltic trade. It further prospered in the 18th and 19thC when it was visited by ships of the Hudson Bay Company. Also a major whaling centre, and in the late 19thC it flourished as a herring fishing port. Daily ferries to the Scottish mainland.

Round church, Orphir

Broch of Gurness, Orkney

Other places of interest nearby: the Round Church at Orphir to the south east; the early 12thC church of St Magnus dominating the small island of Egilsay; the Ring of Brogar, a Stone Age circle in a wilderness of lochs; Broch of Gurness, ruins of a fortified tower IstC BC; Birsay, straggling village with ruined 16thC palace; St Margaret's Hope, attractive harbour village on south Ronaldsay with houses press-ganged jaggedly together.

St Margaret's Hope, South Ronaldsay

The Shetlands　　　　3 O　8
Fingers of the sea (voes) thrust their way deep into the land, and from the air the islands of the Shetland group look like the pieces of a jigsaw which has been abandoned because no one could quite sort out the blue bits from the green and brown ones, and there are no 'straight edges' to help. There are nearly 100 islands of which Mainland is the largest, but the best known is the Fair Isle—its knitting patterns are world famous.

Fair Isle, Shetland

Shetland only became part of Britain at the end of the 15thC when their ruler, Christian I of Denmark, having 'pawned' the group was unable to produce the money to redeem his pledge. The culture remains basically Scandinavian and all the place names and local dialect (Shorn) have Norse origins. The islands lie on the same line of latitude as the tip of Greenland and Siberia, and experience the same long summer daylight hours and the interminably long winter nights. They do not have to undergo the rigours of the Arctic climate because their shores are washed by the Gulf Stream, but the low moorland landscape is frequently lashed by fierce gales. Predictably the land is treeless and not notably fertile, though it is being improved and the peat bogs are slowly being reclaimed. There are some crofters who rear the hardy Shetland breed of sheep and the famous ponies, but the islands lie in the midst of some of the best fishing grounds in the world, and most of the men look to the sea for their living. Few places are more than a mile away from the sea: it is without doubt the most dominating feature of the Shetlanders' lives. People eager to escape from the urban antheap and to revel in the seascapes, to fish, to sail and to observe the bird life are visiting the islands in increasing numbers; a boon to the tourist industry but a self-destroying process. Access by air and by ferry from Aberdeen and Leith. Swimming is only safe from bays, which provide protection from strong currents.

Aith (Shetlands)　　　　3 O　8
Pop 100. Hugging the end of a narrow sea loch, its sturdy crofts stand firm in a rolling blanket of bleak, uninhabited moorland.

Aith

Cunningsburgh (Shetlands)　　　　3 O　9
Pop 100. Crofting community perched on scattered shelves of land carved out of the low hills sloping down to the sea.

Hillswick (Shetlands)　　　　3 N　7
Remote settlement on the banks of a narrow inlet, overshadowed by a dark wall of cliffs.

Lerwick (Shetlands)　　　　3 O　9
Pop 6,300. The capital of Shetland, and the home of more than half the population. A maze of narrow paved streets twists down to the waterfront. Although one might expect

Lerwick, Shetland

the inhabitants of such a remote town to have an insular approach to life, in fact more than 50% of the population have visited most of the major ports of the world. For centuries the port has been the meeting place of seafaring folk: the Viking warriors used to meet here between raids; in the 17thC the Dutch were frequently in the harbour (the houses which overhang the waters of the harbour are a testimony to the fact that their visits were not altogether confined to fish trading: the arrangement was ideal for secret landing of contraband) and today trawlers from all over the world, not to mention the international oil men, maintain the cosmopolitan tradition.

Scalloway (Shetlands)   3 O 8
Pop 900. Quiet cobwebbed world of houses jammed tight round the ruins of a 16thC castle, that stands on a podium of land between a lush green valley and a magnificent sweep of bay. This fishing village was the ancient capital of Shetland. The sheltered harbour is still a colourful fishing centre.

Voe (Shetlands)   3 O 8
Gentle hotch-potch of rows of thatched roofed cottages mixed with bungalows and modern timber houses. It grips the banks of a narrow inlet sheltered by green, brutish hills.

Walls (Shetlands)   3 O 8
Pop 100. Tiny fishing hamlet in a crevice of land amid a heather wilderness with lochs and burns.

Inland towns & villages

Canisbay Highland   3 M 5
Caithness. South east of John O'Groats, a plain village with a bold, simple parish church of harled walls built in the 15thC. The font, as in the Dutch tradition, is positioned beside the pulpit—a particularly rare feature in Scotland.

Contin Highland   3 H 7
Ross & Cromarty. Pop 200. Straggling village built along the banks of the River Blackwater. The bridge was built by Telford. The simple rectangular parish church was built in 1796 on the site of a church burnt by the MacDonalds in 1492, along with the women and children who had sought sanctuary there.

Halkirk Highland   3 L 5
Caithness. Pop 700. Handsome village spread generously by the River Thurso and surrounded by lush, green countryside. It was planned by Sir John Sinclair as a communal venture in self-sufficiency in the late 18thC.

Lairg Highland   3 J 5
Sutherland. Pop 1,100. EC Wed. Though probably the largest of Sutherland's inland villages, Lairg is little more than a hamlet clustered around the eastern shores of the

Lairg, Sutherland

Little Loch—a reservoir created by the damming of the head of Loch Shin and the narrows of the River Shin with its spectacular waterfall. It lies at the junction of the roads leading north and west and is basically a touring centre, with a market. The 'Great Plough', a monument found about 3 miles north of the village, commemorates the large scale land reclamation instigated by the Duke of Sutherland in the 1870s.

Rogart Highland   3 K 5
Sutherland. The heart of a thriving crofting community—it is a colourful wash of houses cradled in a fertile trampoline of land.

Strathpeffer Highland   3 H 7
Ross & Cromarty. Pop 1,100. EC Thur. A prosperous town basking luxuriantly in the shelter of the encircling hills. From the 1770s until after World War I Strathpeffer was a fashionable spa; members of the Royal Family came to take the waters of the nearby chalybeate and sulphur springs. Today it has become a popular touring centre, famous for its smoked salmon. With its abundant trees and shrubs and its chalet-type architecture the town seems like a cross between Bournemouth and a Swiss mountain resort. The Continental atmosphere is reinforced in the evenings, when the shops stay open late and visitors saunter round the square.

Watten Highland   3 M 6
Caithness. Pop 400. Clinging to the eastern bank of Loch Watten, it is a quiet pastoral village marooned in rich farmland.

Regional features

Many of the features mentioned here also apply to the previous section on the **Scottish Highlands and Islands.**

Brochs
A triumph of drystone walling, these bell-shaped towers are found only in the north of Scotland, the Outer Hebrides, Orkney and Shetland. It is thought that they were built by the Picts as defensive structures during the 1st and 2ndC. Typical features include a central courtyard, a low-roofed entrance passage and a spiral staircase built within the outer and inner walls to allow access to the upper galleries. In all there are over 500 brochs in the far north of Scotland and its islands; the best preserved examples are at Mousa and Clickhimin (both on Shetland) and Carloway (Lewis).

The Broch, Carloway, Lewis

Burghs
Burghs were originally created in Scotland by King David (1124–53) in order to confirm and define rights of trading, and thereby strengthen them by the process of monopoly. A rampart or wall was set up as protection for the privileged traders, and sometimes a Royal castle as well. The burgh and its men—burgesses—were partly self-governing, and in return for the advantages gained for a town being created a burgh, burgesses paid customs duties on important exports, and a rent. Some burghs were called Royal, either because they were the King's own burghs or

because they contributed to Royal funds. A Royal burgh had privileges which included the right to trade abroad, whereas the lesser burghs were confined to the home market only. Between 1450 and 1516, 51 lesser burghs were founded, each of which had its own privileged area with the monopoly on buying and selling and craftwork.

By the 1830s, town government in Scotland was undergoing complete reform and in 1833 the Burgh Reform Acts were passed because the form, scale, nature and powers of burghs were completely unsuited to the needs of the new age.

Clans

The word clan originates from the Gaelic 'clann' meaning children, hence kinship, leading to the modern term family. The clan system was at its peak during the 16thC and the order of family precedence was strictly observed.

Theoretically a clan is headed by the chief or father of the family, followed by his immediate family who would inherit land and lease it out on long-term 'tacks' to middlemen or 'tacksmen', who in turn leased it out to their tenants. Thus a clan was built up under the protection of its chief who was held responsible for the conduct and welfare of his clansmen.

The clan system started to die in the 18thC and was abruptly suppressed by the English after the 1745 rebellion. They believed that the clan system with its fierce internal loyalties lay at the root of the Highland disturbances. However the old loyalties could not be totally destroyed, and something of the clan spirit has survived right through to the modern day, aided by the efforts of clan societies who acquire land and property, establish museums and, above all, maintain the famous clan spirit.

Crofters

Originally the land in the North of Scotland and the Western Isles was considered to be the property of the local clan; exceptions occurred in the Orkney and Shetland Isles, where sturdy Vikings admitted no overlordship save that of Almighty God! But gradually ownership passed to the great lairds and noblemen, and the common people had to be content to remain as tenants, paying a minimal rent.

19thC crofters home, Clachtoll, Sutherland

improved cottage, 19thC

By the late 18thC, sheep farmers from the Scottish Borders were offering substantial annual cash rents for Highland grazing land, and from one glen and island after another the clansfolk were driven out and their homes destroyed. Those who remained were offered 'crofts', small farms along the coast, where they could raise some crops and keep a few livestock, fish the seas, or start cottage industries like knitting and weaving. Later legislation, around 1880 and 1950, gave the crofters firm tenure of their limited lands. Though they rarely own either ground or house, they and their families cannot again be evicted.

This explains the pattern of landscape that visitors encounter in Scotland's north and west, where expanses of open, uninhabited country lead suddenly to settlements of neighbouring small farms. Many crofts have vanished, and are perpetuated only by the ruins of stone cottages. But many still survive, for today's crofter holds tenaciously to his ancient birthright. Also in recent years many crofts have been taken over by

Englishmen, some are used merely as holiday homes, but some of the new owners have adopted this way of life permanently. It is still an open question as to whether these newcomers will revitalise the system or hasten its disintegration.

Daylight hours

Caithness is almost 9° of latitude nearer the Arctic than Cornwall; this has a radical effect on the length of daylight hours. During May and June the day never seems to end—it is often light enough to read at midnight. Conversely in winter the days are extremely short: on the 21st December, the sun only appears for 5 hours, 52 minutes. However the interminable hours of darkness are sometimes brightened by displays of the aurora borealis—the northern lights.

Gaelic

Gaelic is one of the oldest languages in Europe; by the end of the 11thC it had spread across most of Scotland, and in the Highlands it was spoken as the first and often the only language. However its use has slowly disappeared over the years since the end of the 18thC and the decline of clanship.

Street names in the Outer Hebrides are sometimes bilingual as in Stornoway on Lewis, and Gaelic songs are still sung in the 'ceilidhs' (pronounced 'kayli'), the informal gatherings for singing and story-telling that are very much part of the self-contained way of life of the Highlander.

Today there are 75,000 Gaelic-speaking people in Scotland, of which about 900 speak no English. For those interested in increasing these figures, there is an Association in Scotland called 'An Commun Gaidhealach' which is dedicated to the furtherance of Gaelic throughout the Highlands.

Hydro-electricity

The North of Scotland Hydro-Electric Board was established by an Act of Parliament in 1943, in order to provide electricity supplies in the under-populated areas by developing water-power resources. The development of hydro-electricity has brought many important changes to life in the Highlands and Islands. Hydro-electric schemes have to be approved by the Secretary of State for Scotland and laid before Parliament. The Board must 'have regard to the desirability of preserving the beauty of the scenery and any object of architectural or historic interest, and of avoiding as far as possible injuries to fisheries and to the stock of fish'; to this end there are Amenity and Fisheries Committees to advise the Board, and in fact a lot of research has been undertaken with regard to fisheries.

Cruachan dam, Argyll

The Hydro-Electric Board is unique in that it does not merely produce and supply electricity: it is also involved in the economic and social improvement of North Scotland, a duty which includes research into raw materials and agricultural experiments, thereby encouraging new industry in the north.

An example of the extent of the Board's work may be seen at the Conon Valley development, which took 15 years to complete, involving 7 generating stations, 7 main dams, 20 miles of tunnels, 15 miles of aqueducts, a main-line railway station, 2 miles of track and 30 miles of roads. There are small hydro-electric schemes on various islands, and the Board has diesel-engined power stations on the islands without water-power resources, as at Kirkwall, Lerwick and Stornoway. In order to supply electricity to the islands, over 50 miles of submarine cables have been laid: a fact which helps to illustrate the immense problems involved in the distribution of electricity in such remote areas.

Lack of inland towns and villages

Even the most cursory inspection of a map of the Northern Highlands and Islands will reveal the fact that while the coast is lined with towns and villages, inland they are a rare feature. Those which do exist tend to be sited at the intersection of major routes. A partial explanation of this phenomenon lies in the native Celtic dislike of living cheek by jowl with his neighbour. (This is not to say that the people are anti-social; the feeling of community within each rural parish is extremely strong.) This is reinforced by the economic impracticality of living on top of one another in farming areas where the soil is poor: some members of the community would have to travel long distances to reach their land.

The Highland Clearances of the 18th and 19thC were the main underlying cause of the lack of inland towns. After the 1745 rebellion the English broke down the clan system extremely efficiently and the lairds no longer felt under the obligation of kinship to care for their tenants. When it was realised that the best return from the infertile moorlands and mountainsides was derived by the development of extensive sheep farming or sporting estates, the tenants were ruthlessly evicted. Some were murdered, thousands sailed to the colonies, others were driven to the coast. Of course, there were humane men who did their best to help the victims to their feet again.

For example, Sir John Sinclair tried to exploit the resources of the sea. Many of the rivers which drained to the east coast had carved natural harbours where they met the sea; the eastern coastal waters were rich in herring—all seemed set for the fishing boom. Unfortunately many of these harbours also had natural disadvantages: they were either often blocked by rock and sand, washed down when the rivers were in spate, or they were not tidal and, worst of all, the shoals of herring mysteriously disappeared from the eastern coastal waters. Hence the many decayed harbours found along the east coast, as at Dunbeath, Janetstown, Lybster, and Staxigoe.

Lighthouses

There are many lighthouses on the windswept headlands of the north coast of Scotland: the seas are stormy and difficult, and the coastline is notoriously rocky. It is worth making a detour to some of the many headlands for the views on clear days are magnificent, and many different birds may be seen nesting on the cliffs.

Many of the lighthouses in Scotland are situated in remote areas, and some keepers are glad to see visitors and may often be prevailed upon to show people round at reasonable hours; some have a considerable knowledge of the local wildlife. The most northerly lighthouse in the British Isles is at Muckle Flagga, Shetland, situated on a rock, one mile north-west of the entrance to the Barrafirth. In fine weather, a boat may be hired at Barrafirth, to view the lighthouse and the stacks of Hermaness—the promontory west of the firth which is now a seabird sanctuary.

The lighthouse at the Butt of Lewis is situated at the northernmost point of the Outer Hebrides: 100 feet high, it is surrounded by impressive cliffs and rock pinnacles—the haunt of seafowl.

The Flannan Islands, or 'Seven Hunters' off Lewis are famous for the mysterious

Dunnet Head, Caithness

disappearance in 1900 of 3 lighthouse keepers. The lighthouse is now automatic and, on climbing up the circular stairs to the balcony, one is either stunned by the view or knocked sideways by the wind.

The windows of the lighthouse at Dunnet Head are said to have been broken, on occasion, by stones hurled from the sea 346 feet below; nonetheless the views across the Pentland Firth to Orkney are worth the visit. Another lighthouse that should be visited for the views is at Scalpay Glass Island, off Harris. The lighthouse stands sentinel over the Minch at the south east end of the island, with views across to Skye, Lewis, Harris, the Uists and the mainland.

The lighthouse at Duncansby Head—the north east promontory of Scotland—commands a fine view of the Orkneys, the Pentland Skerries and the headlands of the east coast. To the north, at the entrance to the Pentland Firth, the Boars of Duncansby may be seen: a reef whose name suggests the fierceness of the sea. To the south are the 3 Stacks of Duncansby—towering pinnacles of rock rising from the sea—and home of a myriad of seagulls.

Machair

Large areas of grass abutting the white shell-sand of the beaches of the Outer Hebrides on which a wide variety of wild flowers flourish. Many rare species can be found but the soft scent of clover which drifts through the air in summer is the best feature of the machair lands.

North Sea oil

Geographically, Scotland is ideally placed to take advantage of North Sea oil developments. Tankers, storage tanks and platforms are the new landmarks of the north east coast. One obvious benefit from the discovery and drilling of oil is that it has opened up wide-ranging opportunities for industry, services and communications in Scotland; thereby halting the drift of population. Certainly, with the decline of the shipbuilding industry in Clydeside and the subsequent loss of jobs, North Sea oil has helped to revitalise the economy, by bringing both employment and rich rewards to other parts of the country. Aberdeen has undergone dramatic changes with the oil boom, but smaller places like the Orkneys and Shetlands have also felt the impact of the sudden influx of industry and quick money.

North Sea oil drilling platform

Although a lot of thought and consideration has gone into protecting the environment from the less attractive consequences of heavy industry, it is, perhaps, inevitable that some areas of Scotland's magnificent coastline have been adversely affected in both scenic and social terms. Still that's progress for you!

Peat
Ten per cent of the land surface of Scotland is covered with peat: a composite of soil mingled with half decayed vegetable material—the remains of reeds, sedges, moss or heath. It varies in consistency from being highly fibrous to a shapeless black substance, depending on age and the type of vegetation. It is still forming in the Island of Lewis, but is receding in other parts of the Highlands. In 1949 the Scottish Peat Commission was set up to investigate the possible exploitation of peat in Scotland, which led to a survey of peat bogs in the Highlands and Islands, and research into the use of peat in the generation of electricity. An unsuccessful attempt to generate electricity from a closed cycle peat-burning turbine was made in 1959 at the Attnabreac Bog in Caithness. Peat has been used as a fuel in Scotland throughout her history: it burns with a subdued heat but has the advantage of being almost smokeless, and it is still widely used as a domestic fuel in the Outer Hebrides. Its various uses were first exploited in 1844 by Sir James Matheson who, having bought the Island of Lewis, attempted to extract paraffin wax. Peat was also being used at that time for salt evaporation, fish and meat curing, lime burning, charcoal making and metal working. Nowadays, however, it is used mainly for whisky distillation, fish curing and domestic fuel; evidence of the last may be seen piled high beside the Highland cottages, providing a long-familiar landmark.

The Sabbath
Still very much a day of rest in the Highlands and Islands of Scotland, particularly in the Outer Hebrides where religion plays an important part in the lives of the people. The inhabitants of Lewis, Harris and North Uist are Protestant, and lay a great emphasis on the Sabbath observance.
At Stornoway, on Lewis, a 6-day week is observed on public transport: this includes the ferries, which is worth bearing in mind in order to avoid being stranded on the island over the weekend. Licensed premises and other amenities are also closed on Sunday.

Shielings
During the summer months the livestock were taken to graze the higher pastures; this ensured that the unfenced fields of crops around the townships were able to ripen without risk of being eaten or trampled upon. The crofters built themselves temporary huts, usually with drystone walls and heather-thatched roofs. The ruined remains of these shielings (Gaelic 'hut') are dotted around the landscape of the far north of Scotland and its islands. The aptly named beehive huts at Kinloch, Isle of Lewis, are a striking version of the shielings. The crofters enjoyed the respite from their daily chores and the idyllic weeks of the summer were eagerly anticipated and have been fondly recorded in folk songs and poems.

Tartan
Traditionally the wearing of a tartan kilt is the distinguishing mark of the Highlander. The custom dates back to the 13thC when the Highlanders were brightly coloured clothes of checked material known as 'breacan'. In 1747 the English Government forbade the wearing of Highland dress as part of their successful efforts to crush the rebellious spirit of the Highlanders by destroying the clan tradition. Inevitably when the Act was repealed in 1782 there were few who could recall the expertise required to weave and dye the setts, or patterns. However, the demand for clan

Highland piper

tartans was revived in 1822 by George IV who wore a kilt at Holyrood, and it has continued up to the present day. There are now over 250 tartans.

Tweed
The Outer Hebrides is the only place in the world where genuine Harris Tweed is made. The tweed was originally woven by the islanders for their own use but the Dunmores of Amhuinnsuidhe Castle in Harris realised its potential and helped to create a demand for the cloth, and today it is the Harris Tweed industry which supports the islanders 'cottage industry'.
In 1909 the Harris Tweed Association was set up to protect the industry from imitators of their unique product, and a 'Genuine Harris Tweed' label now means it was made from pure virgin Scottish wool, spun and dyed in the Outer Hebrides and hand woven by islanders in their homes in Lewis, Harris, Uist and Barra.

Weaving Harris tweed

The process involved in producing a piece of cloth bearing this famous label is complicated and slow: raw Scottish wool is shipped to Stornoway in bales; it is then taken to the mills for dyeing, blending carding, spinning and hand warping. Lorries take the spun yarn to the crofters and return later for the woven tweed, which is left lying at the roadside for collection: a familiar sight, and sure proof of its durability. In the region of 7 million yards of tweed are woven a year, in over 5,000 different colours and designs.

Famous people

J. M. Barrie (1860–1937)   **3** B 4
Loch Voshimid, 8 miles NW of Ardhasaig Bridge on the island of Harris. The island on this loch is reputed to have provided inspiration for Barrie's play 'Mary Rose'. He wrote much of it at Amhuinnsuidhe Castle, on the coast road of West Loch Tarbert. The castle, a magnificent structure, was built by the Earl of Dunmore in the 19thC (not open to the public). There is a river beside the castle where the salmon leap several feet

over a sheer rockfall into the upper waters, and the hills to the north of the castle are rich in red deer: a setting which Barrie must have enjoyed while writing his famous play.

Bonnie Prince Charlie (1720–88) **3** D **2**
The legend of Bonnie Prince Charlie began when he reached Scotland in 1745 in an attempt to win the English throne for his father, the son of the deposed James II. He soon had the support of over 2,000 Highland clansmen who helped him to his first victory, at the Battle of Prestonpans. By December his army of loyal Highlanders had grown to 5,000, but they were defeated against George II at Derby, and the Prince retreated again to Scotland. He gained another victory at Falkirk, but his Highland army was finally outnumbered and overthrown at Culloden Moor in 1746 by an army headed by the Duke of Cumberland—King George's son. In the months that followed he was pursued mercilessly by Cumberland, but was never betrayed by his loyal supporters in spite of a considerable price on his head.
The Highlands and Islands played a major part in the legend of Bonnie Prince Charlie; he set foot on Scottish soil for the first time in July 1745, on the Island of Eriskay in the Outer Hebrides. In 1746 he was on the mainland, and spent a day in Kintail eluding the redcoats. He hid in a forester's hut between the mountains Hekla and Ben More on South Uist from May to June 1746, and in the same year he landed at Ardvourlie Bay on the island of Lewis, from whence he was forced to walk 20 miles back to Arnish. 'Prince Charlie's Cairn and Loch' is a monument on Arnish Moor, near Arnish Lighthouse at Stornoway, which records the fact that he spent some time there while on the run after his defeat at Culloden. In June 1746 he set sail from Creagorry on the island of Benbecula with Flora MacDonald, famed for taking the fugitive Prince 'over the sea to Skye', dressed as her maid. He finally left Scotland for France in September 1746, but his legend lives on in the Scottish Highlands and Islands.

HM Queen Elizabeth   **3** M **5**
the Queen Mother
Castle of Mey, off A838, nr village of East Mey. In 1953 Queen Elizabeth the Queen Mother purchased the Castle of Mey for use as a summer home. Originally called Barrogill Castle, it was built in 1568 by the 5th Earl of Caithness, and remained in the family for over 350 years. *There are special day openings of the castle in aid of charity during Jul and Aug, and the grounds are open to the public on certain days.*

Famous travellers
People have always hankered to travel to the Highlands and Islands, attracted by the remoteness, the scenery and the different way of life of this part of the British Isles. Many travellers through the centuries have written down their impressions, but none more expressively than Johnson and Boswell, as may be seen in Johnson's 'Journey to the Western Isles of Scotland' and Boswell's 'Journal of a Tour to the Hebrides': written as a result of their trip to explore the Highlands and Islands in 1773. Queen Victoria visited Loch Maree in Ross and Cromarty in 1887: an event which is commemorated by a stone with an inscription in Gaelic. The same year Anthony Trollope visited St Kilda—the lonely group of islands west of North Uist in the Outer Hebrides. Keats, on sailing home from Cromarty after his visit to Scotland, was 'heartily sickened of accursed oatcakes', but otherwise appeared to have enjoyed his visit.

Flora MacDonald (1722– 90)   **3** C **8**
Fionnghal MacDonald met Bonnie Prince Charlie in 1746 at her brother's shieling of Alisary (at Milton, 18 miles from Carnan, in South Uist), where it was suggested that the safest way of escape from the Duke of Cumberland and his army would be for

Flora to disguise the Prince as her maid: 'one Betty Burke, an Irish girl and a good spinster'. Although reluctant to partake in such a dangerous adventure, she eventually agreed to the plan, and set to sewing a suitable dress for her 'servant'. Charles wanted to wear a pistol under his petticoat, but Flora said if he were searched the pistol would give him away, to which he replied; 'Indeed, Miss, if we shall happen with any that will go so narrowly to work in searching me as what you mean, they will certainly discover me at any rate'.
They finally left for Skye on the 18th June and arrived safely the next day, when Flora took leave of Prince Charles, having risked her life for 'her king', never to see him again.

Robert Louis Stevenson (1850– 94) **3** M **6**
There is a plaque over the Customs House at Wick in Caithness recording the months the author spent there. His father, Thomas Stevenson, designed and built a breakwater as part of a scheme to improve the harbour, but a storm washed it away (the remains can still be seen near the lifeboat shed).
RLS was employed to improve the harbour in 1868 but found the work unsuited to his health.
In retaliation to the townsfolks' scornful words about his father's workmanship, the author of 'Treasure Island' described the town as the 'bleakest of God's towns on the baldest of God's bays'.

Thomas Telford (1757–1834)   **3** M **6**
In 1803, as engineer to the Society of British Fisheries, Telford was asked to produce a report examining the possible ways in which the communications system could be improved to enable the Highlands and Islands to be opened up to economic expansion. The Government acted on his suggestions and he was put in charge of a vast civil engineering project which took over 18 years to complete and led to the construction of over 1,000 bridges, 920 miles of roads, the improvement of 280 miles of military roads and numerous harbour modernisation schemes.
In 1815, at a cost of £9,600, he built The Mound; a 1,000-yard-long embankment carrying his road from Wick across the head of Loch Fleet, thereby reclaiming the marshy valley of the River Fleet. Finally, in 1824 he designed a number of churches and manses in the Highlands which were built at the Government's instigation. Telford's churches can still be found on Lewis, Harris, North Uist, Quarff (in the Shetlands) and North Ronaldshay (in the Orkneys). Telford's brilliant engineering skills enabled a social revolution to take place in the previously inaccessible Highlands and Islands of Scotland. In terms of historical importance and sheer magnitude, this work must represent the greatest achievement of his extremely succesful career.

Cathedrals, abbeys & churches

Croick Church Highland   **3** K **6**
Sutherland. North of Balnapaling, the church stands in a district notorious during the Highland Clearances, when the crofters were cleared from the land to make way for sheep. Many, their crofts burned, took refuge in the tiny church in 1845. The names and comments they scratched on the church windows are still there today and, like concentration camp graffiti, a harrowing reminder of man's inhumanity to man—made more terrible in the empty silence of the bleak landscape around.

Dornoch Cathedral Highland   **3** K **6**
Dornoch, Sutherland. Begun in 1224 by Bishop Gilbert de Moravia, the cathedral is on the probable site of a Celtic foundation. It was badly damaged in 1570 and

subsequently neglected. The nave was rebuilt in 1835–37 for the Duchess of Sutherland, and further restoration work took place in 1924 when, happily, some of the 13thC stonework was revealed. Sixteen Earls of Sutherland are said to lie in the cathedral; at the west end there is a statue by Chantrey of the 1st Duke of Sutherland. In the cathedral graveyard, and closely resembling a tombstone, is a 'Plaiden Ell': this was used for measuring cloth at fairs and markets.

Fortrose Cathedral Highland   **3 K   7**
Fortrose, Ross & Cromarty. Founded by David I of Scotland in the 12thC, the remaining fragments of this cathedral stand in a superb green close surrounded by yew trees; a perfect foil for the deep red tones of the sandstone. Cromwell is said to have ordered the use of many of its stones to build Inverness Castle.

Gilchrist Mausoleum Highland   **3 J   8**
Ross & Cromarty. West of North Kessock, the church dates from the 13thC. Disused since 1780, it is the only church in this part of Scotland with a pre-Reformation piscina and sacrament house. The sacrament house was a cupboard where bread and wine were stored between the services.

Old St. Peter's Church, Thurso

Old St Peter's Highland   **3 L   5**
Thurso, Caithness. Founded in the 13thC by Gilbert Murray, Bishop of Caithness, the church was in use until 1832 but is now roofless, after a fire. The nave and transept are 16th and 17thC, and the churchyard has a tombstone possibly dating from the 14thC.

St Clements Western Isles   **3 B   5**
Rodel, Isle of Harris. A stolidly handsome piece of 16thC architecture looking composedly out to sea; its intrinsic beauty is heightened by the loveliness of its setting. Effective use has been made of natural stone, with black crystals glowering in the nothern transept.
There are strong stylistic connections with Iona Cathedral, notably the use of Celtic carving—as seen for example in the tower. (Freely accessible to the visitor who is prepared to scale a few ladders.) The tombstones are great fun; they too display a free use of Celtic motifs, in some cases the iconography has clearly not been drawn from Christian sources!

Probably built in 1528 to house the tomb of the 8th chief of MacLeod, which is set into the south side of the choir. The church was restored in 1873.
The key has to be fetched from Rodel Hotel; this however permits a glimpse of a superb relic of a by-gone era.

Tomb, St Clements

The Cathedral of St Magnus   **3 N   3**
Kirkwall, Mainland, Orkney. Dedicated in 1137 to the memory of his saintly uncle by Earl Rognavald, the Norse ruler of Orkney,

St Magnus, Orkney

this impressive sandstone building represents the zenith of the Norse civilization in Orkney. It is the only cathedral, apart from the one in Glasgow, to have survived without structural damage from the pre-Reformation period.

Ui Chapel   **3 E   2**
Eye Peninsula, Lewis. The roofless and neglected 14thC chapel of St Columba at Ui, or Eye, was the traditional burial place for the chiefs of the Clan MacLeod. It contains an armed effigy of Roderick MacLeod, and a memorial to his daughter Margaret MacFingone (died 1503), mother of the last abbot of Iona. Some of the Seaforth Mackenzies are also buried here.

Castles & ruins

Ardvreck Castle Highland   **3 G   4**
Loch Assynt, Sutherland. On N bank of Loch Assynt, off A894. A ruin of 3 storeys, built about 1490 by the MacLeods of Assynt. It was here that the Marquis of Montrose was captured and confined after his defeat at the battle of Culrain.

Badbea Tower Highland   **3 L   7**
Badbea, Caithness. 3 miles SW of Berriedale off A9. A small tower near the cliffs, built from the stones of a cottage belonging to John Sutherland, one of the early 19thC lay religious leaders. It is the only remaining part of a village inhabited by crofters who were driven off their lands in nearby Ousdale. The tower was used for shelter, and it is said that the children and cattle had to be tethered to prevent them hurtling down the steep cliff.

Ballone Castle Highland   **3 K   6**
Portmahomack, Ross & Cromarty. Ruins of a magnificent 16thC tower house, with tall stone keep and projecting towers on the diagonal angles, enriched by corbelled corner turrets. Two projecting turreted staircase towers give access from the first floor hall to the floors above.

Earl's Palace, Kirkwall

Bishop's Palace and Earl   **3 N   3**
Patrick's Palace
Kirkwall, Orkney. The ruined Bishop's Palace, south of Kirkwall Cathedral, was founded in the 13thC and altered by Bishop Reid in the 16thC. King Hakon of Norway died here in 1263 after his ill-fated Scottish invasion. To the east is the ruined Earl's Palace, built 1600–07 for Earl Patrick Stewart and described as 'the finest relic of domestic Renaissance architecture in Scotland'. Both ruins are scheduled Ancient Monuments.

Carbisdale Castle Highland   **3 J   5**
Ardgay, Ross & Cromarty. 3½ miles NW of Bonar Bridge off A9. A turreted mansion resembling a Rhine Schloss, built in the 1900s by a former Dowager Duchess of Sutherland. It is now a youth hostel.

Dunrobin Castle Highland   **3 K   5**
Golspie, Sutherland. On a natural terrace near the sea, the castle originally consisted of a

Dunrobin Castle

keep built by Robert, 2nd Earl of
Sutherland, in 1275 and called Dun Robin
after him. It was enlarged in 1844–48 by Sir
Charles Barry, and altered by Sir Robert
Lorimer in 1921 after a fire. Part of the
castle has been used as a school since 1965.
Gardens laid out in the formal style of
Versailles.

Eilean Donan Castle Highland   3 E 9
Dornie, Ross & Cromarty. Built in 1220 by
Alexander II on a superb site overlooking
Loch Duich, the castle was blown up in
1719 by an English warship, but was
restored 1912–32. For generations a
stronghold held by the MacRaes, it serves as
a war memorial to the clan. Relics of the
Jacobites and Dr Johnson may be seen
inside. But the exterior is more deserving of
a visit; the castle's best feature is its
magnificent siting.

Kinkell Castle Highland   3 J 7
Ross & Cromarty. South east of Conon
Bridge, it is a fine z-plan tower house built
in 1594 by John Rory Mackenzie, a
descendent of Red Hector of Kintail.
Recently restored, but private.

Kisimul Castle, Barra

Kisimul Castle Western Isles   3 A 9
Castlebay, Barra, Outer Hebrides. The castle
dates from 1030 and apart from the 200
years leading up to 1938, it has always been
inhabited by the Macneils of Barra. The
family has a reputation for eccentricity and
independence: this is illustrated by their
alleged rejection of Noah's offer of a place in
the Ark because 'the Macneil had a boat of
his own'. *Closed winter.*

Eilean Donan Castle, Loch Duich

Fairburn Tower Highland   3 J 8
Ross & Cromarty. South west of Marybank,
it is a grim towering stone keep, rectangular
in plan with a projecting stair tower. 17thC
stronghold of the Mackenzies, its entrance,
on the first floor, was defended by a sliding
bar.

Fort Charlotte   3 O 9
Lerwick, Shetland. Begun in 1665 to protect
the Sound of Bressay against the Dutch, the
massive fort was burned by them in 1673. It
was rebuilt in 1781, and garrisoned during
the Napoleonic War.

Castles Girnigoe   3 M 6
and Sinclair Highland
Caithness. 3 miles NE of Wick off A9.
Spectacularly situated together on a rocky
ledge above the sea at Sinclair's Bay, the two
castles appear at first glance as one ruin.
Sinclair, built in the 17thC, is now a
complete ruin but the remains of Girnigoe
dating from the 15thC, include the dungeon
where the 4th Earl of Caithness murdered
his son the Master of Caithness after 6 years'
imprisonment between 1570 and 1576. Both
castles were deserted and in ruins by the end
of the 17thC.

Castle of Old Wick Highland   3 M 6
Caithness. 1 mile SE of Wick, ⅓ mile E of A9.
Known as 'The Old Man of Wick', standing
on a narrow spine of rock projecting into the
sea, the remaining ruined tower was besieged
and taken by the Master of Caithness in
1569. The castle, the oldest in Caithness,
dates from the 12thC.

Redcastle Highland   3 J 8
Ross & Cromarty. Brooding ruin standing on
the northern banks of the Beauly Firth. It
was built in 1178 by William the Lion so
that he could better control the violent
anarchy of the Norsemen of the Black Isle.
He built 2 other castles at Dingwall and
Dunskaith.

Scalloway Castle Western Isles   3 O 9
Scalloway, Mainland, Shetland. The castle
was built in 1600 by the wicked Earl Patrick
Stewart. Legend has it that warriors' blood
and maiden's hair were used as cement. Its
ruins may be visited.

Skelbo Castle Highland   3 K 5
*Loch Fleet, Sutherland. 3½ miles N of Dornoch
off A9.* The ruined keep and walls dating
from the 14thC command fine views of Loch
Fleet from the grassy hillock on which they
stand. The castle itself is not open to the
public.

Thurso Castle Highland   3 L 5
Thurso, Caithness. The ruins of the 17thC
castle, rebuilt in 1872, overlook the harbour.
The original castle of 1660 was said to be
close enough to the sea to fish from the
windows. *Not open to the public.*

Harold's Tower Highland   3 L 5
*Thurso, Caithness. 1½ miles NE of Thurso off
A836.* Harold, Earl of Caithness was buried
here after the Battle of Clairdon, 1196. The
tower was built over his grave in the mid
18thC by Sir John Sinclair, the agriculturist
(1754–1835) as a family burial place.

Castle Sinclair, Caithness

Unusual buildings

Cairns Highland   3 M 5
Auckingill, Caithness. To the north of
Nybster are a series of cairns built in the
19thC by an eccentric local who decorated
them with statuettes like a birthday cake.

Classic piece of folk art to rank with the legendary Watts Towers, Los Angeles, for its poetic and lyrical intensity.

Dounreay Nuclear   3 L 5
Reactor Highland
Dounreay, Caithness. 10 miles W of Thurso on A836. This remarkable installation can be seen for miles, perched on the clifftops looking like a giant golf ball waiting to be teed off into the Atlantic. Fortunately it is restrained by the maze of cables and pylons that lead off inland. The world's first 'fast-breeder reactor', it is a prototype nuclear power station that 'breeds' as much fuel as it uses in the production of electricity. *A permanent exhibition is open to the public during summer.*

Italian Chapel   3 N 3
Lamb Holm, Orkney. 6¼ miles S of Kirkwall. An attractive chapel built in a Nissen hut by homesick Italian prisoners of war in 1943. The concrete structure, completely transformed with beautiful decorations and intricate wrought-iron work, is an impressive monument to Italian workmanship.

Strathpeffer Pump   3 H 7
Room Highland
Strathpeffer, Ross & Cromarty. The present pump room was built in 1909. With its green and white tiles it has a chilly atmosphere—and a remarkable resemblance to a dairy. Any hopes of achieving a return to the elegance of the 18thC as you gently sip the waters are shattered at the self-service counter where you may unceremoniously help yourself to a bottle of sulphur water. However, a leisurely stroll across the svelte lawns waiting outside should restore your poise.

Bonar Bridge, Sutherland

Telford's bridges   3 J 6
The engineer Thomas Telford (1757–1834) spent 18 years in the Highlands on a government programme of improving communications in the region. Apart from the great Caledonian Canal, most of his work involved the construction of roads and bridges, and Wick Bridge, Helmsdale Bridge, Bonar Bridge and a host of minor bridges were all Telford's, as well as the great Craigellachie Bridge further south. Most of his bridges still stand intact, but inevitably some are succumbing to today's heavy road traffic and are being replaced. Telford's arched and typically castellated Bonar Bridge has recently gained a worthy neighbour in the delicate modern structure that now stands beside it.

Whalebone arches   3 D 2
A novel feature of the far north of Scotland and its isles. The arch at Bragar, Isle of Lewis, was clearly erected in a spirit of triumph: the harpoon which killed the mammal still dangles from it. Another of these arches is found leading into a field beside the A9 about a mile north of Latheron, Caithness. It was made from the

remains of a whale washed ashore in 1869. Note: basking whales can sometimes be seen off the northern coasts, and during the 19thC the Shetlanders made an abortive attempt to establish the beginnings of a whaling industry.

Houses & gardens

Many people open their gardens to the public once or twice a year; it is impossible to give details here, but do make a point of enquiring locally as they are well worth seeing. For details write to Scotland's Garden Scheme, 26 Castle Terrace, Edinburgh.

Dundonnell House Highland   3 G 6
Ross & Cromarty. 10 miles NW of Braemore. Superb private gardens only occasionally open to the public, with rare and oriental shrubs. There are also aviaries of exotic birds.

Dunrobin Castle Highland   3 K 5
Nr Golspie, Sutherland. With lovely views over the Moray Firth, this is a formal garden laid out in the best 17thC French manner. *Closed winter.*

Fairburn Highland   3 H 7
Ross & Cromarty. 6 miles NW of Muir of Ord. An attractive garden with azaleas, rhododendrons and specimen trees. *Limited opening.*

Inverewe Gardens Highland   3 E 6
Poolewe, Ross & Cromarty. A garden of enormous interest, started in 1862 by Osgood Mackenzie on an exposed, barren site beside Loch Ewe. He planted Corsican pines as windbreaks, gradually adding

Inverewe Gardens, Ross & Cromarty

eucalyptus, Monterey pines, Chinese and Himalayan rhododendrons, azaleas and camellias. The garden is informally laid out; the 'Bambooselem' section is devoted to bamboos and a wonderful collection of hydrangeas. There are also many lilies, spring bulbs and alpines.

Lael Forest Garden Highland   3 G 6
Ardcharnich, Ross & Cromarty. 4 miles SE of Ullapool. The garden on the edge of Inverlael Forest contains some 150 different shrubs and trees. There is an explanatory Forestry Commission leaflet available.

Langwell Highland   3 L 7
Berriedale, Caithness. A splendid garden which well illustrates what can be achieved in exposed areas. *Limited opening.*

'900 Roses' Rose Garden Highland   3 K 6
Tain, Ross & Cromarty. The garden was laid out to celebrate the 900th anniversary of the Burgh of Tain receiving its Royal charter.

Rovie Lodge Gardens Highland   3 K 5
Rogart, Sutherland. 8 miles NW of Golspie. The house is situated in the valley of Strath Fleet with wonderful lawns sloping down to Torbreck Burn. There are fine herbaceous borders and heaths, and a water garden. *Closed winter.*

whale bone arch, Bragar

Traditional dwellings

Black Houses

A characteristic house in the north is the Hebridean black house, roof thatched with heather and weighted down with boulders. The walls are built of enormously thick dry stone, often up to 9 feet in depth but on average about 6 feet thick and 6 feet high. The plan consists of living quarters with a byre leading off it. Many such houses were replaced in the 19thC by more substantial white houses, built by the crofters themselves, with chimneys, stones cemented together and slate roofs.

Black Homes, Lewis
Triple combination

Hebridean Black House

The black houses probably owe their name to the fact that there was no chimney to allow the escape of smoke from the central peat fire. As it found its way out through what openings were available, the smoke gradually blackened most of the interior. Like those in Skye, the houses here were designed to withstand the fierce Atlantic winds. A characteristic feature of those built on Lewis, Harris and the Outer Islands is the exposed broad ledge of wall-top extending around the house. The walls, constructed of boulders found in abundance on the hillsides, were built as 2 separate structures with a 2-foot-wide cavity. The outer wall is canted inwards and the cavity filled with earth or gravel. The roof was raised on the inner face of the wall to avoid eaves. The exposed wall-top was turfed over, often with room for sheep or lambs to graze. Because the roofs frequently had to be rethatched, and because few crofters had ladders, steps were occasionally formed in the wall by projecting stones.

The rainwater discharged from the roof would filter through the gravel or earth 'infill' of the cavity, forming it into a damp blanket that acted as a barrier against the winds, which would have otherwise penetrated the stone walling. The boulders of the inside wall were inclined upwards to form a primitive kind of damp proof course that prevented any excess rainwater penetrating the interior. Again the corners of the buildings are rounded.

The black houses of the Orkneys and Shetlands consist generally of a long rectangle with an entrance through the byre at the lower end, the byre being separated from the dwelling by a stone cross wall. On Lewis, the house plans often consisted of 3 irregularly shaped buildings comprising barn, byre and living quarters, joined together. The thatched roof was usually roped down with heather and tied to stones to secure it from the Atlantic winds.

Few houses had windows. Where windows were inserted they had reveals of 4 feet or more in breadth. Many had bed recesses built into the thickness of the walls. On the mainland, timber box beds were more common.

The peat fire was originally lit in a central stone hearth, the smoke either drifting out through the thatched roof or through a smoke hole. Later the hearth was moved to the end walls and a chimney built. The floor of the house was invariably of beaten earth. In order to accommodate the manure, the byre floor was set lower than that of the living room. When sufficient manure had accumulated, it was removed and then used as a fertilizer for the crops.

Of interest are the Black Houses at Arnol (14 miles south of Stornoway, Isle of Lewis) and near Eochdar (Isle of South Uist). They have been converted into museums and may be visited.

Burgh Houses

Typical burgh houses of the late 16thC and 17thC are to be found in Kirkwall in the Orkneys. Most are built of local flagstone laid in clay mortar and roofed with heavy stone slates. The house fronts are narrow and they are also usually gabled.

Cruck Houses

As in the Scottish Highlands and Islands, the typical structure is the cruck frame. Here in the north, however, many crucks are raised off the ground and spring from a wall plate on a low wall. Where timber was scarce as in the old counties of Sutherland and Caithness, many crucks were constructed from ships' timbers.

Dalriadic Houses

In Sutherland many of the early 19thC crofters' cottages are modelled on the Dalriadic type of black house, with fireplaces and chimneys built at both gable ends.

White Houses

Many of the black houses were gradually replaced in the 19thC by white houses. They are generally 2 storeys in height with grey cemented walls and asbestos or bitumen felted roofs. The old black houses are now used as byres or weaving sheds.

Museums & galleries

Carnegie Museum Highland   **3** M 6
Wick, Caithness. Generously endowed by the industrialist Andrew Carnegie, the museum contains collections of local antiquities and natural history specimens.

Cottage Museum Western Isles   **3** A 7
South Uist, nr Bualdubh Eochair, Outer Hebrides. On Eochair to Ardvaicher road W of A865. This little museum has only recently been opened and displays old husbandry utensils, local costumes and other items of interest.

Croft Museum   **3** N 9
Voe, Dunrossness, Shetland. A croft house which has been restored as a museum.

Hugh Miller's Cottage Highland   **3** K 7
Cromarty, Ross & Cromarty. The birthplace of this eminent 18thC writer, naturalist, theologian and geologist. Now a museum, its exhibits include his collection of geological specimens. The fossils are particularly worth seeing. The cottage has been furnished with early 18thC furniture by the National Trust for Scotland. *Closed winter.*

Shawbost Museum   **3** C 2
Western Isles
Shawbost, Isle of Lewis. A folk museum set up by the local school children in a disused church. It is now under the aegis of the National Trust for Scotland. The exhibits

reflect many aspects of the islanders' life centring round the traditional activities of fishing, crofting and weaving. Well worth a visit.

Shetland County Museum 3 O 9
Lerwick, Mainland, Shetland. Housed above a library containing a special 'Shetland Room', the museum contains a variety of interesting relics depicting the Shetlands' past.

Stromness Museum 3 M 3
Alfred St, Stromness, Mainland, Orkney. Good botanical and ornithological collection; also a display of boats and model ships, and an exhibition of traditional agricultural tools.

Tankerness House Museum 3 N 3
Broad St, Kirkwall, Mainland, Orkney. A 16thC farmhouse with a collection of prehistoric and historic relics of the Orkneys; also occasional travelling exhibitions and art shows.

Thurso Museum Highland 3 L 5
The Town Hall, Thurso, Caithness. Local geological, zoological and botanical exhibits. Houses a collection of fossils, plants and mosses gathered by Robert Dick (1811–66), a Thurso baker with a flair for natural history.

Nature trails & reserves

Beinn Eighe National Nature 3 F 7
Reserve Highland
Ross & Cromarty. W of Kinlochewe via A832. An outstanding Highland reserve with fine mountain plants, native pine forest, golden eagles, pine martens and wildcats. Nature trail at Glas Leitire, otherwise enquiries to the Warden at the reserve or to Nature Conservancy Council, 12 Hope Terrace, Edinburgh.

Dale of Cottasgarth and Birsay 3 M 2
Moor
Orkney. Two almost adjacent RSPB reserves on the mainland with typical moorland. Parts are visible from the minor road joining A986 and A966. Consult RSPB representative, Easter Sower, Orphir, Orkney, for further details.

Glas Leitire Nature Trail Highland 3 F 7
Ross & Cromarty. Part of Beinn Eighe National Nature Reserve. 1 mile. Pine forest on Loch Shore with associated wildlife. Fine scenery. Start from car park/picnic site (clearly signposted) on A832, where guide is available.

Inverpolly National Nature 3 G 5
Reserve Highland
Ross & Cromarty. 10 miles N of Ullapool. A landscape of mountains, lochs, rivers, moors, crag and cliff covering 27,000 acres. Superb fishing especially at Loch Sionascraig. The haunt of the pine marten, wildcat, golden eagle and deer.

Slattadale Nature Trail Highland 3 E 7
Ross & Cromarty. On Gairloch-Kinlochewe road, A832. Forest trail along Loch Maree. Fine scenery and good all-round wildlife interest. 1–5 miles. Guide from Forestry Commission, 21 Church St, Inverness.

Torridon Nature Trail Highland 3 E 7
Ross & Cromarty. Superb mountain scenery with deer, feral goats, golden eagle, peregrine, falcons and interesting upland plants. Information centre and car park. Self guided walks—full details at the information Centre, Torridon; or from National Trust for Scotland, 5 Charlotte Square, Edinburgh.

Birdwatching

Dornoch Firth Highland 3 K 6
Ross & Cromarty. The large area of this firth is exceptionally good for autumn waders and grey geese, whooper swans and other wildfowl in winter—but a summer visit is likely to be equally rewarding. The A9

provides good access to Tarbae Ness, via B9165 south of Tain; Edderton Sands and Ferry Point, north from A9 from about 3 miles west of Tain (waders and wildfowl); Skibo Inlet, south from A9 at Clashmore and right to Ferrytown (wildfowl); and Cuthill and Dornoch Sands via the road from Clashmore across Cuthill Links.

Dunnet Head Highland 3 L 5
Caithness. Via B855 from Dunnet on the A836. As well as being the most northerly point on the British mainland, Dunnet Head boasts a lighthouse, superb cliffs and a large, mixed seabird colony where puffins are a particularly noteworthy attraction. It is also a good area for great and Arctic skuas and twite, and red-throated divers can usually be seen from the B855.

Fair Isle 3 O 10
Shetland. This island, famed for its migration studies, is one place all serious birdwatchers visit sooner or later. Accommodation is available at Fair Isle Bird Observatory. Enquiries to: The Warden, Fair Isle Bird Observatory, Fair Isle, Shetland.

Kyle of Tongue, Sutherland

Kyle of Tongue Highland 3 J 2
Sutherland. W of Tongue. Much of this area can be seen from the A838; it is within easy reach of the Loch Loyal. The tidal estuary is good for waders at passage times while most seabirds, including skuas, black guillemots and Arctic terns occur offshore. The minor roads to Talmine on the west and Skerray on the east give good access to the coast nearby. Storm petrels nest on Eilean nam Ron opposite Skerray and wintering barnacle geese (visible from the mainland) linger there well into spring.

Loch Loyal Highland 3 J 3
Sutherland. An area of spectacular loch and mountain scenery crossed by the A836 from Altnaharra to Tongue, which can be covered from the road but is best explored on foot. The massif of Ben Loyal is good for mountain birds, including golden eagle, raven and ring ouzel, and possibly peregrine, while the low-lying ground at the south east and north east ends of Loch Loyal itself is good for breeding birds such as red-throated diver and greenshank. Both black-throated diver and grey lag goose are worth looking out for in this area.

The Orkneys and Shetlands
It is difficult to do justice to these two island groups but both are exceptionally rich in seabirds and some of our most northerly breeding species are famous for their migration. Visitors should contact the RSPB representatives for advice and help at Easter Sower, Orphir, Orkney, or Redfirth, Mid Yell, Shetland.

Summer Isles Highland 3 F 5
Ross & Cromarty. These delightful islands at the mouth of Loch Broom are regularly visited by boats from Ullapool and Achiltibuie; anyone holidaying in this area should not miss them. Breeding birds likely to be seen include grey lag goose, red-throated diver, Arctic tern, black guillemot and buzzard. Storm petrels breed on at least one island and wintering barnacle geese may still be about in April.

Fossil hunting

Visit the local museum. Its fossil collection usually states where individual fossils have been found. When visiting quarries always seek permission to enter if they look privately owned or worked. Be careful of falls of rock.

Mainly unfossiliferous highly-altered rocks. The Cambrian Durness limestone of Durness, Sutherland, has yielded some trilobites. Devonian rocks contain few fossils but there are fish-bands in the rocks of Thurso, and Caithness in general, and around Dingwall and on the Black Isle in Ross & Cromarty. Around Brora, Sutherland, are Upper Jurassic beds with ammonites, belemnites and bivalves, together with a coal-bed, and Lower Jurassic (lias) occurs at Applecross, Ross & Cromarty on the west coast.

Forests

Birch and oak forests
Remains of these ancient forests can be found in various parts notably at Letterewe in Wester Ross and the northern edges of the Great Glen.

Deer forests
Of the 2 million acres of deer forest (nearly all over 2,000 feet) in the Highlands most is unfit for grazing. The red deer is a thriving animal and needs to be kept in check. The largest area of deer forest in Scotland is that north and west of the Great Glen where it is possible to walk through 100 miles of continuous forest. In Scotland the deer are used to living outside their normal wooded haunts and herds can often be seen across the moorland.

Mountains

Arkle and Foinaven Highland   3 G 3
Sutherland. Away to the north of Laxford Bridge the twin hills of Arkle, 2,580 feet, and Foinaven, 2,980 feet, extend their terrific ranges of white Torridonian sandstone crags. As the last major range of the Highlands here in the far north west they create a vivid sense of space and isolation.

Ben Loyal, Sutherland

Ben Wyvis Highland   3 H 7
Ross & Cromarty. Ben Wyvis raises its vast bulk to a height of 3,423 feet, just north of the town of Dingwall. Its gracefully curving slopes, a landmark from all directions, are rimmed at the summit with snow-wreaths for most of the year, and there are proposals to start a skiing ground on the rarely seen northern side where deep snow fields linger. Easily climbed in summer from Strathpeffer. The western slopes of Ben Wyvis carry the huge 7,000-acre Torrachilty Forest of the Forestry Commission, and here there are car parks and splendid waterfalls where in June and July leaping salmon can be seen.

Coigach Highland   3 F 5
Ross & Cromarty and Sutherland. In the far north western corner of Ross and Cromarty, peaks of the pinkish white Torridonian sandstone tower up from the Highland plateau in fantastic shapes. From north to south the tally of outlandish names runs:

Beinn Eighe, Ross & Cromarty

Quinag (highest at 2,652 feet), Canisp, Sulven, Cul Mor and Cul Beag, Stac Polly and Ben More Coigach. All can be seen in clear weather from the main road north A835, then A837, and their ascent involves a tough scramble amongst a wilderness of rock and peat.

Kintail Highland   3 F 9
Ross & Cromarty. This is the wild high mountain area where the Scottish mainland faces Skye across the Kyle of Lochalsh and the Sound of Sleat. Here two broad sea lochs, Loch Carron and Loch Duich, run deep into the hills, their slopes clad in waving forests of pine, spruce and larch trees. The Five Sisters of Kintail, steep peaks set in a rhythmic pattern, tower over Glen Shiel. They now belong to the National Trust for Scotland; highest is Sgurr Fhuaran, at 3,505 feet. For the finest views take the tricky Mam Ratagan by-road due west from Shiel Bridge.

Maiden Pap, Morven and   3 L 7
Scaraben Highland
Caithness. This shapely trio of peaks springs up from the broad tableland of southern Caithness, providing landmarks visible from the whole area. Indeed in clear weather they can be plainly seen from Moray away to the south, across the 40-mile expanse of the Moray Firth. Morven, the 'great mountain' is the westernmost and highest at 2,818 feet. Maiden Pap, 1,917 feet has the comely shape its name suggests. Scaraben, literally the 'scarred mountain', 2,054 feet in altitude, has a long jagged skyline. All three lie in Langwell Forest, wild and rocky deer-stalking country with scattered birch woods.

Rivers & lochs

Dornoch Firth Highland   3 K 6
Sutherland. This long narrow arm of the sea runs inland for a total of 15 miles, though mostly less than 1 mile wide. At Bonar Bridge it is crossed by the main road and becomes the Kyle of Sutherland. Both sides of the Dornoch Firth are heavily wooded, and there are fine views across it, especially from Struie Hill.

Corrieshalloch Gorge Highland   3 G 6
Ross & Cromarty. Eleven miles south east of Ullapool you will find this stupendous gorge close to the oddly named Braemore Junction on the A835 road towards Inverness. First take the A832 road towards Gairloch for ¼ mile to see, from the car park, the breathtaking view over the Lael larchwoods towards Loch Broom in its deep glen. Then walk back to the entrance to the gorge, which belongs to the National Trust for Scotland and is clearly signposted. A good path leads down through the larches to a slender suspension bridge (only 6 people at one time) slung over the deep cleft in the rocks where the Falls of Measach swirl and tumble in their wild cascades. A viewpoint a 100 yards lower down the gorge gives an even better view of this tree-hung defile, which incidentally taxes the photographer's skill to its utmost.

Cromarty Firth Highland   3 K 7
Ross & Cromarty. This remarkable long inlet of the sea has a narrow cliff-bound entrance

Cromarty

between two headlands called the Sutors of Cromarty. It broadens out to the muddy tidal sandbanks called the Sands of Nigg, then runs south west like an estuary, scarcely a mile wide, to Dingwall and Beauly; total length 18 miles.

Helmsdale Highland   **3** K   3
The River Helmsdale, near the borders of Caithness and Sutherland springs from Loch nan Clar, one of several trout-rich waters in an inland, upland region of peaty moors, diversified by steep, isolated and rock-girt peaks. It flows south eastwards, quickly dropping into a 15-mile-long, narrow vale called the Strath of Kildonan. Many conifer plantations have been made along this lovely curving hollow amid the hills.

Loch Broom Highland   **3** F   5
Ross & Cromarty. This broad arm of the sea, 10 miles long by ⅓ mile wide, runs deeply inland in a south easterly direction from the open west coast of Ross and Cromarty. All along its shores crofting settlements lie as green oases, often high up the slopes. Following the loch shore south towards Inverness you find the flat fields of Lael—a Norse word meaning 'low country'. Little Loch Broom, 8 miles long, near Inverewe is a parallel sea loch of wilder aspect, with steeper slopes and more remote crofts. Above it on the south towers An Teallach, 3,480 feet high and usually stormswept.

Loch Maree Highland   **3** F   7
Ross & Cromarty. Loch Maree lies beside the A832 Dingwall-Gairloch main road. Twelve miles long by 1 to 2 miles wide, it runs from Kinlochewe straight north west to its outlet, down the River Ewe to the sea at Poolewe. On its northern shore, Slioch, a tremendous wedge-shaped mountain of bare blue-grey rock, rises to a height of 3,217 feet. On the south is the Nature Conservancy Council's large National Nature Reserve of Beinn Eighe, which preserves native Caledonian Scots pine woods and their associated plant and animal life.

Loch Shin Highland   **3** H   4
Sutherland. Fifteen miles long, though only ½ mile across, this upland freshwater loch runs north west through the heart of Sutherland. Shin Forest, a vast 75,000 acres lies a little to the east. South of Lairg the River Shin, which drains the loch, plunges amid forests through the deep Achany Glen with impressive waterfalls where salmon leap, to reach the sea near Bonar Bridge.

Loch Torridon Higland   **3** E   7
Ross & Cromarty. A fine sea loch, 12 miles long by 2 miles wide, running deeply south east into the wild coast of Wester Ross. Around it stand the gaunt, bare, rocky hills of the ancient Torridonian sandstone. Beinn Eighe, 3,309 feet to the east has a dazzling white summit of white quartzite rock; it is now part of a large nature reserve. A fascinating single track road from Kinlochewe-Dingwall-Gairloch main road leads to the seashore crofting villages of Torridon and Shieldaig, both with hotels. To the south lies the even hillier Applecross Peninsula with a tricky hairpin-bend road climbing across bare Beinn Bhan to Applecross village.

Moray Firth   **3** K   2
Deep-sea fishermen regard the Moray Firth as the great bight of the North Sea between the coasts of Moray on the south and Sutherland to the north, 30 miles across. This narrows to a wedge-shaped bay, still 10 miles across, north of Nairn, which forms a foreground to the grandest distant prospects in Northern Scotland. From the south you gaze across the Moray Firth to the far Sutherland and Caithness highlands. From the shores of Ross and Cromarty to the north you get an equally immense view towards the Cairngorms in the central Grampian highlands. Nearer to Inverness the great firth narrows to the straits then broadens out into an inner Moray Firth, still 2 miles across by 10 miles long, with steep, though sheltered, shores often wooded. Running west again, beyond the Kessock Narrows, the tidal waters become the Beauly Firth fringed by broad mudbanks where shelducks breed each spring.

Strath Naver Highland   **3** J   3
Sutherland. Loch Naver, 5 miles long by ½ mile wide, lies in the wilderness of northern Sutherland, close to the road north from Lairg. Above it towers Ben Klibreck, 3,154 feet high. The by-road that follows the loch's shores runs on for a dozen miles down Strath Naver, once a densely-peopled, well-farmed glen, but deserted since the 'Clearances'.

Strath Oykell Highland   **3** G   4
Sutherland and Ross & Cromarty. The River Oykell rises high on Ben More Assynt, a great mountain, 3,273 feet high in western Sutherland. In its 30-mile course east to reach the sea near Bonar Bridge it flows through a broad, almost uninhabited, strath past huge forests and isolated sheep farms. The main road, from Bonar Bridge to Lochinver on the west coast, gives a fine impression of this lonely yet lovely countryside.

Archaeological sites

Callanish Stones Highland   **3** C   2
Isle of Lewis, Ross & Cromarty. 9 miles S of Arnol. Callanish is one of the major British antiquities of the Bronze Age. The great circles of free-standing stone uprights are undoubtedly religious, and associated with the group of burial cairns which forms part of the monument. The stone circle, built of large stones, is an accessory to the religious function of the site.

Callanish Stones, Lewis

Camster Cairns Highland   **3** M   6
Camster, Caithness. A fine group of Neolithic long cairns, with narrow stone built chambers and projections at each end resembling horns.

Cairn of Get Highland   **3** M   6
6 miles SW of Wick, Caithness. A Neolithic burial chamber in which, during excavations in 1866, several skeletons, ornaments and leaf arrowheads were found.

Clickhimin Broch   **3** O   9
Nr Lerwick, Shetland. This site began as a stone built courtyard house, and was later fortified with a ring wall along the edge of the island. This was commanded from a strong blockhouse, which also provided housing; other shelter was provided by penthouses inside the perimeter wall. A rise in the water level made change necessary, and a late Iron Age broch was constructed, with characteristic galleried wall.

Dun Carloway Broch Highland   **3** C   2
Isle of Lewis, Ross & Cromarty. The broch at Dun Carloway is one of the finest of these Iron Age defensive towers, and survives to a height of over 20 feet.

Dwarfie Stone 3 M 3
Hoy, Orkney. The only Neolithic tomb in Britain to be cut into rock rather than built free-standing. It is a vast sandstone block containing 2 hollowed out cells.

Holm of Papa Chambered Cairn 3 N 1
Westray, Orkney. A fine group of Neolithic long chambered cairns, including one with a corridor-like chamber with mural cells, and another of the 'stalled' type where the long chamber is divided into cells with upright slabs.

Jarlshof, Shetland

Jarlshof 3 O 10
Sumburgh, Shetland. During the Bronze Age the site at Jarlshof was occupied by settlers living in courtyard houses but, as elsewhere in the north of Scotland, the need for shelter against the strong winds, and the availability of good building stone, led to the development in the Iron Age of a dwelling known as a 'wheelhouse'.
This is a round structure, between 20 and 35 feet across with a thick outer wall, probably roofed with a corbelled vault. A number of radial walls ran from the outer wall in plan like the spokes of a wheel but stopping short of the centre; this formed 8 or so compartments, roofed by slabs or corbelling. The central area was some 10 feet across, and may have been left open. Some wheelhouses have a passage or 'aisle' inside the outer wall, and others have connecting doorways between the radial rooms.
A fine broch tower, with the characteristic galleried wall, is probably the latest Iron Age structure on the site. The Dark Age settlement that followed was succeeded by a Viking settlement, with Scandinavian longhouses and smaller attendant structures.

Kintradwell Broch Highland 3 K 5
6 miles N of Brora, Sutherland. This drystone tower was used as a fortification by the Picts between 200BC and AD50. There are many Pictish remains in this area.

Knowe of Yarso Chambered Cairn 3 N 2
Rousay, Orkney. The cairn at Knowe of Yarso is of a type peculiar to the Orkneys. A Neolithic long cairn, it contains a long chamber divided into several lateral cells. Others of this 'stalled' type can be seen on Rousay, at Blackhammer, Knowe of Rowiegar, and Mid Howe (which also has an Iron Age broch).

Langwell Wag Highland 3 L 7
Langwell, Caithness. The type of monument found at Langwell, known as a wag, is of a type apparently unique to Caithness, and is a variation of the 'wheelhouse' type of Iron Age dwelling. The basic house is a strongly built circular hut, to which has been added a stone built oval chamber about twice as large, with its floor excavated below ground level. This contains an arrangement of stalls built from large slabs of stone, and was perhaps also roofed with slabs. Wags have been interpreted as shelters to protect cattle from wolves.

Maes Howe Chambered Cairn 3 M 3
Mainland, Orkney. Maes Howe is the most important monument of its type in north western Europe, a Neolithic round cairn with a corbelled roof built from the local laminated stone; the roof survives intact. The cairn is abnormally large, and has links with the great cairns found in Ireland. It also has the unique feature of a surrounding ditch 35 feet wide.

Mousa Broch 3 O 10
Island of Mousa, Shetland. In addition to being the best-preserved, the Iron Age broch on Mousa is also the smallest (some 51 feet in diameter) and the best built, and must be among the latest examples of the type. It is the usual tower, built as a double shell of drystone on a solid foundation, linked with slabs to form a gallery within the wall; the gallery is lit from the interior.

Skara Brae prehistoric village 3 M 2
Mainland, Orkney. The superb Neolithic settlement at Skara Brae was exposed in a storm in 1851. The huts are closely grouped, roughly rectangular in shape with rounded corners; the groups are linked by paved causeways.
The huts are set into the ground, and built from the local stone which splits naturally into long slabs. They contain unique features in drystone masonry, including box-beds made of stone planks, and tanks, probably to hold shellfish.

Skelpick Highland 3 J 2
Sutherland. A group of Neolithic cairns; Skelpick illustrates the variety of forms found in this part of Scotland. It includes plain round cairns, and round and long horned cairns, in which the ends of the cairn are extended to form horn-like projections. Another group of chambered round cairns with horn extensions can be seen at Spinningdale.

Stenness Stone Circles 3 M 3
Mainland, Orkney. A major late Neolithic or Bronze Age henge monument, Stenness has a surrounding earthwork with interior ditch, and two opposed entrances. In addition, there are the stone circles, the Ring of Stenness, the Ring of Bookan, and the Ring of Brodgar. The whole would have formed an important religious site. Associated is a group of burial cairns.

Taversoe Tuick Chambered Cairn 3 O 2
Taversoe Tuick, Rousay, Orkney. A rare type of cairn belonging to the Neolithic period, with 2 chambers built one on top of the other and provided with separate entrances. The remains of another can be seen at Huntersquoy on Eday.

Vementry 3 N 8
Shetland. A Neolithic 'heeled' cairn, a type peculiar to Scotland, in which a chambered cairn is placed on a stone built platform in the shape of a heel. The chamber is cross-shaped, with its entrance sited at the concave part of the heel to give the effect of a forecourt.

Regional sport

Many of the sports mentioned in the previous section, **Scottish Highlands and Islands,** also apply to this part of Scotland.

Climbing and hill walking 3 F 6
The northern highlands include many of the finest mountains in Scotland, and even the lower peaks do not lack for character. There are 3 outstanding mountains above Loch Torridon: Beinn Alligin (3,232 feet), Liathach (3,456 feet) and Beinn Eighe (3,309 feet). Stac Polly (2,009 feet) to the north of Ullapool is easily climbed from the roadside between Drumrunie Lodge and Achiltibuie, but watch out on the soft sandstone.

Fishing 3 H 7

The north of Scotland offers little coarse fishing, but with salmon and trout fishing costing so little, who's fussed about variety. A salmon permit for Loch Achonachie near Strathpeffer will cost a small amount per day or per week. The islands tend only to offer trout, though there is salmon to be fished on Lewis, Harris and North Uist.

Sea fishing round the Orkneys and Shetlands is in some respects the finest in Europe. The European Record Skate (226¼ lbs) was a fish taken in the Shetlands. In 1971 the European Sea Angling Championships were held out of Scrabster, Caithness, when 25,000 lbs of fish were caught.

Golf 3 M 6

Obviously the further north one goes the fewer golf courses there are, but as this is Scotland there are still a lot. Charges are all very low; the courses at Dornoch, Wick and Stornoway are good; other courses, and also not expensive, include Tain, Muir of Ord, Thurso, Kirkwall and Golspie.

Ullapool, Ross & Cromarty

Pony trekking 3 G 5

There are riding establishments all over Scotland, licensed by local authorities who offer this means of exploring wild country. The ground is often rough and the treks lead across moors and mountains, along forest paths, through burns and rivers. For further details contact the Ullapool Pony Trekking Centre, Ullapool, Ross & Cromarty and the Tower Farm Trekking Centre, Urray, Muir of Ord.

Stalking 3 F 5

The season for stalking red deer begins on the 1st July, although in practice stalking seldom starts much before the beginning of September, when the stags' antlers are in prime condition, and ends on the 20th October. This is an expensive sport. The following hotels offer stalking (some also offer grouse, pheasant and rough shooting): Summer Isles Hotel, Achiltibuie, Ross & Cromarty; Lochdhu Hotel, Altnabreac, Caithness; Forsinard Hotel, Forsinard, Sutherland.

Special attractions

Cheese Factory 3 K 4

Highland Fine Cheeses, Tain, Ross & Cromarty. With the depopulation of the Highlands the art of making traditional cheeses was almost lost. Fortunately their manufacture has now been taken up commercially. See the making of Highland cheeses from start to finish, with free tasters afterwards.

Click Mill 3 M 2

Orkney. NE of Dounby off B9057. Old machinery is always interesting, but perhaps this rare example of a very old horizontal water wheel of Norse design is more interesting than most because it is the only one still working today.

Kirkwall Ba' Games 3 N 3

Mainland, Orkney. A football match between the 'Up-the-Gates' and the 'Down-the-Gates' is played in the streets of the town. *1st Jan and 25th Dec.*

Tweed Weaving 3 K 5

Dickson's The Tartan Flag, Benarty, Brora, Sutherland. Left of the main road N from Brora. See the looms and ancillary equipment; warping and weaving methods demonstrated. The manufacture of woollen cloth is one of the few industries, apart from North Sea oil, in this part of Scotland.

Shetlanders celebrate their Norse past

Up Helly Aa Festival 3 O 9

Lerwick, Shetland. This picturesque ceremony, which welcomes the return of the sun, reaches its climax with the burning of a replica of a Norse galley. It dates back to Viking times when the bodies of dead chieftains were sent to Valhalla in blazing ships. Some 300 men in fancy dress, each bearing a lighted torch, follow the Guizer Jarl (dressed as a Viking chieftain) behind the 30-foot model galley. After dark the galley heads a procession down to the sea. While the band plays 'The Norsemen's Home', the torches are flung into the galley which then sinks in a mass of flames. Sadly this lavish, ceremonial destruction only takes place once a year on the *last Tue in Jan.*

Regional food & drink

Lobsters and crab

Mostly exported from the catching area, but local delicacies such as Parton Bree—a crab soup thickened with cream—are still available.

Mutton hams

A leg of mutton is cured and smoked over a peat and wood fire to produce this local delicacy. Beef, pork, duck and goose are also similarly cured.

Scones and oatcakes

The girdle is a popular cooking utensil here as in Wales and Ireland, and such fine things as oatcakes and Scottish dropscones are produced on it.

Shortbread

One of the true delicacies of the Scottish kitchen, this is traditionally baked in a round flattish mould.

Trout

Though caught and sold throughout Scotland, trout is best when just caught. It is often cooked in tossed oatmeal.

Highland whisky

The word whisky is derived from the Gaelic 'uisge beatha', 'water of life'. The main ingredients—fresh mountain air, pure burn water, locally-grown barley and aromatic peat are all, happily, provided free by nature. There are 3 main types of Scotch whisky: malt, grain and blended. Malt whisky is made from a watery extract of malted barley, the peat fire over which it is dried providing the smoky flavour for which all genuine Highland whisky is famous. It can take up to 15 years in oak casks to mature properly, although it may legally be sold after only 3 years. Grain whisky is usually made from imported maize, but barley and oats can also be used. It is lighter in colour and chemically purer than malt whisky, but the flavour is less distinctive. Today it is used for blending with malt whiskies and not usually drunk on its own. Blended whisky is a mixture of 3–5-year-old malts and grain whiskies, combining the best of both. Many happy hours may be spent touring those distilleries open to the public in order to select a favourite brand of Highland whisky. Bear in mind, however, the old Highland saying: 'There are two things a Highlander likes naked and one is whisky'.